Etowah

Etowah

The Political History
of a Chiefdom Capital

ADAM KING

A Dan Josselyn Memorial Publication

THE UNIVERSITY OF ALABAMA PRESS
Tuscaloosa and London

In memory of my teacher, mentor, and friend
James W. Hatch

Copyright © 2003
The University of Alabama Press
Tuscaloosa, Alabama 35487-0380
All rights reserved
Manufactured in the United States of America

Cover and Text Design by Ander Monson

Typeface: Bembo

∞

The paper on which this book is printed meets the minimum requirements
of American National Standard for Information Science–Permanence of
Paper for Printed Library Materials, ANSI Z39.48-1984.

Library of Congress Cataloging-in-Publication Data

King, Adam, 1965–
    Etowah : the political history of a chiefdom capital / Adam King.
        p.   cm.
"A Dan Josselyn Memorial Publication."
Includes bibliographical references and index.
    ISBN 0-8173-1223-4 (cloth : alk. paper) — ISBN 0-8173-1224-2
(pbk. : alk. paper)
    1. Etowah Indian Mound State Historic Site (Ga.) 2. Mississippian
culture—Georgia—Etowah River Valley. 3. Chiefdoms—Georgia—
Etowah River Valley. 4. Mississippian pottery—Georgia—Etowah River
Valley. 5. Social archaeology—Georgia—Etowah River Valley. 6. Etowah
River Valley (Ga.)—Antiquities. I. Title.
    E99.M6815 .k56 2003
    975.8'35—dc21

                                                            2002008020

British Library Cataloguing-in-Publication Data available

Contents

Illustrations   vi

Tables   vii

Acknowledgments   viii

1. Mississippian Chiefdoms and Political Change   1

2. The Etowah River Valley and Its Mississippian
   Archaeology   26

3. A Political History of Etowah   50

4. The Rise and Fall of Etowah Valley Chiefdoms   84

5. Understanding Etowah Valley Political Change   107

6. Summary and Future Directions   139

Appendix: Radiocarbon Dating the Occupations at Etowah   145

References Cited   155

Index   175

Illustrations

1. The Etowah site   2
2. The Etowah River valley in northwestern Georgia   27
3. Mississippian period complicated stamped motifs   31
4. Mississippian mound sites of the Etowah River valley   37
5. Plan map of the Etowah site   51
6. Early Etowah phase buildings beneath Mound C   56
7. Plan map of Larson's Structure 8   58
8. Changes in the Etowah site structure through time   61
9. Plan map of Structure 3   65
10. Construction history of Mound C   67
11. Embossed copper plate from Rogan's Burial a   69
12. Clay staircase on the face of Mound A's ramp   72
13. Final ring of Mound C burials   76
14. Marble statues from Larson's Burial 15   79
15. Chiefdom capitals in the Etowah River valley   87
16. Northern Georgia mound centers, A.D. 900–1300   109
17. Plan map of the Macon Earthlodge   110
18. SECC exchange corridor through northern Georgia   124
19. Northern Georgia mound centers, A.D. 1300–1550   127
20. The Paramount Chiefdom of Coosa   137

Tables

1. Ceramic phase sequences of the Etowah River valley 29
2. Context and number of sherds used for ceramic
   assemblage analyses 98
3. Etowah site assemblage diversity through time 101
4. Diversity of Etowah and secondary center assemblages
   compared 102
5. Similarity of assemblages from Etowah and a secondary
   center 103
6. Distribution of grave goods in the Funeral Mound
   excavations 112
7. Etowah site phase sequence 146
8. Radiocarbon dates from Etowah period contexts 147
9. Statistically significant date groupings 149
10. Radiocarbon dates from Wilbanks contexts 150
11. Mound C radiocarbon series 152

Acknowledgments

This volume is based on research I conducted for my dissertation, which was funded through a Dissertation Improvement Grant from the National Science Foundation, a Hill Fellowship from the Department of Anthropology at Pennsylvania State University, and the generosity of John C. Burns and Charlotte A. Smith. Special thanks go to John Scarry and James Brown for their thoughtful reviews of the book, to Keith Stephenson for his insightful comments on earlier drafts, to George Wingard for expertly drafting the figures, and to Farrah Brown for creating the index.

Although the interpretations presented in this book are my own, they could not have been committed to paper without the help of many people (any errors of fact are my own). First and foremost, I would like to thank James W. Hatch. From my first field experience as an undergraduate to my dissertation defense, he has been my teacher, my mentor, and my friend. Thank you for getting me into this business and seeing me through it. I would also like to thank the rest of my dissertation committee, including Peter Gould, David Hally, Joe Michels, and George Milner, for their time, effort, and input. A very special thanks to David Hally for all of the opportunities and support that he has given me, and for teaching me the archaeology of chiefdoms and the Etowah River valley. I would also like to thank Lewis Larson for allowing me to use his data from the Etowah site, sharing his knowledge of Etowah River valley archaeology, and continuing to advise and support my research.

In completing this volume, I spent a great deal of time at museums and universities examining collections. During that time I had the opportunity to work with some old friends, and I also had the great pleasure of making some new ones. My work at the University of Georgia's Laboratory of Archaeology could not have been possible without the assistance of Mark Williams, David Hally, and John Chamblee. Thanks also to Sharon Pekrull of the South Carolina Institute of Archaeology and Anthropology for making my efforts there both productive and enjoyable. While I worked at

Tulane University, Kathi Trujillo and Will Andrews of the Middle American Research Institute, T. R. Kidder of the Center for Archaeology, and Evan Charles of housing all helped me in many ways. The hospitality and assistance provided by Jim Bradley and Leah Rosenmeier of the R. S. Peabody Museum of Archaeology in Andover will not be forgotten. A special thanks to David Rosenthal of the Smithsonian Institution's Museum Support Center for taking the time to lead me to the Etowah site treasure housed there. Finally, a very special thanks to Lewis Larson, Sharon McCormick, Dave Davis, and Allen Freeman for their assistance and friendship during my long stay at West Georgia College's Antonio J. Waring Laboratory of Archaeology.

I also had the chance to conduct limited testing at the Horseshoe Bend site (9CK4). I would like to express my great appreciation to Dick Hamby for allowing a stranger to dig in his hay field. As part of that effort several people willingly, and at no cost to me, spent their weekends working in the hot sun. To Guy and Jennifer Harris, Gordon Martin, Tom Pluckhahn, J. C. Salyer, Karen Smith, and Sammy Smith I owe a special debt of thanks.

Behind every project that takes this long to finish there are a group of people who provide the support, friendship, and encouragement that make it possible. This, of course, has always been true of my parents and brother, who have looked on what I do with respect, interest, and enthusiasm. It is also true for John Burns, Jennifer King, Jennifer Harris, Guy Harris, J. C. Salyer, Sammy Smith, and Keith Stephenson. You have all been my friends, my teachers, and my support and I appreciate that more than you know. Finally, a very special thanks to my wife, Jennifer. Next to myself, she has suffered the most at the hands of this undertaking and I thank her for her patience, support, and love.

Etowah

I

Mississippian Chiefdoms
and Political Change

The Etowah site, located in northwestern Georgia (Figure 1), is one of the most famous Mississippian period mound centers in the Southeast. No doubt its prominence stems in part from the impressive nature of the site's layout and monumental architecture. Etowah contains six mounds, including one of the largest ever built in North America, arranged around what appear to be two open plazas and surrounded by an impressive defensive ditch. To a large degree, Etowah's fame also derives from the fantastic array of native art objects recovered from the site's elite burial mound, Mound C. These items belong to the suite of ceremonial objects and symbolic themes known as the Southeastern Ceremonial Complex, and the collection from Etowah is one of the largest and best documented in the Southeast.

Etowah's prominence stems from more than just big mounds and fancy artifacts. It also derives in no small measure from the nature and quality of its archaeological record. That record has played an important role in creating our current understanding of Mississippian chiefdoms. Work done under the direction of Cyrus Thomas (1894) and later Warren K. Moorehead (1932) was influential not only in shaping conceptions of Mississippian cultures (Griffin 1985), but also in formulating ideas about the Southern Cult (Waring and Holder 1945). The data generated by Lewis H. Larson's later excavations led to a fuller exploration of Mississippian symbolism and elite status (Brown 1989; Knight 1986; Muller 1989), while Larson's (1971a) classic paper on social stratification at Etowah still stands as one of the few clear examples in the Southeastern literature of a hierarchical ranking structure expressed through mortuary data.

Figure 1. The Etowah site. Image reproduced with permission of Aerial Photo Service, Inc. ©

Despite these contributions, the full scholarly potential of Etowah's record has yet to be realized. Although more than a century of archaeological research has been conducted at the site, no comprehensive treatment of Etowah's history and its place in the prehistory of the Southeast has been produced. Efforts at synthesizing data recovered from Etowah have been hindered by two all too common problems. The first of these is an overabundance of excavated data and a relative lack of analysis and interpretation. A second problem is that most attempts to place the site in a broader social and historical context have been completed without the aid of absolute dating methods, whether by choice or necessity (Brain and Phillips 1996; Larson 1993; Little 1999; Moorehead 1932). As a result, issues of chronology still cloud full understanding of Etowah's history.

From what has been published about Etowah, it is apparent that exploring its history can help to address issues important to not only Mississippian scholars but also those interested in the emergence and operation of ranked societies generally. For example, the dating of the site's first Mississippian component, at around A.D. 1000–1100 (Hally and Langford 1988), suggests that Etowah may have been one of the first places in Georgia (after Macon Plateau; see Hally 1996) where social ranking and the chiefdom social structure emerged. The large quantities of Southeastern Ceremonial Complex goods removed from Etowah's Mound C (Larson 1971a; Moorehead 1932; Thomas 1894) show that the site's inhabitants participated heavily in the exchange of exotic materials, an undertaking that was apparently fundamental to the operation of chiefdoms during the Middle Mississippian period. Finally, recent interpretations of the route of Hernando de Soto (DePratter et al. 1985; Hudson 1997), buttressed by the presence of sixteenth-century European goods at Etowah (Brain and Phillips 1996; Larson 1989; Smith 1976), indicate that the site was visited by those Spaniards, and therefore experienced some of the earliest contact with Europeans in the Southeast.

In this book, I summarize all that is known currently about Etowah and trace its history as a Mississippian political center. Ultimately, my goal is to place Etowah in its proper social and historical context, and then to attempt to understand the causes behind the political changes experienced by Etowah and its associated chiefdoms. Two themes run through this effort: an interest in the nature of chiefdom political economies and an emphasis on interaction as an important cause of social change.

The ways that chiefdom social and political structures are justified, operationalized, and materialized differ depending on how political economies are organized. This in turn impacts how those polities are structured, the nature of the archaeological record they leave behind, and the kinds of stimuli that are most likely to bring about political change. Ultimately, the nature of the political economy is an axis of variation that is as important to the study of Mississippian political change as settlement system hierarchies and evidence for social ranking. Blanton et al.'s (1996) Dual Processual Theory provides a framework for recognizing differing political economic strategies, and I will use it throughout this study.

In addition to seeking an understanding of the nature of political economies, I will also focus explicitly on the role of local- and regional-scale interaction in the course of political change at Etowah. Etowah's political history has a context that reaches beyond the Etowah site. Acknowledging this, I will examine archaeological information at three increasingly broader scales: the Etowah site, the Etowah River valley, and northern Georgia. Ultimately, it will become apparent that, while Etowah may provide valuable information for more general comparative studies of chiefdoms, its political development was part of a unique historical process that was closely linked to other people and centers across the Southeast.

Since much of this volume will be devoted to the identification of different organizational forms of chiefdoms and explaining changes in that organizational structure, I will dedicate the rest of this chapter to discussing chiefdom organizational variability, how chiefdoms can be identified in the archaeological record, and possible causes behind political change in chiefdoms.

CHIEFDOMS AND THEIR ORGANIZATIONAL VARIABILITY

As the title of this book shows, I use the term *chiefdom* to refer to the most common form of social organization found in the interior Southeast during the Mississippian period (A.D. 1000–1600). Over the past 20 years, the chiefdom concept (along with neoevolutionary classification schemes in general) has been criticized roundly for being arbitrarily defined, not representative of the actual variability in social groups exhibiting social ranking but lacking social stratification, and creating an emphasis on social classification (Feinman and Neitzel 1984; Spencer 1987). In a discipline that purports to be comparative in its approach, labels like *chiefdom,* when separated from undesirable connotations, serve the all-important purpose of facilitating comparison. Following other recent volumes dealing with North American chiefdoms (Anderson 1994; Blitz 1993; Knight and Steponaitis 1998; Milner 1998; Muller 1997; Pauketat 1994), I will use the term *chiefdom* while acknowledging the great variation in organization of societies that may be included in this category, and without the evolutionary undertones included in its original definition (see Service 1962).

The term *chiefdom* first came into use during the late 1950s (Oberg 1955; Steward and Faron 1959) and was most formally defined and applied as a general concept by Service (1962) in his influential work on the evolution of human social organization. Unlike less complexly organized social forms, chiefdoms are characterized by institutionalized social ranking and the presence of permanent political offices. Social ranking is guided by kinship rules and political leaders receive the right to rule by virtue of their birth. Since the office of chief is permanent, there is a certain amount of legitimacy and authority vested in the office that transcends the individual officeholder. Quite often the legitimacy of chiefly rule is sanctioned by a religious ideology, and chiefs often take pains to reinforce actively that legitimacy through conspicuous displays in terms of dress, consumption, and treatment. Unlike leaders in states, chiefs do not hold an institutionalized monopoly on the use of force. Although chiefs may have the greatest access to the use of force, there are usually several individuals or parts of society holding that right jointly (Earle 1973:27).

Redistribution was an integral part of the chiefdom form of organization, as it was originally defined. According to Service (1962:145–152), the redistributive economy developed out of the need to integrate settlements or social groups living in ecologically diverse settings. Labor and surplus were collected and pooled by the chief to be redistributed for the benefit of all members of the polity. More recently it has been recognized that most settlements in chiefdoms are relatively self-sufficient and do not re-quire redistribution to remain viable (Peebles and Kus 1977). There is no doubt that the chiefdom structure encourages surplus production and serves to mobilize that surplus. Quite often, however, surplus labor and production are not returned directly to the producers but are used to fund public construction, sponsor important feasts, support military ventures, and fund the conspicuous consumption of the chief. How much individual producers benefit from participation in the system depends in large part on the size and complexity of the chiefdom (Johnson and Earle 1987).

While several different classification schemes have been developed to account for the wide variation in chiefdom organization (Earle 1978; Goldman 1970; Sahlins 1958; Steponaitis 1978; Wright 1977), the most widely used classification system divides all chiefdoms into simple and complex forms (Anderson 1994; Earle 1978; Steponaitis 1978; Wright 1977). In general, the simple/complex chiefdom dichotomy is based on the number of levels, above the local community, in a chiefdom's political administrative hierarchy, but the definitions of each class of chiefdom also include some characterization of the polity's political economy. For example, according to Steponaitis (1978) simple chiefdoms have only one level of superordinate political office, and individuals who serve as chief are part-time administrators not exempt from subsistence production. Status differences between chiefs and commoners generally are not very great and usually are not accompanied by great differences in material wealth. In these polities a chief's household is expected to be self-sufficient, so surplus collected by the chief is usually distributed back to the contributing pro-ducers. In fact, as Steponaitis (1978:420) indicates, "The chief, in living up to his role as a superiorly generous kinsman, is often forced to give away more than he takes in, the difference being made up by his household hav-ing to work harder at production."

In contrast, complex chiefdoms have two or three levels in a political hierarchy, and elite statuses are clearly and markedly distinct from the status of commoner (Earle 1978; Steponaitis 1978; Wright 1977). Higher-ranking chiefs hold political authority over lesser chiefs, who in turn hold sway over particular territorial units. In complex chiefdoms, political control translates into a right to collect tribute, and tribute flows up the political hierarchy from the primary producers to the paramount chief. Because elites are exempt from subsistence production, the vast majority of surplus produce flowing up the political hierarchy is consumed by elites for subsistence needs or political ends. Consequently, little is left to be redistributed to primary producers. Obligations to reciprocate are fulfilled by the elites' performing religious or secular duties that commoners cannot, or by presentations that are more symbolic than substantive.

Recently, it has become increasingly apparent that there are different paths to political complexity, and those paths involve different political economic strategies designed to reproduce the political structure. Given this, I intend, as much as possible, to separate definitions of political complexity, based on number of levels in an administrative hierarchy, from the nature of the political economic strategy that produced and reproduces that particular political structure. Each will be examined separately as different elements of chiefdom organizational variability as I attempt to reconstruct and explain instances of political change in the chiefdoms of the Etowah valley.

Strictly in terms of political complexity, I will call a simple chiefdom a polity that has one level in its political administrative hierarchy (above the local community) and a complex chiefdom a polity that has two or three levels (above the local community) in its political administrative hierarchy. Chiefdoms are essentially political economies in which surplus labor and produce are mobilized, in some manner funneled through the political structure, and "spent" in ways that serve to reproduce that political structure. From this perspective, administrative hierarchies exist mainly to facilitate the mobilization of surplus. I agree with Muller (1997), who takes exception to the use of the term *tribute* to describe surplus mobilized by Southeastern chiefs, because it implies the presence of coercive power where such power may not have existed. Exactly how individual chiefs justified their right to mobilize and spend surplus was determined by the larger set of strategies they used to gain access to political authority.

Recent archaeological and ethnohistoric research in the southeastern United States suggests that it may be useful typologically to identify the paramount chiefdom as a specific kind of complex chiefdom (Hally et al. 1990; Hudson et al. 1985). Like other complex chiefdoms, paramountcies have two or three levels in their political administrative hierarchy, but they are defined on the basis of spatial parameters. These polities incorporate spatially discrete simple and complex chiefdoms into a single polity and often cover vast areas. For example, the sixteenth-century Coosa paramountcy located in northwestern Georgia and adjoining parts of Tennessee and Alabama consisted of 7 to 10 simple and complex chiefdoms and incorporated an area about 500 km in length (Hally et al. 1990).

Several researchers have suggested that the limit of effective political control in prestate political formations is dictated by transport and communication technology (Earle 1987; Hally 1993; Johnson 1982, 1987; Renfrew 1975; Steponaitis 1978). While the distance may differ given the nature of physical environments and available technology, this limit appears to be on the order of 20 km in many areas of the world where chiefdoms once existed (see Hally 1993). By incorporating spatially distinct polities over vast areas, paramount chiefdoms extend political authority beyond the limits up to which military force or exchange of bulk goods can be used to maintain sustained, direct political control.

Political complexity, expressed in terms of the number of administrative levels, does not necessarily correlate with the degree of centralization in political decision making. Muller (1997, 1998) has argued that Mississippian chiefdoms were not as centralized as some models of complex chiefdoms might suggest. Using ethnohistoric evidence from the sixteenth century and historical information from the seventeenth and eighteenth centuries, he shows that few Southeastern chiefs exercised power as individuals. At least during the Protohistoric and early Historic periods, most important decisions were made only after consultation with other important members of society (presumably representatives of constituent corporate groups or polities). It has long been recognized that chiefs, regardless of the size of their polity, needed the backing of supporting populations for political decisions (Service 1962). Even in Hawaii, which may have developed into one of the most centralized chiefdoms described historically, exalted chiefs could not maintain policies that did not have the support of the common people (Kirch 1984). Southeastern chiefs operated under the same constraints. Ultimately, however, the degree to which political decision making is controlled by a few individuals or a larger corporate body will depend on the strategies used by leaders to access and maintain sources of power and control.

Blanton et al. (1996) have recently argued that all strategies used in the maintenance and exercise of political authority can be divided into two general categories. They refer to these as network and corporate strategies, with the former being exclusive and competitive and the latter being inclusive and integrated. While these strategies are not necessarily mutually exclusive within any social formation, one usually becomes dominant in the operation of the political structure. As Blanton et al. (1996) outline, these different strategies have different legitimizing ideologies and require political actors to use surplus labor and produce in different ways to reproduce the political structure. As a result, the nature of the strategy used will affect surplus production and mobilization, the actions of political leaders, and the content of the legitimizing ideology. Given this, the political economic approach employed will have important implications for the overall organization of polities, how that organization is materialized and reflected in the archaeological record, and the nature of the causal factors that may transform it.

In the network strategy, individual political actors reach preeminence by creating or tapping into networks of social ties. Through these social ties, individuals gain access to knowledge, prestige goods, and labor that are used to establish or maintain political control. In most respects, polities organized around this strategy correspond to Renfrew's (1974) conception of individualizing chiefdoms. The application of a network strategy usually leads to the development of a prestige-goods system in which scarce or technologically complex goods are substituted for food or utilitarian items as important elements in social reproduction and intergroup exchange. Elites then attempt to monopolize access to the prestige goods and the political advantage gained from their manipulation. Fundamentally, this approach is an example of wealth finance as defined by D'Altroy and Earle (1985). In the network strategy, the ability of individuals to easily shift allegiance to competing factions in a social network is limited through an ideology stressing strong household, descent, or ethnic ties, while the appropriation of produce and labor and differential access to prestige goods are justified by a strong system of ranked corporate groups. Blanton et al. (1996) refer to these structures as patrimonial rhetoric.

Where the network strategy becomes successful, individual participants become not only exchange partners but also competitors for political domination over other network participants. Under these circumstances, a shared symbolic vocabulary, or what Blanton et al. (1996) call an international style, often develops. The international style facilitates the movement of goods and information across social boundaries and serves as a marker of elite status recognizable in local polities and in the wider network. While possessing widespread similarities in symbolism, international styles have no single center of origin, and no single political center controls their content.

Polities structured through a network strategy are likely to exhibit greater differences in individual wealth and prestige, and individual leaders are likely to be highly visible because a great deal of the mobilized surplus will be used to aggrandize them. Prestige goods are likely to figure prominently in these efforts, and, as a result, the fate of individual leaders and their polities may be affected by changes in access to prestige goods. In general, network polities will tend to be unstable and more likely to go through cycles of formation and dissolution. This is because the exclusionary tactics of leaders encourage factionalism and competition between political actors within and outside of local polities. Also, other actors in the networks that provide social power can be unpredictable, making it difficult for leaders to control those sources of power. Because the network strategy emphasizes the individual, political viability also will be directly affected by the abilities of leaders. Finally, network polities are likely to be more limited in scale because their legitimizing ideologies are exclusive and difficult to extend over great distances to incorporate diverse social groups.

Corporate approaches are more inclusive and emphasize the importance of the social group at the expense of individual wealth and status. Fundamental to these kinds of strategies is "a cognitive code that emphasizes a corporate solidarity of society as an integrated whole, based on natural and immutable interdependence between subgroups, and in more complex societies, between rulers and subjects" (Blanton et al. 1996:6). Conceptually, polities operating within a corporate strategy correspond to Renfrew's (1974) group-oriented chiefdoms. These kinds of polities are capable of achieving a high degree of political complexity and creating massive public works, but the approach to meeting those ends is decidedly group-oriented in nature. Within these systems, hierarchically graded roles and statuses are defined and organized so as to limit the importance of individual achievement in political preeminence, thereby thwarting the effort of individuals to dominate the political system. Rather than relying on personal wealth and prestige-goods consumption, corporate political economies are based in what D'Altroy and Earle (1985) call staple finance, which is the production and mobilization of food, tools, and other utilitarian craft items.

Corporate polities are likely to exhibit fewer wealth and status differences, and political leaders as important personages will be less visible archaeologically. Prestige goods are likely to be relatively unimportant, and mobilized surplus will be used to create large spaces for communal, solidarity-building activities. Since mobilization of staples forms the primary basis for the political economy, corporate polities are more likely to be associated with innovations in subsistence technology and subsistence production intensification. Where the limits of intensification are few corporate polities are more likely to expand, while in areas where the potential for intensification is limited so is the potential for political expansion. Corporate polities are also more likely to be destabilized by subsistence shortfalls due to environmental fluctuations or overexploitation, or overturned by overburdened supporting populations. Overall, however, corporately organized polities are likely to be more stable because they limit factionalism by promoting social solidarity and institutionally limiting the ability of individuals to control sources of power. In addition, compared with network polities, corporate strategies are more likely to be associated with larger and more expansive polities. This is because the corporate strategy is based on an inclusive ideology, stressing transcendent themes like world renewal, which can more easily accommodate elements of other ideologies and facilitate the incorporation of diverse groups.

RECOGNIZING THE POLITICAL
COMPLEXITY OF CHIEFDOMS

As the discussion above indicates, in attempting to reconstruct and explain sequences of political change, I will focus on two elements of chiefdom organizational variability: political complexity and political economic strategies. By political complexity I mean the number of levels in the administrative structure above the local community, which is used to differentiate simple from complex chiefdoms. A great many studies have attempted to identify chiefdoms in the archaeological record, and out of these efforts have come a series of archaeological correlates of chiefdoms (Creamer and Haas 1985; Earle 1987; Peebles and Kus 1977; Renfrew 1973; Wright 1984). The most important of these include ascribed social ranking, which may be visible in the mortuary record as well as in the size and location of residential architecture; a well-defined decision-making hierarchy reflected in settlement hierarchies; and supra-household mobilization of surplus labor and produce utilized for the good of the political structure.

Comparatively fewer studies have focused specifically on differentiating between simple and complex chiefdoms, and in the majority of those cases settlement data provided the primary means of reconstructing political complexity (Hally 1993; Kowalewski et al. 1989; Peebles and Kus 1977; Renfrew 1973; Sanders and Price 1968). In the following chapters, I also will rely primarily on settlement data to identify organizationally different forms of chiefdoms. Because of the nature of paramount chiefdoms, it may not be possible to recognize them using settlement data alone (Hally et al. 1990). Therefore as an additional means of identifying the political structure of paramount chiefdoms, I will use changes in the composition of ceramic assemblages at each of the political centers in the Etowah River valley. The rationale behind these approaches is outlined below.

Settlement Data

In the southeastern United States, it is generally accepted that Mississippian period mounds functioned as important civic-ceremonial structures, and sites with platform mounds represented social and political capitals of chiefdoms (Hally 1996). Ethnohistoric accounts make it clear that the residences of chiefs and temples for chiefly ancestors were placed on mounds (DePratter 1991), and archaeological evidence shows that elites in Mississippian society were preferentially buried in or near mounds (Hatch 1974; Larson 1971a; Peebles and Kus 1977). Hally (1996:97) sums up the critical importance of mounds to Southeastern chiefs in the following statement:

> His exalted status was symbolized by the location of his residence on top of the mound. His divine nature was demonstrated by the bones of his ancestors stored in the mortuary temple located on the mound. Succession to the office of chief may have been symbolized by the addition of mound stages and rebuilding of summit structures. And a number of the duties that he had as chief were carried out on the mound or in temple structures on its summit. In short, the platform mound and accompanying summit structures were essential elements of the chief's role as political and religious leader, and they served to legitimize and sanctify the office of chief and the incumbent's claim to that position.

Given the clear significance of mounds to chiefs, Hally (1993, 1996) has argued that chiefdoms in the Southeast did not exist or exist for long without a mound. Following this logic, the presence of a mound can be used to infer the existence of a prehistoric chiefdom and identify its capital. Further, when mound site hierarchies are constructed that reflect the place of those sites in an administrative network (Peebles and Kus 1977), it is possible to differentiate simple from complex chiefdoms. Simple chiefdoms will have only one political capital (mound site), while complex chiefdoms will have two or three levels of political capitals.

Without some sense of the spatial extent of polities, however, it is difficult to use settlement hierarchies to identify individual chiefdoms. As I noted above, several researchers have argued that the costs of travel and transport limit the spatial extent of effective control over territories in prestate political organizations such as chiefdoms (Earle 1987; Johnson 1982, 1987; Renfrew 1975; Steponaitis 1978). In several different parts of the world, this spatial limit appears to be about 25 to 40 km. For example, in the Middle Formative of the Oaxcaca valley (Kowalewski et al. 1989), the Late Early Horizon and Early Intermediate Horizon in the Santa valley of Peru (Wilson 1988), and the Early Uruk period in southwestern Iran (Johnson 1982, 1987), clusters of sites representing political units measure 25 to 40 km across. Similarly, the average distance separating highest-order centers in Minoan period Crete (Renfrew 1975), the Late Classic period in the southeastern Peten (Hammond 1979), and sixteenth-century Panama (Helms 1979) was also approximately 40 km.

Looking for similar patterns in the spacing of Mississippian political capitals, Hally (1993) examined the straight-line distances between 47 mound sites in northern Georgia. Of that total, 37 had construction stages that were documented and dated through archaeological investigation. All but two were separated by intervals less than 18 km or greater than 32 km. In an attempt to include more mound sites in the study, Hally also examined the distances separating mound sites with contemporary occupations, but not necessarily documented contemporary mound stages. Out of the 141 pairs of contemporary sites examined, 117 adhered to the same spacing pattern.

Using these data, Hally suggests that mound sites separated by distances less than 18 km are, in most cases, administrative centers of a single polity, while those separated by distances greater than 32 km are members of distinct polities. He also acknowledges that the distances separating administrative centers in some of the largest and most powerful chiefdoms may have been as great as 22 km. On the basis of these conclusions, Hally further argues that throughout much of the Mississippian Southeast simple chiefdoms may be identified by the presence of a single-mound site separated from all others by more than 18 km and usually at least 32 km. In contrast, complex chiefdoms can be identified by the presence of two or more mound sites separated by distances that may be as great as 22 km for the most powerful polities, but usually will be less than 18 km.

The spacing of Mississippian administrative centers, according to Hally (1993), reflects the spatial limits placed on effective control in chiefdoms. The exercise of control by chiefs and the participation in the system by supporting populations require a great deal of travel and communication. In order to maintain political influence over subordinates, chiefs often rely on some combination of coercion, gift giving, and demonstration of supernatural and secular powers (Brumfiel and Earle 1987; Earle 1987; Hally 1993), and this often requires travel on the part of chiefs and their representatives. The greater the distance becomes between administrative centers and supporting populations, the more expensive and less effective that political control becomes (Hally 1993; Johnson 1982). Similarly, for supporters to contribute surplus produce and labor and participate in ritual activities, travel and communication also are necessary. As Steponaitis (1978) has shown, when the distance between administrative centers and supporting populations becomes greater, the cost of participating in such a social system increases and the intensity of that participation decreases.

Blitz (1999) points out that some of the patterns in mound distributions found by Hally (1993) do not fit the settlement models for simple and complex chiefdoms. For example, paired or grouped single-mound sites (separated by distances less than 18 km), where there is no evidence for a settlement hierarchy, could be either sequentially occupied capitals of a simple chiefdom or contemporary capitals in a complex chiefdom. In addition, Blitz suggests that isolated multiple-mound sites, because of the amount of civic-ceremonial architecture they possess, seem to indicate the presence of a complex chiefdom, but the associated settlement hierarchy is not apparent.

While Blitz (1999) acknowledges that our ability to interpret these patterns may be a result of temporal control, he suggests they may be explained better as the result of a fission-fusion process such as was witnessed in operation during the Historic period (see Willis 1980). In this process, political units might fuse and fission as a result of demographic pressures, antagonism between constituent units, or hostile relations with other political units in the region. After splintering from the "mother" polity, political units might attach themselves to another, powerful polity, mainly out of concerns for protection. Each political unit within the new polity would maintain its own civic-ceremonial space, consisting of a square ground and round house. Sometimes these might be located in separate settlements in close proximity to each other, and at other times they may have even been in the same settlement.

Taking the Historic period analogy further, Blitz (1999) suggests that Mississippian mounds are analogous to Historic period square ground/round house complexes and, by extension, that each mound represents an associated political unit. From this perspective, clusters of single-mound sites may represent the agglomeration of political units, and isolated multiple-mound sites may represent the same social situation except all units are centralized into one settlement. Rather than being a complex chiefdom with hierarchical relations between the political units, Blitz argues, like Historic period political formations, the polities actually may have been confederacies with fairly egalitarian relations between constituent political units. He goes on to suggest that many of the polities identified as complex chiefdoms actually represent these confederacies on the way to consolidation or in the process of breaking apart.

While I agree that fission and fusion were quite likely commonly applied solutions to certain problems that arose during the Mississippian period, attributing certain "anomalous" mound distributions to confederacies rather than simple or complex chiefdoms mixes distinct elements of political organization (complexity and political economy) that would be better left separate. Essentially, Blitz's model describes possible outcomes in the fusion of political units that operate under a corporate political economic strategy. It seems clear that the strategies used by Historic period leaders, out of which came the confederacies on which Blitz bases his model, were distinctly corporate in nature.

It is entirely conceivable, as the Historic period information discussed by Blitz shows, that as political units following a corporate strategy coalesced, they might maintain distinct, but roughly equivalent civic-ceremonial spaces. If this occurred, in some cases those spaces could have been integrated into one political capital, while in others they remained in separate centers. These behaviors would reflect the inclusive and accommodating nature of corporate strategies. It is important to remember, however, that hierarchy can exist within corporately organized structures, but it is masked by material egalitarianism and ideologies expressing hierarchy as part of an immutable natural order. Even in Historic period groups, where red and white moieties were complementary parts of a larger whole, the white moiety was ranked above the red moiety (Knight 1990).

Separate from the strategy that served to create these polities is their degree of political complexity. In the case in which several political units co-locate their civic-ceremonial spaces in one political capital, the effective result would be the creation of a political administrative hierarchy with a single level above the local community—a simple chiefdom. Similarly, I would argue that in cases in which political units come together to form a new chiefdom, but maintain separate civic-ceremonial complexes, a complex chiefdom would be formed. If the individual units were to act together as a polity, then one settlement would have to serve as the location where polity-wide decisions were made and political action was taken. The resulting administrative hierarchy would have two levels above the local community, and would thus constitute a complex chiefdom.

Schroedl (1998) has raised more general concerns about the use of settlement data, especially the distribution of mound and non-mound sites, to identify prehistoric chiefdoms. This argument is based on Baden's (1987) modeling of Mississippian period agricultural production in eastern Tennessee, which suggests that most Mississippian settlements moved about every 50 to 150 years because of soil depletion and crop failures. Because of these periodic moves, sites assigned to the same archaeological phase may represent sequentially occupied settlements used by the same population rather than contemporary sites. Logically, our ability to recognize settlement shifts should be directly related to the length of archaeological phases. In eastern Tennessee, where Schroedl's critique is directed, Mississippian phases are fairly long, lasting sometimes up to 300 years. In the Etowah valley and throughout much of northern Georgia, however, Mississippian period phases generally last from 50 to 100 years and should therefore be

short enough to capture many of the settlement moves precipitated by ecological factors as modeled by Baden (1987).

In general, Schroedl's critique is a good one. Settlements may have
moved for a variety of reasons, many of which are social and not environmental (see Blitz 1999; Williams and Shapiro 1990), and, because of the
length of phases, those shifts may be impossible to detect in the archaeological record. Given the regular spatial patterning in mound sites identified by Hally (1993, 1996), and the fact that similar spatial parameters hold
for prestate complex societies around the world, the issue of strict contemporaneity does not seem to impact the usefulness of settlement data in lo-
cating prehistoric chiefdoms. It may, in some cases, affect their usefulness
in distinguishing between simple and complex chiefdoms. For example, it
could be argued that mound sites located within 18 km of each other actually represent serially occupied centers of a simple chiefdom rather than
primary and secondary centers in a complex chiefdom. Ultimately, the
problem of contemporaneity has the potential to affect all settlement system studies in archaeology. I, presumably like the many other archaeologists who employ settlement data, take the perspective that only in constructing, applying, and evaluating models that account for regularities in
our data can we advance the goals of archaeological research. Therefore, I
think it is more productive to use a model that assumes general contemporaneity of sites dating to the same phase rather than to abandon the use of
settlement data altogether.

Keeping issues of contemporaneity in mind, I will use Hally's (1993,
1996) spatial models of simple and complex chiefdoms to reconstruct the
political complexity of chiefdoms. I will identify a mound site (single or
multiple mounds) 18 km or more from any other as the capital of a simple
chiefdom. Similarly, when two or more mound sites are located within
18 km of each other, and one is larger and more complex than the others,
I will identify that polity as being a complex chiefdom. In instances where
two or more mound sites of equal size and complexity are located within
18 km of one another, and there are no reasons to doubt contemporaneity,
I will tentatively identify this as a complex chiefdom.

PARAMOUNT CHIEFDOMS AND THEIR IDENTIFICATION

Paramount chiefdoms are essentially complex chiefdoms that have suc-
ceeded in extending political authority beyond the limits of direct political
control imposed by transport and communication technologies. The paramount chiefdom concept was first defined using sixteenth-century descriptions of expansive chiefdoms encountered in the interior Southeast by Spanish explorers (DePratter et al. 1985; Hally et al. 1990; Hudson 1990, 1997;

Hudson et al. 1985). Those descriptions indicate that sixteenth-century Southeastern paramountcies existed in a highly competitive atmosphere in which individual chiefs and their supporters vied with one another, through alliance and warfare, for regional political dominance (Anderson 1994). Essentially, these paramountcies were held together through personal relationships between individual chiefs, and, as a result, were weakly integrated and relatively unstable (Hally et al. 1990).

It appears that leaders of sixteenth-century Southeastern paramount chiefdoms relied on a network political economic strategy to reproduce their political structures (King 1999). Because these particular chiefdoms were used to define the paramount chiefdom concept, there may be the tendency to attribute similar organizational characteristics to all paramount chiefdoms. It is conceivable, however, that paramountcies might also form from the application of a corporate strategy. In such a circumstance, the polity is likely to be integrated by an inclusive ideology that ties disparate groups together as complementary elements in a unified natural order. Blanton et al. (1996) argue that such a polity based in a corporate structure might actually be more stable because of the inclusive rather than exclusive nature of the corporate strategy.

Analyses of the settlement systems of Southeastern paramount chiefdoms like the Coosa paramountcy (Hally et al. 1990) indicate that the distribution of political capitals may not provide clues to the existence of an overarching political structure (Blitz 1999; Hally et al. 1990). For example, the capital of the Coosa paramountcy was neither the largest and most complex mound center nor the only multiple-mound center in the polity (Hally et al. 1990). According to Hally (Hally 1994; Hally et al. 1990), paramount chiefdom administrative structures are not reflected in settlement systems because paramountcies were weakly integrated and unstable, and therefore rarely lasted long enough to impact settlement distributions.

Given the potential that corporately organized paramountcies are more stable, it is possible that their administrative structure might be visible in settlement distributions. The Cahokia complex chiefdom, which Trubitt (2000) argues was based on a corporate strategy, may represent one possible example of such a polity. According to Milner (1990, 1998), the Cahokia political system incorporated a series of political centers and their associated populations distributed over a 100-km stretch of the Mississippi River valley. In Cahokia's settlement system, the Cahokia site is by far the largest and most complex center, surrounded by dozens of politically equivalent secondary centers apparently positioned to take advantage of ecologically favorable locales (Milner 1998). At least to the south, the boundary of that system can be discerned by a gap in settlement as well as a marked difference in pottery decorative style (Milner 1990). This gap may represent a buffer zone like those described by early Spanish explorers in the Southeast (Hudson 1997). If Cahokia was a corporately organized paramountcy, then it may provide a model for such a polity's settlement hierarchy: one massive political center, surrounded by a series of secondary centers continuously distributed across a large area, and flanked at its edges by a buffer zone.

As the above discussion indicates, it may not be possible, especially in the case of network-oriented polities, to identify all paramount chiefdoms with the use of settlement data alone. Because of this potential problem, I will look to economic patterns as an additional means of recognizing paramount political structures. Chiefdoms are not just political entities, they are whole social systems in which political activities are not separable from religious and economic undertakings. In these systems, chiefs and their capitals hold religious and economic importance as well as political importance. Chiefs derive much of their authority by being living intermediaries between the secular and supernatural worlds, and they maintain their legitimacy through the manipulation of flows of goods and labor (Earle 1987, 1991).

As a result, chiefdom capitals were focal points for flows of goods and information as people gathered for ritual, warfare, or important political occasions. As the political roles of individual political centers changed through time, so too did the intensity and direction of these flows, and such changes should be reflected in the composition of ceramic assemblages. Therefore, as an additional means of identifying the formation of paramount chiefdoms, I will use changes in the composition of pottery assemblages from political centers. The rationale behind this approach will be discussed in more detail in Chapter 5.

IDENTIFYING POLITICAL ECONOMIC STRATEGIES

In addition to political complexity, another important element of chiefdom political structures is the strategy used by leaders to access sources of political authority. The nature of the strategy used can affect the structure and stability of the polity, as well as the character of its material record. As a result, I will attempt to reconstruct those strategies as part of my effort to understand political change in the Etowah valley. To do this, I will rely on Blanton et al.'s (1996) distinctions between network and corporate strategies. It is important to stress that the corporate/network distinction does not define types of societies. It is meant to describe general categories of strategies used by political leaders, each potentially capturing a wide range of variation.

Based on Blanton et al.'s (1996) characterization, the following material correlates can be expected of polities operating within a network strategy. In general, there will be marked differences in wealth and prestige between elites and non-elites, and these differences will be most visible in material possessions and the location and elaborateness of architecture and mortuary treatments. Political leaders are likely to be conspicuously visible in these data. Leaders also will be closely associated with nonlocal materials, symbols, or architectural styles, indicating the importance of external contacts to the maintenance of political authority. In many cases, such items may be prestige goods and they also are likely to be recognizable as elements of an international style. Additionally, public works projects, especially monuments, will be designed to aggrandize individual leaders and their kin groups.

In contrast, polities based in a corporate strategy are likely to exhibit fewer differences in wealth and status, as reflected in mortuary programs, material possessions, and architectural arrangements. Mortuary treatments will have a distinctly communal orientation, and public works, especially monuments, will be focused on the creation of large communal spaces. As a result, political leaders will be relatively invisible. Important people or social segments are more likely to be associated, through symbolism or material possessions, with the manipulation of agricultural produce and crafts rather than exotica and prestige goods. Finally, nonlocal goods, symbols, and styles are less likely to be conspicuously associated with leaders.

One of the easiest criticisms to level against the corporate/network distinction is that it is merely a classification scheme that masks important variability in political economies. The corporate and network models do in fact represent a classification framework that, by its very nature, ignores variation. These general models were not developed to replace detailed studies of individual political economies. They were designed as a framework for recognizing different categories of political economies that are structured along different organizing principles. Those organizing principles represent an important axis of variation in human societies that has important implications for the structure and exercise of political control. The corporate/network distinction is merely a classification scheme if it is used only for classification and not for making interpretations or generalizations.

In using these models to understand chiefdom political economies in the Etowah valley, my greatest limitation is the quality of data available. At Etowah, most information about the site has been derived from excavations conducted on or near the mounds. Outside of Etowah, investigations at other mound sites also have focused almost entirely on mound contexts, and there is little information from non-mound sites. While these data are in no way sufficient to reconstruct a full understanding of individual political economic systems, in most cases enough information is available to construct a general characterization of the kinds of principles that organize those systems.

UNDERSTANDING POLITICAL CHANGE IN CHIEFDOMS

In addition to attempting to identify instances of political change, I am also concerned in this volume with suggesting some possible causes of that political change. It is now widely recognized that chiefdoms are relatively unstable political formations (see Earle 1987, 1991; Wright 1984). They have a marked tendency to form, collapse, and reform (Hally 1996), or to cycle between levels of political complexity (Anderson 1994; Wright 1984). Over the past decade, Southeastern archaeologists have focused a great deal of effort on discovering the causes behind this instability and specific instances of political change (Anderson 1990, 1994; Hally 1993, 1996; Milner 1998; Pauketat 1994; Pauketat and Emerson 1997; Scarry 1990, 1996; Williams and Shapiro 1990). Anderson's (1994) exhaustive treatment of the subject has demonstrated that the list of possible causes is long and varied. In most cases, however, those causes can be grouped into one of four broader categories of potential causal factors, including environment and population, ideology, factional competition, and regional interaction.

   Of these potential causes of political change, those relating to environment and population have the longest history of use in anthropology. In these explanations, demographic shifts, increases or decreases in subsistence productivity, and changes in resource availability bring about political change by providing or denying a chiefdom the people and produce needed to function or expand. For example, Milner (1998) has argued that the differential productivity of local environments led to the development of chiefdoms in the American Bottom. Those social groups situated on more productive lands had access to more surplus labor and produce, which was used to extend dominance over less advantageously located groups through military might and the appeal of surplus foods in times of localized food shortages. Following a related line of reasoning, Anderson (1994) has argued that repeated years of poor harvests as a result of lower than average rainfall in the Savannah River valley led to the eventual abandonment of the valley after A.D. 1450. In this case, chiefdoms dissolved as supporting populations lost confidence in their leaders and gravitated toward other centers of power in the region.

   More recently, archaeologists have become interested in the impacts that

regional interaction has on political formations. In many cases, these investigations have been conducted within the context of economic models like
the prestige-goods system (Steponaitis 1991; Welch 1991) and world-system
theory (King and Freer 1995; Kowalewski 1996; Peregrine 1992, 1995,
1996), or broader regional models like Peer-Polity Interaction (McKivergan
1995). Although activities such as the exchange of staple and wealth items,
armed hostilities, and marriage exchanges all constitute kinds of interactions that occurred at the regional scale, warfare and the exchange of prestige goods appear most often as being potential causes of political change
in chiefdoms. For example, Welch (1991:190–197; see also Steponaitis 1991)
has suggested that a loss of access to prestige goods may have contributed
to the collapse of the Moundville complex chiefdom. Similarly, Steponaitis
(1991) has suggested that the reason polities in the Big Black River valley
of Mississippi did not develop into complex chiefdoms is that the growing
Moundville polity diverted away from the region flows of prestige goods
needed by elites to consolidate regional authority. According to Helms
(1979:35–36), many paramount chiefs in sixteenth-century Panama gained
their positions of authority because their polities were located to take advantage of flows of status goods or valued raw materials. Payne and Scarry
(1998) offer a similar explanation for the emergence of the complex chiefdom associated with the Lake Jackson site in Florida. Elites at Lake Jackson were positioned at the interface between the Mississippian and non-
Mississippian worlds, allowing them to parlay control of flows of prestige
goods and information between the two areas into political control.

Archaeologists in the Southeast and elsewhere also have turned to factional competition as a potential cause of political change in chiefdoms
(Anderson 1990, 1994; Brumfiel and Fox 1994; Hally 1993; Scarry 1996).
This interest stems from the recognition that in most chiefdoms, as well as
other centralized political structures, there will always exist competing
claims to positions of political control. The result is competition between
elites and their supporters, both within individual polities and on the regional stage, as they vie with one another for access to positions of authority, or as subjugated populations attempt to break free from overarching political control. Warfare, feasting, prestige-goods exchange, and
marriage exchanges are all interactions that may occur as part of factional
competition.

This factional competition can provide the impetus for increasing political centralization, as leaders attempt to keep their competitors at bay
through expansion. The early seventeenth-century Powhatan paramountcy
apparently was assembled through some combination of threat, warfare,
and alliance in the Coastal Plain of Virginia (Rountree 1989). This same

competition may also serve to dissolve these larger polities. Traditional accounts of the political history of Hawaii contain many instances in which larger polities were broken apart by factional competition within chiefly lineages, and this often coincided with the rule of chiefs who were excessively demanding of the commoners (Kirch 1984:261). Similarly, historical documents indicate that the Napochies, a subjugated polity in the sixteenth-century Coosa paramount chiefdom, attempted to break away from paramount control in 1564, only to be put back in their place with the help of Spanish soldiers (DePratter et al. 1985).

Finally, ideology and its manipulation also have been identified in many cases as the cause of political change. Political leaders in chiefdoms rely on ideology to legitimize their authority and right to appropriate surplus. In addition, the nature of that ideology determines the actions that leaders must undertake in order to reproduce their political roles and the ideology. Therefore, the emergence of chiefdoms may occur as would-be leaders promote an ideology that supports their preeminence and their right to use of surplus labor and produce. Similarly, increases in political complexity may result as leaders reformulate existing ideologies to intensify surplus production and its mobilization, which is then used to expand their political authority. Alternatively, decreases in political complexity or total collapse of a chiefdom may result as intensified demands for surplus lead to environmental degradation or dissatisfaction of supporting populations. Also, ideological structures that rely on the abilities of individual leaders and encourage competitive interactions with elites in a wider region will create factionalism within polities and in the wider region that may result in the unseating of individual rulers and the collapse of polities.

One particular version of this perspective, which incorporates agency theory and Gramsci's (1971) concept of hegemony, has been championed by Pauketat (1992, 1994, 1998; Pauketat and Emerson 1997) in his explanation of the rise and eventual fall of Cahokia. According to Pauketat, the political consolidation that created the Cahokia complex chiefdom occurred only after an ideology supporting the political dominance of elites at Cahokia was widely accepted by other social groups in the American Bottom. This ideology legitimized the rule and right of Cahokia's elite to appropriate surplus labor and produce. According to this perspective, ideologies become dominant not through force but through accommodation and reconciliation with alternative ideologies, a process that occurs within the context of ritual. Following a related line of reasoning, Nassaney (1992) has argued that the demise of social ranking in the Plum Bayou culture of Arkansas was ultimately caused by the failure of emerging elites to completely replace an ideological structure based in kinship with one that allowed appropriation of surplus produce and labor outside of the strictures of kinship obligations.

POLITICAL ECONOMY AND THE REGIONAL PERSPECTIVE IN IDENTIFYING CHANGE IN THE ETOWAH VALLEY

In attempting to understand political change in the Etowah River valley, rather than choosing a single set of related causes a priori, I intend to take a broader perspective. Chiefdoms are essentially political economies that consist of three important elements: (1) surplus labor and produce, (2) the decisions and actions of political leaders, and (3) an ideology that supports that political structure. Ideology serves to rationalize social ranking and the political and social advantages that accompany it. That ideology is reproduced by the actions of political leaders, who perform the functions and roles prescribed by the ideology. Those actions, such as feasting, funding public works, orchestrating important ritual, conducting warfare, directing the production and exchange of prestige goods, and so on are all in turn funded by mobilized surplus produce and labor. Therefore, anything that impacts the production of surplus, a leader's ability to mobilize surplus, a leader's ability to perform his/her specified duties for society, or the ideological structures that justify the leader's position and ability to mobilize surplus has the potential to bring about political change.

Only rarely does environmental change alone affect the elements of chiefdom political economies listed above. In most cases, it is the decisions of people acting as members of social groups that serve to transform their own social structure and that of others. From this perspective, social change is rooted in those elements of a social formation that encourage people to act in ways that bring about change. Chiefdoms have centralized decision-making structures wherein the right to make certain polity-wide decisions is willingly granted by supporting populations to a limited segment of society. Since that social segment is responsible for making decisions that affect the operation of the political structure, their actions (and the reactions of supporting populations) should be the ultimate source of political change. Therefore, in attempting to understand political change in the Etowah valley, I will pay close attention to the nature of political economic strategies used and how they may have served to create political change.

I (King and Freer 1995), along with others (Kowalewski 1996; Peregrine 1992, 1995), have argued that the Mississippian period Southeast was an interconnected system of social groups that can be best understood as a world-system. Although world-systems ideas have great potential to help archaeologists understand prehistoric social change, few researchers have explicitly embraced the perspective. Peregrine (1996) argues that this is because archaeologists have confused the world-system perspective with world-system theory. The former is a way of viewing social groups and social change that emphasizes the importance of economic interdependencies between autonomous social units created through sustained interaction. The latter defines the nature of the interactions creating interdependencies.

From this perspective, there may be many world-system theories that define many different types of world-systems. Wallerstein's (1974) theory was defined to understand the development and operation of the modern capitalist world-system, and as such is not appropriate for understanding other world-systems not based in capitalist accumulation (see Schortman and Urban 1987:58–59). To facilitate general world-system theory building, Chase-Dunn and Hall (1991, 1993; Hall and Chase-Dunn 1996) have recently reformulated many of Wallerstein's original concepts so that they may be used in the creation of general world-system theory.

They define world-systems as "intersocietal networks in which the interaction (trade, warfare, intermarriage, information, etc.) is an important condition of the reproduction of the internal structures of the composite units and importantly affects changes which occur in these local structures" (Hall and Chase-Dunn 1996:13). While non-capitalist world-systems will have differentiated cores and peripheries, the relations between them may not always be hierarchical and exploitative (Chase-Dunn and Hall 1991:18–19; Hall and Chase-Dunn 1996). In addition, the interdependencies between cores and peripheries in non-capitalist settings may be created by interactions besides the exchange of bulk goods, such as the exchange of wealth items or prestige goods (Kristiansen 1987; Peregrine 1992; Schneider 1977), warfare, intermarriage, or information flows (Chase-Dunn and Hall 1993; Hall and Chase-Dunn 1996; King and Freer 1995; Kowalewski 1996).

The Mississippian Southeast was one such non-capitalist world-system (King and Freer 1995; Kowalewski 1996; Peregrine 1992, 1995). It consisted of the area traditionally defined as the Mississippian culture area, but also included, at varying times, non-Mississippian regions like central Florida and portions of the Plains, the Upper Midwest, and the Middle Atlantic (see Kowalewski 1996). Included within this system were simple and complex chiefdoms, spatially extensive paramount chiefdoms, and, at the edges of the system, less complexly organized societies that may have even gone through cycles of centralization and decentralization. The impetus for interaction was determined by the nature of the prevailing political economic strategies used by leaders, but, in general, prestige-goods exchange and political-military conflict (warfare and alliance formation) were the most important for linking social groups (King and Freer 1995; Kowalewski 1996; Peregrine 1992, 1995). Core-periphery differentiation was rooted in demography, character of local environmental settings, and access to exchange routes and prestige goods. Dominance of cores, if achieved, was likely expressed in terms of political domination, and, given the instability of chiefdoms in general, was likely to be short-lived and tenuous (see Hall and Chase-Dunn 1996).

In order to be a system, its parts had to be linked through flows of energy, matter, or information, and they had to be interdependent. That matter flowed across these areas is indicated by the widespread distribution of pottery vessels, a variety of raw materials (Brown 1985; Brown et al. 1990), and numerous decorative styles (Brown 1989; Phillips and Brown 1978). Evidence for the flow of information is equally abundant in the form of widespread symbolic themes, such as world renewal as seen in mound construction (Knight 1986, 1990), falcon imagery (Brown 1976; Phillips and Brown 1978; Waring and Holder 1945), and rattlesnake representations (Brain and Phillips 1996; Hally et al. 1990). Information flow is also indicated by the apparent existence of a shared architectural grammar of Mississippian towns (Lewis and Stout 1998).

In addition, for the world-system perspective to be relevant, that system of interconnected social groups must also be interdependent, such that change in one part of the world-system has the potential to cause change in other parts. The most compelling way to demonstrate that interdependence is through what Kowalewski (1996) has called concordant, macroregional change. One of the most dramatic instances of concordant change in this region was the emergence of social ranking, which occurred widely after A.D. 900–1000 (see Smith 1990). Another was the appearance at around A.D. 1250 of a shared suite of symbolic themes and ceremonial objects, associated with the Southeastern Ceremonial Complex, along with extensive exchange networks that served to distribute those goods widely (Brown 1976, 1985, 1989; Phillips and Brown 1978). The disappearance of large, multiple-mound political centers after A.D. 1450 may be yet another example of concordant change in the Mississippian world-system (Anderson 1994; King 1996).

If it is accepted that the Mississippian Southeast constituted a connected world-system, then individual polities and their leaders were linked to others in the region through exchange and political-military conflict. Therefore, while political economic strategies were applied by local political actors, the implications of their decisions reached beyond the local polity to the wider region. Given this, in order to understand the causes of political change in the Etowah valley, it will be important to view those polities and their associated political economic strategies within the context of a larger regional system. For my purposes here, I will not attempt to include the entire Mississippian system, but will limit my investigation to northern Georgia and adjacent portions of surrounding states.

THE CHAPTERS THAT FOLLOW

In the chapters that follow, I apply the theoretical and methodological approaches discussed above to reconstruct and understand political change in the Etowah River valley. Chapter 2 presents the natural, temporal, and archaeological context of Etowah River valley Mississippian and includes a summary of archaeological research conducted at all mound sites in the valley. Because so much work has been done at Etowah and so little of it has been published, Chapter 3 will focus exclusively on the political history of Etowah. That political history is then placed in a larger context in Chapter 4, where political change in the Etowah River valley is considered. In Chapter 5, those changes are viewed within the context of northern Georgia, as I attempt to suggest some possible causes of political change in the Etowah valley. The final chapter summarizes the results of these efforts, discusses their limitations, and suggests directions for future research.

2

The Etowah River Valley and Its Mississippian Archaeology

The focus of this study is the Etowah site and associated chiefdoms located in the Etowah River valley of northwestern Georgia (Figure 2). For the purposes of this book, I define the Etowah River valley to include the entire length of the Etowah River along with that stretch of the Coosa River that runs between Rome, Georgia, and the Alabama border. Defining the study area boundaries using a modern administrative border is somewhat arbitrary. Archaeological research indicates, however, that there is a substantial gap in the distribution of chiefdom capitals along the Coosa River to the west of the Alabama border (see Hally 1996). Therefore, the Etowah River valley, as I have defined it, captures a spatially discrete set of prehistoric chiefdoms.

In this chapter, I outline the context within which this research is conducted. In the first section I briefly describe the physical setting of the Etowah River valley, and this is followed by a discussion of the temporal framework used to understand its Mississippian occupation. In addition, I briefly discuss the history of Mississippian research conducted in the valley and summarize the results of investigations conducted at each of the mound centers.

THE PHYSICAL SETTING

As figure 2 shows, the Etowah River begins in the Blue Ridge province of north-central Georgia and flows southward and westward through the

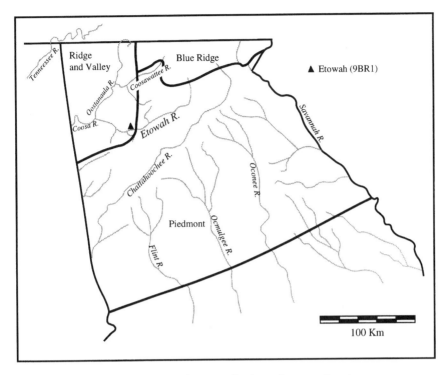

Figure 2. The Etowah River valley in northwestern Georgia.

Piedmont and into the Ridge and Valley province. At the present-day town of Rome, Georgia, the Etowah River joins the Oostanaula to become the Coosa River, which flows into Alabama and eventually the Gulf of Mexico. The distribution of known mound sites in the valley shows that the Piedmont and Ridge and Valley portions were most intensively used in the late prehistory of the area.

The late prehistoric people of the Etowah valley practiced a mixed subsistence strategy that included corn agriculture and the exploitation of various wild plant and game species and naturally available raw materials. Both the Piedmont and Ridge and Valley portions of the Etowah valley provided inhabitants with pockets of rich and periodically renewed floodplain soils. The Oak–Hickory climax forest provided access to a variety of nuts and fruits as well as deer, bear, and many small game species. The Etowah River contained abundant aquatic wildlife such as fish, turtles, and shellfish (Wharton 1978).

Although similar in many general respects, there are some physical dif-

ferences between the Ridge and Valley and Piedmont physiographic prov-
inces that influenced human settlement. The Ridge and Valley province
consists of a series of long parallel river valleys, separated by narrow ridges.
It contains some of the best agricultural soils in the state of Georgia (La-
Forge et al. 1925), and its sedimentary geology provided abundant sources
of chert for prehistoric tool manufacture (Goad 1979). In contrast, the
Piedmont is characterized by more rugged topography and more upland
areas that were probably wooded prehistorically. Its valleys are narrower
and more deeply cut, and pockets of good floodplain soils occur but tend
to be more restricted (Wharton 1978). Because the geology of the Piedmont is dominated by metamorphic and igneous rock (Clark and Zisa
1976), it contains lithic raw materials not found in the Ridge and Valley
that were important to prehistoric people, such as galena, ochre, mica,
graphite, quartz, schists, and slates.

According to Hally (1989), in all but one case, chiefdom capitals in the
Etowah valley were located on substantial expanses of floodplain soils, suggesting that access to prime agricultural land was very important and must
have influenced choices about where to locate political capitals. The largest
center in the valley, the Etowah site (9BR1), is located on the first patch of
floodplain soils along the Etowah River below the point where it flows out
of the Piedmont and into the Ridge and Valley. Larson (1971b) and Hally
(1989) both have argued that this location was chosen because it gave the
site's inhabitants access to some of the best agricultural land in the valley
(USDA 1926). At the same time, because the location is only 4 km from
the Piedmont, it also provided ready access to resources in both the Piedmont and Ridge and Valley.

THE TEMPORAL FRAMEWORK

Chronology is a fundamental concern that runs through this entire volume.
The validity of all arguments I make in the following chapters about political change at Etowah and in the Etowah River valley is directly depen-
dent on understanding the dating of site occupations and mound construction histories. Given the importance of dating, this section reviews the
ceramic sequence of the Etowah River valley. Readers wishing to delve
more deeply into the Etowah River valley ceramic sequence are referred
to Hally and Langford (1988) and King (1997).

The Etowah valley phase sequence is the culmination of over 60 years
of archaeological research aimed at chronology building and refinement.
The earliest work in the valley concerned with issues of chronology was

Table 1. Ceramic phase sequences of the Etowah River valley

Date (A.D.)	Period	Regional Period Designation	Phase
1500–1625	Late Mississippian	Lamar	Barnett
1475–1550	Late Mississippian	Lamar	Brewster
1425–1475	Late Mississippian	Lamar	Mayes (provisional)
1375–1425	Late Mississippian	Lamar	Stamp Creek
1325–1375	Middle Mississippian	Savannah	Late Wilbanks
1250–1325	Middle Mississippian	Savannah	Early Wilbanks
1200–1250	Middle Mississippian	Savannah	Unoccupied
1100–1200	Early Mississippian	Etowah	Late Etowah
1000–1100	Early Mississippian	Etowah	Early Etowah

undertaken by Robert Wauchope while working for the Works Progress Administration in the late 1930s. Wauchope (1948, 1966) conducted a massive survey and excavation project that encompassed much of northern Georgia, and in the process he visited most of the mound sites in the Etowah River valley. These efforts were augmented by results from surveys and excavations conducted in the late 1940s in preparation for the creation of the Allatoona Reservoir in the Piedmont portion of the Etowah valley (Caldwell 1957; Miller n.d.; Sears 1958a). By the early 1950s excavations conducted by William Sears (1958b), Arthur Kelly (Kelly and Larson 1957; King 2001), and Lewis Larson (Kelly and Larson 1957; Larson 1971a, 1972) at Etowah also began to contribute to the Etowah valley sequence. Recently, many of these older collections have been reanalyzed or analyzed for the first time (Hally and Langford 1988; Hally and Rudolph 1986; King 1996, 1997, 2001), leading to the Etowah valley phase sequence as it currently exists.

As Table 1 shows, the Mississippian occupation of the Etowah River valley spans the period from about A.D. 1000 to 1600 and is subdivided into the same Early, Middle, and Late Mississippian periods used throughout the Mississippian Southeast. In Georgia and adjoining parts of Alabama and South Carolina, these Early, Middle, and Late subdivisions have regional period designations (Etowah, Savannah, Lamar) that were defined to recognize regularities in ceramic sequences seen over this entire area. I will use both sets of period designations throughout the rest of this volume.

What follows are brief descriptions of the pottery assemblages associated with each phase.

The Early Mississippian Etowah period occupation of the Etowah valley is divided into two phases: the Early Etowah phase and the Late Etowah phase. In general, Etowah period ceramic assemblages consist primarily of complicated stamped, burnished, and plain pottery with minor amounts of incised and painted ceramic types. Complicated stamped designs are fine-lined and fairly well executed and consist mainly of a variety of concentric diamond motifs, the filfot cross, and the lineblock motif (Figure 3). Late Etowah assemblages are distinguished from those of the Early Etowah phase on the basis of differences in temper types, frequencies of complicated stamped motifs, and occurrence of certain minority types. In Early Etowah collections, the ladder-base diamond is the predominant motif and shell is the most common tempering agent. In Late Etowah collections two-bar diamonds and grit tempering are more common, and the filfot cross motif, Etowah Incised, and Hiwassee Island Red on Buff all first appear.

The Middle Mississippian Savannah period in the Etowah valley also is divided into two phases. At the beginning of the period, however, there appears to be a gap in the occupation of the Etowah River valley. While components dating to the early Savannah period have been recorded in other river valleys, no contemporary site occupations have been recorded along the Etowah River.

Savannah period assemblages are dominated by plain and complicated stamped types, but compared with pottery of the Etowah period, sherds are thicker, with bolder and sloppier complicated stamped designs. Stamped designs include the concentric circle, figure 9, figure 8, and quatrefoil. Also, a series of minority types occur in Savannah period assemblages, including brushed, corncob impressed, cord marked, and check stamped. Coarse grit is the predominant tempering agent.

Late Wilbanks phase assemblages are distinguished from those of the Early Wilbanks mainly by the presence of a series of minority types and vessel modes. Late Wilbanks assemblages contain Rudder Comb Incised, Dallas Incised, Pisgah-like types, and sherds resembling Lake Jackson Deco-rated. In addition, a small percentage of vessels are tall-neck jars, have peaked and noded rims, or exhibit various forms of appliqués. A percentage of Late Wilbanks sherds appear to be thinner than their Early Wilbanks

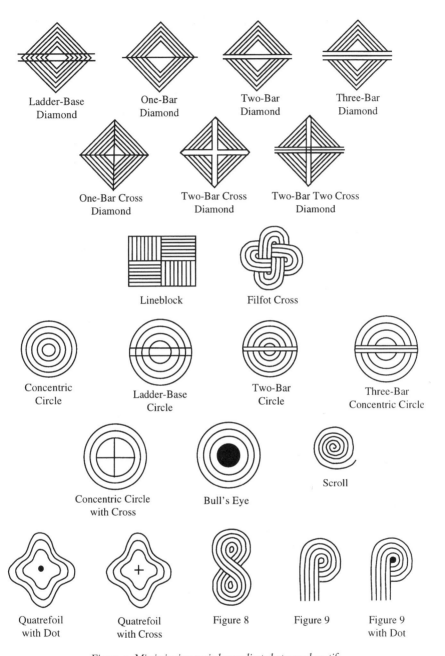

Figure 3. Mississippian period complicated stamped motifs.

counterparts, and their stamped motifs have narrower and more clearly defined lands and grooves.

THE LAMAR PERIOD (A.D. 1375 TO 1625)

The Late Mississippian Lamar period in the Etowah River valley is divided into four phases. In general, Lamar ceramic assemblages consist of three major types: complicated stamped, plain, and incised. Probably the single most distinguishing characteristic of Lamar assemblages is the modified rim. These occur almost exclusively on jars and consist of an additional strip of clay added to the rim, which is then pinched, individually sculpted, or formed into nodes.

Stamp Creek assemblages are distinctive in their absence of the type Lamar Incised. In terms of stamped motifs, minority types, and vessel shapes Stamp Creek assemblages are similar to Late Wilbanks collections. Rim modifications are found on the majority of Stamp Creek jars, and these consist of rows of individual nodes or narrow, deeply cut pinches on thickened or unthickened rims. The Mayes phase, provisionally defined using Wauchope's collections from Long Swamp and Horseshoe Bend, does include Lamar Incised vessels, which exhibit boldly executed one- to three-line designs. Mayes phase modified rims are somewhat wider than those of the Stamp Creek phase, and complicated stamped motifs are evenly divided between curvilinear (figure 9, filfot cross) and rectilinear (lineblock) motifs.

There are two roughly contemporary late Lamar phases in the Etowah valley, the Brewster and Barnett phases. In the Brewster phase, Lamar Incised vessels are common and exhibit motifs with more and somewhat narrower lines than seen in the Mayes phase. The rims of all jars and some bowls are modified with pinched and folded applied strips or notched fillet strips, and on average rim folds are wider than seen in the Stamp Creek and Mayes phases. Stamping is at its sloppiest, with most motifs being unrecognizable. Rectilinear stamped designs, such as the lineblock and simple-stamped variations, are the most common, followed by curvilinear designs such as the figure 9 and filfot cross.

The Barnett phase is temporally equivalent to the Brewster phase, but is found only in those parts of the Etowah valley (as defined in this volume) located on the Coosa River below Rome, Georgia. Like Brewster phase collections, Barnett phase pottery collections exhibit all of the hallmarks of classic Lamar assemblages (complicated stamped pottery, Lamar Incised, pinched and folded jar rims). They differ from Brewster phase collections in having much higher percentages of shell-tempered types such as Dallas Plain, Dallas Incised, and Dallas Filleted (Hally 1979).

A BRIEF HISTORY OF MISSISSIPPIAN
ARCHAEOLOGY IN THE ETOWAH VALLEY

Archaeological investigation of Mississippian period sites by professional archaeologists began in 1883, when agents of Cyrus Thomas of the Bureau of American Ethnology visited the valley. John Rogan directed the investigation of several mounds at Etowah and recovered some of the first fantastic burial goods from Mound C (Thomas 1894:292–312). Testing, presumably directed by Rogan, also was conducted on the mound at the site now known as Conyers Farm (9BR40), located across the river from Etowah (Thomas 1894:312). From 1925 to 1927, Moorehead (1932) conducted additional investigations at Etowah, where he again tested Mounds B and C, as well as many non-mound portions of the site. Like Rogan before him, Moorehead recovered a veritable treasure trove of burial artifacts from Mound C. In 1928 Margaret Ashley, while working with Moorehead (1932:157), investigated the mound at the site now called Plant Hammond (9FL3).

In 1938 and 1939, Wauchope (1948, 1966), while working for the WPA, conducted a massive survey and excavation project that encompassed much of northern Georgia. During this work, Wauchope and his crew visited most of the Mississippian mound sites in the valley, including Etowah (9BR1), Two Run Creek (9BR3), Free Bridge (9BR6), Wilbanks (9CK5), Long Swamp (9CK1), and Horseshoe Bend (9CK4), as well as many non-mound sites. Most of the work was limited to testing, but the results contributed significantly to the construction of the Etowah valley ceramic sequence. Also, many of the sites Wauchope visited have been destroyed, so his artifact collections represent the only archaeological information available for those sites.

In 1948 and 1949, surveys and excavations were conducted in preparation for the creation of the Allatoona Reservoir in the Piedmont portion of the Etowah valley (Caldwell 1957; Miller n.d.; Sears 1958a). As part of this project, Sears (1958a) excavated major portions of the mound at the Wilbanks site (9CK5) and Caldwell examined several important non-mound sites including Stamp Creek (9BR139) and Woodstock Fort (9CK85). In addition to making major contributions to the valley's cultural chronology, these excavations produced important information about Mississippian mortuary patterns, site structure, and residential architecture.

The emphasis shifted in the 1950s from major survey and testing projects to intensive investigations focused on the Etowah site. In 1952 and 1953 Sears (1958b) excavated a series of test units across major portions of the site. While the results were never published, they represent the only information available on the distribution of Mississippian components in the heart of the site. From 1954 to 1958 Kelly (Kelly and Larson 1957; King 2001) investigated the western flank of Mound B and adjacent non-mound areas, producing valuable information about site chronology and the construction history of Mound B. Larson's (Kelly and Larson 1957; Larson 1971a, 1989) complete excavation of the Mound C remnant also began in 1954 and continued until 1962. In addition to recovering an incredible collection of elaborate burial goods, Larson also gathered the information required to reconstruct the construction history of Mound C. Continuing from 1962 through 1973, Larson also conducted excavations in many non-mound portions of the site, producing valuable information about Lamar period domestic architecture.

Outside of Etowah, Plant Hammond was revisited in 1967 as part of salvage excavations conducted by students under the direction of Arthur Kelly (Chamblee et al. 1998). The project produced important details about the mound's stratigraphy and construction history. In 1973 and 1974 archaeologists excavated approximately three-fifths of the King site (9FL5), a late Lamar period village on the Coosa River (Garrow and Smith 1973; Hally et al. 1975). The remaining portions were investigated by a field school from the University of Georgia in 1992. The information recovered has provided one of the most detailed records of the domestic architecture and structure of a Mississippian period village (Hally and Kelly 1998; Kelly 1988). Comparative data were collected by Hally and three University of Georgia field schools during their investigation of a late Lamar village located at the Leake site (9BR2) (see Hally and Langford 1988).

In 1985, the Army Corps of Engineers funded a survey of the shoreline of Lake Allatoona (Ledbetter et al. 1987), where many of the important sites investigated during the original Allatoona Reservoir survey were revisited. To investigate settlement in upland areas around the reservoir, Ledbetter and Smith (1986) conducted surface surveys in areas clear-cut during timber harvesting. These upland settlement data were augmented when Ledbetter (1992) conducted additional surveys and testing in similar settings on the Vulcan tract near Lake Allatoona. The combined results of these surveys have helped to refine our understanding of the Mississippian settlement system in the Piedmont portion of the Etowah valley (King and Ledbetter 1992). Southerlin's (1993) survey of floodplains within 5 km of the Etowah site served to provide similar information on Mississippian settlement in the Ridge and Valley.

In the 1980s and 1990s, work resumed at Etowah. Morgan (1980) tested areas immediately to the north of the site in preparation for the construction of a new visitors' center and museum, and results indicated that Mississippian use of this area was quite limited. In 1987, Morgan R. Crook (personal communication 1995) and a group of students from Georgia State University conducted systematic surface collections in recently plowed areas along the eastern third of the Etowah site. These collections represent the only systematically recovered archaeological information available for study from that portion of Etowah. Unfortunately, until recently (King 1996), those artifacts had not been analyzed. In 1994, the Georgia Department of Natural Resources sponsored testing at the summit and base of Mounds A and B in preparation for the construction of new visitor access stairs (King 1995). The results of these excavations have helped to refine the construction histories of both mounds. In 1995, another crew from the Georgia Department of Natural Resources investigated an area on the northern edge of the palisade ditch, in preparation for the construction of a new bridge crossing the ditch. Although the results remain unreported, they contain important information about the dating and structure of the palisade wall.

Recent extensive excavations at two sites in the Piedmont portion of the valley have contributed to our understanding of Savannah period subsistence practices, domestic architecture, and site structure. Cable et al. (1994) uncovered portions of a palisade as well as structural remains and roasting pits at the Lake Acworth site (9CO45) along the margins of the Allatoona Reservoir. In addition, several isolated Savannah period buildings and associated domestic features were exposed at the Hickory Log site near Canton, Georgia (Paul Webb, personal communication 2000).

While a great deal of archaeological research has been conducted on Mississippian sites in the Etowah valley, the preceding paragraphs show that the data produced are not without their limitations. Many of the investigations were completed before modern excavation and recording techniques were used, so the information produced is minimal. Also, research results generally are difficult to access and summarize because they have not been published or they have been under-published in limited-distribution reports. Most of the settlement surveys conducted in the valley have not been systematic, so a great deal is not known about whole Mississippian settlement systems. In addition, comparatively little is known about the range of non-mound sites on the landscape because most of the sites chosen for intensive investigation have been mound sites. Finally, most excavation projects focused more on small-scale testing rather than large-scale excavations, so more information is available on site chronologies than their internal structure. The upshot of all of this is that the Etowah valley Mississippian period data are richest and most representative when they deal with the distribution and dating of mound sites. These problems have limited the kinds of data that are available for addressing anthropological questions and have, to a certain extent, shaped the methodological approach used in this volume.

THE ARCHAEOLOGY OF ETOWAH VALLEY MOUND CENTERS

A total of 10 Mississippian period mound centers have been recorded in the Etowah River valley, and most of these have been investigated at some level by professional archaeologists (Figure 4). The methods I use to identify chiefdoms and changes in their organizational structure require a detailed understanding of the dating and use of political centers. What follows are summaries of the results of investigations conducted at each of these centers, with the exception of Etowah, which is the subject of the next chapter. Because much of this information has never been published or represents a reconsideration of old data, I will discuss it in some detail. Where relevant, I cite the source of unpublished information and indicate the location of artifact collections I analyzed. Lists of the specific artifact lots analyzed and the sherd counts produced from these analyses can be found in King (1996).

Seven of these mound sites were investigated by Robert Wauchope during his survey of northern Georgia, sponsored by the WPA. Most of the artifacts from these investigations are currently housed at the Middle American Research Institute at Tulane University, although smaller portions are also curated at the Laboratory of Archaeology at the University of Georgia and the Center for Archaeology at Tulane. Unfortunately, all of the field documentation and most of the analysis forms and notes pertaining to this huge undertaking are currently missing. The only written materials that remain are Wauchope's typed progress reports submitted to the WPA from 1938 through 1940 (Wauchope 1938, 1939a, 1939b, 1939c, 1939d, 1940a, 1940b). Also, a substantial percentage of the artifacts collected were discarded after the original analysis was performed. This is especially true of plain and unidentifiable complicated stamped pottery. What remains are essentially type collections composed of unique sherds and representative examples of more common types. Perhaps the most damaging problem with the collection is that it is not currently possible to associate individual sherds with specific contexts at the sites investigated. While this information was certainly recorded, it has been lost with the rest of the documentation. As will be seen, even with these limitations Wauchope's collections contain valuable information.

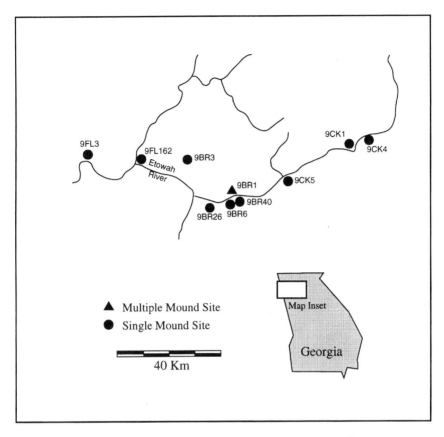

Figure 4. Mississippian mound sites of the Etowah River valley.

THE PLANT HAMMOND SITE (9FL3)

The Plant Hammond mound is the western-most mound site included in this study. It lies on the north bank of the Coosa River, which is formed when the Oostanaula and Etowah flow together at the modern town of Rome, Georgia. In 1928 Margaret Ashley visited this mound and village site, at the time called the Coosa mound, and described it as having a ditch that surrounded a single mound and village areas (Moorehead 1932:157). These features were still visible in 1943 when the USDA took aerial photographs of the region (Chamblee et al. 1998). The brief discussion of Ashley's investigations (Moorehead 1932:157) indicates that the mound present in 1928 was a "domiciliary, composed of river sand and clay."

This site later became part of the Georgia Power Company's coal-burning electric plant known as Plant Hammond. In 1967, when it was learned that Georgia Power planned to destroy the mound as part of the construction of a canal, A. R. Kelly of the University of Georgia initiated salvage excavations at the site (Chamblee et al. 1998). These investigations consisted of stratigraphic tests and block excavations both on and off of the mound. Near the close of the project, two east-west trenches also were excavated through the mound with the use of a bulldozer.

In the block excavated adjacent to the mound, Kelly's crew uncovered a single structure (Structure 3), while at the mound they found evidence for at least two construction stages with associated buildings (see Chamblee et al. 1998 for a slightly different interpretation). The first stage is represented by the fills lying beneath the area designated as Structure 2, while the second includes the fills over Structure 2 and beneath Structure 1. The profiles also give some indication that there may have been more fills on top of Structure 1, possibly representing a third stage. Chamblee et al. (1998) have argued that there may have been two stages beneath Structure 2 and that a small terrace may have been added to the east side of the mound near the end of its construction history.

Pottery collections recovered by Kelly's crew from Plant Hammond are currently housed at the University of Georgia's Laboratory of Archaeology in Athens. In 1995 I examined part of this collection (King 1996) and shortly thereafter the entire collection was analyzed by Chamblee et al. (1998). The following inferences about the dating of Plant Hammond are drawn from the results of both analyses. Beneath the mound Kelly's crew recorded a thick Swift Creek midden (Chamblee et al. 1998). On top of this midden and throughout the mound, crews recovered Wilbanks pottery. Among those sherds were many examples of narrow, neatly impressed complicated stamped sherds diagnostic of the Late Wilbanks phase. In addition, many examples of the type Rudder Comb Incised, another Late Wilbanks diagnostic, were found beneath the mound and in association with each of its summit structures. Finally, a single example of a Late Wilbanks modified rim was recovered from one of the features located off of the mound (King 1996:153). It seems clear that the Mississippian occupation of the Plant Hammond site, including the construction of its mound, dates to the Late Wilbanks phase.

The Nixon Site (9FL162)

Approximately 16 km up the Coosa River from Plant Hammond there was once a mound site located at the confluence of the Etowah and Oostanaula rivers (Jones 1873). This site apparently was destroyed sometime during the late nineteenth century, probably in conjunction with the growth of Rome, Georgia. Among the collections that I examined at the

Smithsonian Institution's Museum Support Center in Suitland, Maryland, are artifacts listed as deriving from the Nixon mound and burial place, near Rome. According to the accession records at the Museum Support Center, these artifacts came into the possession of Dr. Roland Steiner sometime in the 1880s or 1890s (possibly between 1894 and 1897) and were sold to the U.S. National Museum in 1898. Steiner was an avid collector and amateur archaeologist who acquired collections through his own excavations and through purchase. Exactly how Steiner acquired the Nixon collection remains unclear.

In the records housed at the Museum Support Center, the Nixon mound is described as being located at the confluence of the Etowah and Oostanaula rivers, while the burial place was located "opposite Rome." This suggests that the two areas, although both owned by the Nixon family, were distinct sites located on opposite sides of the river. Given this, it seems probable that the burial place was actually the Coosa Country Club site (9FL161), which is located below the confluence of the Etowah and Oostanaula rivers and across the Etowah River from Rome. On the basis of extant surface collections, Hally and Langford (1988) identified Late Etowah and Barnett phase occupations at the Coosa Country Club site, and this fits well with the set of diagnostics included in the Steiner collection.

The Steiner collection from the Nixon mound is not rich in diagnostics, but those that are present indicate that the mound was used at least during the sixteenth-century late Lamar period. The collection from the mound includes a number of flaked and ground stone celts, projectile points, shell beads, pearl beads, shell pins, bear teeth, and a shell gorget. The gorget is decorated with a stylized rattlesnake and is clearly an example of a Citico-style gorget (Carters Quarter in the classification scheme of Brain and Phillips 1996). Gorgets of this style are commonly found in sixteenth-century contexts throughout northwestern Georgia, eastern Tennessee, and northeastern Alabama (Hally et al. 1990). In addition, among the celts in the Steiner collection from Nixon there is an example of a perforated spatulate celt, which is an artifact form also found in sixteenth-century contexts in northwestern Georgia (Smith 1987:52).

THE TWO RUN CREEK SITE (9BR3)

Moving eastward up the Etowah River, Two Run Creek is the next known Mississippian mound site in the valley. It consists of a small mound and village that are located on the south bank of Two Run Creek, 8 km above its confluence with the Etowah River. In the spring of 1939, when Wauchope visited the site, the mound stood 2.5 m high and village areas extended

150 m to the north and northeast of the mound. At that time, Wauchope (1939b:5–12, 1966:223–231, 446–450) was granted permission to conduct excavations in both of these areas, where he found occupations dating from the Archaic through the Historic periods.

As part of granting permission to work at the site, the owner asked that the mound be leveled so the area could be more easily plowed. Wauchope and crews excavated two bisecting trenches through the mound to expose stratigraphy, and using this information, proceeded to strip off layers horizontally until the mound was almost entirely excavated. In the process, nine construction stages and several associated buildings were recorded.

At the base of the mound crews uncovered part of a building that appeared to be rectangular in plan. Above this the inhabitants of the site built a small mound (Stage 1) and placed a rectangular building on top. This platform was rebuilt three more times (Stages 2–4), and each time a new building was placed on its summit. Each new construction consisted of "a dark brown earthen platform . . . capped with a layer of bright, greenish yellow viscous clay" (Wauchope 1966:446). After the fourth rebuilding of the platform, the mound measured 4.9 by 4.7 m and stood about 60 cm high.

The addition of Stage 5 nearly tripled the area covered by the mound but left its height unchanged. On top of this new stage the site's inhabitants placed a larger building, which had two burned areas located at the middle of the north and south ends of the structure. More clays were added to the northern edge of this platform (Stage 5a) and were eventually covered with charcoal. Wauchope suggests that this represented a localized expansion of the mound added sometime during the use of Stage 5.

Eventually the entire mound was again covered (Stage 6) and a new rectangular building was placed on the summit. The addition of this stage doubled the height of the mound, but did not change its horizontal extent. At the base of the southern slope Wauchope (1966:448) found what he interpreted to be the remains of a circular, earth-embanked structure. If his identification is correct, then a rectangular structure occupied the summit of the mound, while a circular building stood at the foot. This same pattern is repeated with the construction of Stages 7, 8, and 9. In each case the platform was enlarged, a new rectangular building was placed on the summit, and a circular, earth-embanked structure was built at the base of the southern flank. During Stage 8, however, the circular building at the base of the mound was rebuilt a second time before construction on Stage 9 began.

Interestingly, Kelly found a series of earth-embanked structures (one circular) adjacent to Mound B at Etowah (King 2001:28–34). These were apparently built on a prepared surface and rebuilt with each successive Wilbanks mound construction stage. If it is accepted that the summit of Mound B supported rectangular buildings (the more common Wilbanks architectural form), then the architectural pattern at Two Run Creek matches that seen at Early and Late Wilbanks phase Etowah.

According to Wauchope, all of the mound construction at Two Run Creek (including the premound structure) occurred during the Wilbanks phases. In my own reanalysis of what remains of Wauchope's collections I found several Late Wilbanks diagnostics (King 1996:157–158). While their stratigraphic position within the mound cannot be reconstructed, they do indicate that at least some of the nine mound stages built at Two Run Creek date to the Late Wilbanks phase.

THE RACCOON CREEK SITE (9BR26)

Still farther east up the Etowah River is Raccoon Creek. This is a small mound and village site located on the south bank of the Etowah River at its confluence with Raccoon Creek. No excavations have been conducted at this site, although Wauchope (1939b:2, 1966:236–237) and David Hally both visited and made surface collections in 1939 and 1988, respectively. The vast majority of the collection Wauchope made no longer exists, but the published description shows that the site was used from the Early Woodland through late Lamar periods, with the main component dating to the Early Wilbanks phase. The presence of a Rudder Comb Incised sherd in Hally's collection (King 1996:158–159), housed at the University of Georgia's Laboratory of Archaeology, refines this sequence by including a Late Wilbanks component. Given the occupational history of the site and the strength of the Wilbanks (Early and/or Late) component, it seems likely that mound construction dates to one or both of the Wilbanks phases.

THE FREE BRIDGE SITE (9BR6)

Approximately 1.5 km downriver from the Etowah site on the south bank of the Etowah River is Free Bridge. This is another small mound and village that was visited by Wauchope (1939c:5–8, 1966:245–250, 450–452) in the summer of 1939. At that time the mound stood 2 m above the ground surface and measured 26 m in diameter. Wauchope's investigations were limited to 12 tests in non-mound areas and a single trench excavated through the mound. The non-mound units were placed in areas where artifacts were scattered on the surface, but, according to Wauchope (1966:246), in these tests crews "found no other implications of an occupation." The trench through the mound revealed that prior to mound construction a rectangular building had occupied the location. The mound itself was constructed in at least two stages, with the possibility that a third had existed but was destroyed by plowing or flooding. The summits of Stages 1 and 2 each supported a rectangular building, and the structure on Stage 1 was also surrounded by a low clay wall.

As with Two Run Creek, the premound building and each of the mound construction stages at Free Bridge were built during one or both of the Wilbanks phases. Unfortunately, Wauchope's ceramic collections from the site are no longer available for study, so it is difficult to apply recent refinements in the ceramic sequence to the collection from Free Bridge. However, there is some reason to believe that at least one of the mound stages at the site dates to the Late Wilbanks. First, in a surface collection made at the site in 1988 (housed at the University of Georgia's Laboratory of Archaeology) there appears a single sherd with the Late Wilbanks diagnostic peaked and noded rim (King 1996:161). Second, Wauchope (1966:242) lists only five Lamar diagnostics in his collections from Free Bridge. Four of these are Lamar specialized rims and are described as being decorated with "horizontal row of diagonal slashes (1), spikes (1), lumps or nodes (2) on the exterior or just below the lip." None of these sound like classic Lamar pinched and folded rims, but any could fit the description of Late Wilbanks modified rims.

THE CONYERS FARM SITE (9BR40)

Directly across the river from Etowah, on the south bank of the Etowah River, is a small mound and village known as the Conyers Farm site. This site was first investigated by an agent of Cyrus Thomas (presumably John Rogan) as part of the Bureau of Ethnology's mound explorations (Thomas 1894:312). At that time, the site was known as the Edwards Mound and was described as having a single mound, oval in form, that was 24 m long at the base, 16.8 m wide, and flat on top. Some 40 years later, the site was investigated by Moorehead (1932:90) during his exploration of the Etowah mounds. Moorehead's crews augered the mound at Conyers Farm and uncovered several houses in non-mound areas. The most useful comment Moorehead makes concerning these investigations is that the pottery found at Conyers Farm is similar to that found at Etowah.

In 1939, Wauchope (1966:260) also visited the site and made a surface collection. This collection is no longer available for study, but the published description indicates that it contains Mississippian diagnostics from the Etowah phases (n = 70), the Wilbanks phases (n = 419), and the Brewster phase (n = 77). Wilbanks materials are predominant and include the Late Wilbanks diagnostic Rudder Comb Incised with a peaked and noded rim

(Wauchope 1966:fig. 222). Given this, it seems likely that mound construction took place during one or both of the Wilbanks phases.

THE WILBANKS SITE (9CK5)

Moving eastward out of the Great Valley and into the Piedmont portion of the Etowah valley, the next Mississippian mound is at the Wilbanks site. This is a mound and village located in a crescent-shaped piece of floodplain on the southeast bank of the Etowah River. In 1949, when the Allatoona Reservoir was created, the Wilbanks site was flooded. Prior to construction of the reservoir, Wilbanks was visited at least twice by professional archaeologists and numerous times by looters. The first intensive investigation of the site was conducted by Wauchope in 1938 (Wauchope 1939a:18–23, 1966:280–289, 453–455). At that time, the mound stood about 2 m tall and village areas were located to the east, west, and south of the mound. Wauchope and his crew excavated several test units and a long trench in village areas and placed a trench into the center of the mound. In 1948, as preparations were being made for the creation of the Allatoona Reservoir, additional excavations were conducted at the site by William Sears (1958a). Sears excavated a series of trenches into the flanks of the mound and then horizontally stripped individual strata. Artifacts recovered by Wauchope and Sears show that the primary occupations of the site date to the Early and Middle Woodland periods and the Early through Late Mississippian periods.

The mound profiles recorded by Wauchope (1966:fig. 201) and Sears (1958a:fig. 6b) show that the Wilbanks mound was built in three or possibly four construction efforts. The first was interpreted by Sears (1958a) to be an earth lodge that measured 14 m on a side, was surrounded by a low clay wall, and had a roof made of wood and perishable thatching covered with a layer of earth. The roof supports rested on the clay wall and were held in place at the base by an earth embankment, and they were lashed at the peak to a ridge pole. Sears found no clear evidence for central support posts, an entranceway, or an interior hearth. After the structure was destroyed, the area between its walls was filled and leveled to form the first stage of a platform mound. A second stage was built later that extended the mound 4.9 m to the south and raised the summit an estimated 45 cm above Stage 1. It is possible that the outermost fills on the mound represent a third construction stage, but neither Wauchope nor Sears investigated this possibility fully.

The nature of the Wilbanks earth lodge has been the subject of some discussion. Rudolph (1984) has argued that rather than a true earth lodge, the structure excavated by Sears was more likely an earth-embanked building without an earth-covered roof. In Larson's (1994) critical appraisal of Southeastern earth lodges, he echoes Rudolph's doubts about the existence of true earth-covered buildings in the region. Larson further suggests that not only was the Wilbanks earth lodge not earth covered, but also it may not have been a building at all. Drawing parallels with his own work at Etowah's Mound C, Larson suggests that the arrangement of clay, rocks, and wooden beams uncovered by Sears at Wilbanks was actually part of the mound construction process rather than the remains of a building. As evidence supporting his assertion, Larson cites the lack of support posts, an entrance, and a hearth at Wilbanks.

While Larson's argument holds logical appeal, his Mound C analogy may not fit with the evidence uncovered by Sears. Larson references material that was placed on the slope of an existing mound stage, presumably to help stabilize new construction fill placed on a sloping surface. According to Larson, the beams came from a palisade that surrounded Mound C and was dismantled as part of the new construction effort. At Wilbanks, the beams and rock were found lying flat at the base of the mound within the area enclosed by a clay wall. In this case, there is no obvious source for the beams and their placement at the base of the mound cannot be justified by the need to stabilize a sloping mound deposit. Under these circumstances, it is possible that the beams found at the base of the Wilbanks mound were the remains of a building that had been dismantled. Such premound buildings are very common throughout the Southeast. Its size and configuration, however, may never be understood clearly.

According to Wauchope (1966:282), the premound structure (Sears's earth lodge) and first construction stage of the Wilbanks mound date to the Etowah period. The second construction stage dates to the Savannah period, and the possible third dates to either the Savannah or Lamar period. Portions of the ceramic collection recovered by Wauchope are still available for study, but at this time it is not possible to connect individual sherds with specific mound strata. The diagnostics that are present in the collection, however, do indicate that the site was used during the Late Etowah phase and the Early and Late Wilbanks phases, the Stamp Creek or Mayes phase, and the Brewster phase (King 1996:165–166).

Pottery collections recovered by Sears are now maintained at the University of Georgia's Laboratory of Archaeology. In my analysis of selected lots in that collection (King 1996:167–172), I found that the premound midden and structure (earth lodge) and first mound construction stage all date to the Late Etowah phase. Midden on the flanks of Stage 2 contained Wilbanks pottery, with no Late Wilbanks diagnostics, indicating that it was constructed during the Early Wilbanks phase. The collections taken from midden accumulations and wash on the outer surfaces of the mound contain a mix of Etowah, Wilbanks, and Lamar pottery. The Wilbanks ceramics are the most common and contain Late Wilbanks diagnostics. On the basis of these data, if a third stage was added to the Wilbanks mound, it probably dated to the Late Wilbanks phase. As in Wauchope's collections, the Lamar pottery recovered by Sears appears to contain a mix of early and late Lamar diagnostics (especially rim forms). Although it is difficult to determine with certainty, the absence of stratigraphic evidence for a fourth construction stage and the low frequency of Lamar sherds in the upper mound contexts suggest that no stages were built during the Lamar period.

Several years before and after Wauchope's visit, floods exposed a number of burials in village areas at the site. It was reported that one of the skeletons in these graves held a monolithic ax in each hand (Wauchope 1966:281). In another grave collectors found a pair of carved stone ear spools (Sears 1958a). At least four or five of the burials exposed by the floods and four of the burials located by Wauchope were stone-lined graves, which is a burial form found in the Early Wilbanks construction stages of Etowah's Mound C. The motif depicted on the stone ear spools from one of the washed-out graves is very similar to those found at Spiro and is securely dated to the Spiro III phase (A.D. 1250–1350) (Brown 1996). This cross date lends support to the notion that most of these graves, and probably a substantial portion of the non-mound occupation at the site, date to the Early Wilbanks phase.

The Long Swamp Site (9CK1)

Continuing upriver from Wilbanks, the next Mississippian mound site in the valley is located where Long Swamp Creek flows into the Etowah River. This site is known as Long Swamp and consists of a village and the remains of a small mound. Wauchope (1939a:8–13, 1966:301–314, 455–458) worked at this site in the fall of 1938, at which time the mound stood only 1.2 m high. The owner at the time remembered the mound standing 1.8 to 2.4 m high in 1908, and Wauchope estimates that it stood as high as 3 to 4 m after its final construction stage (Wauchope 1966:301). In 1949 Lewis Larson, under the direction of A. R. Kelly, conducted more excavations at Long Swamp. According to Larson (personal communication 1995), at the time of his visit the mound was no longer a visible feature at the site.

During their visit, Wauchope and his crew conducted fairly extensive investigations in non-mound areas of the site. As part of this effort crews dug 17 test pits, and in one (Pit 2) uncovered portions of a structure (House 2) containing a fired hearth area and heavy deposits of burned timbers and daub. In a long trench excavated adjacent to a gully created by floods, Wauchope's crew found a refuse pit (Refuse Pit 1) that measured 3.3 m in diameter and 43 cm deep. Above this crews recorded portions of another building (House 1) that contained a hearth area, had a red clay floor, and measured approximately 6 to 8 m across. In an attempt to connect non-mound and mound stratigraphy, Wauchope also excavated a narrow trench between the gully and the mound. In this, crews uncovered a heart-shaped clay house floor designated as House 6. Stratigraphically, Houses 2, 5, and 6 and Refuse Pit 1 were the first Mississippian features created at the site, and these were followed by the construction of House 1 and the mound.

At the mound, Wauchope reported finding 10 strata that represented three construction stages. Beneath the mound, excavators recorded a roughly circular scatter of posts (House 5) that had a burial without grave goods associated with it. Above this the occupants of the site built a small platform 55 cm high and placed a circular structure on its summit (House 4). House 4 measured 6.8 m in diameter, had a puddled clay hearth in the center, and was surrounded by a shallow ditch. Its floor was covered with a rich midden containing pottery, animal bone and freshwater shell, bone and stone tools, and broken clay pipes (Wauchope 1966:457–458). In his published account, Wauchope (1966:303) refers to this building as a "round house or earth lodge," but he gives no justification for using those terms. After the occupation of this house, a second stage was added to the mound and a new structure was placed on the summit (House 3). According to Wauchope, the mound was enlarged a third time but the summit and any evidence for the existence of a summit structure had been destroyed by many years of plowing.

According to Wauchope (1966:304), sometime after the third stage had been built the entire site was flooded and blanketed with a layer of river sand. Beneath this flood deposit, crews recovered only Etowah period pottery. The high occurrence of the filfot cross motif, the presence of cross bar diamonds, and the relatively low occurrence of ladder-base diamonds in Wauchope's Table 41 (Wauchope 1966:306) all argue for a Late Etowah assignment for all six houses and three mound stages constructed at Long Swamp. Above the flood deposit Savannah and Lamar ceramics appeared for the first time, but only as a small minority compared with Etowah period pottery. Since these sherds appear only after the flood deposit, the three stages added to the Long Swamp mound must have been built during the Late Etowah phase.

Results of my re-examination of what remains of the Long Swamp collection are consistent with these observations (King 1996:173–177). As

Wauchope's counts show, the Etowah period pottery dates to the Late Etowah phase. In the Savannah period collections there are two Rudder Comb Incised sherds and several complicated stamped sherds with the circle with cross motif, suggesting that there is a Late Wilbanks component at the site. As I discussed previously, the Lamar ceramics from Long Swamp date to the Mayes phase of the early Lamar period.

The Horseshoe Bend Site (9CK4)

The eastern-most recorded Mississippian mound in the Etowah valley is known as Horseshoe Bend. This site is located on the west bank of the Etowah River near the western border of Cherokee County and is situated on a level terrace overlooking the river floodplain in a large horseshoe-shaped bend. Wauchope visited the site in the winter of 1939 and conducted excavations in the village areas and on the mound (Wauchope 1939a:13–18, 1966:323–330). At the time of this visit the mound stood only 60 cm high and several stone slabs were visible on the surface in village areas 100 m to the north. To investigate these features Wauchope's crew excavated 10 test pits in village areas and a long trench that bisected the mound.

In the village areas, where the stone slabs had been exposed by plowing, crews uncovered four burials (Test Pit 1). The stratigraphy in this area consisted of a plow zone followed by a thin layer of red earth and clay (probably part of a house floor), a relatively thick midden, and sterile red clay (Wauchope 1939a:14). Two of the graves (Burials 2 and 4) originated at the surface of the midden, a third (Burial 3) began in the plow zone, and the fourth (Burial 1) originated at the surface of the red clay floor. The latter two had grave offerings consisting of a shell earplug and a conch shell, respectively.

In another excavation (Test Pit 9) closer to the mound, Wauchope and his crew exposed and dug portions of a large refuse pit (Refuse Pit 1) that measured at least 3 m across and was 43 cm deep. This feature was filled with sherds, charcoal, and animal bone, and originated from the surface of the midden encountered near the burials (Wauchope 1939a:15). Crews also uncovered parts of a second midden-filled pit (Refuse Pit 2) on the western side of the mound. Exposed areas of this feature measured 2.4 m by 1.2 m and 80 cm deep.

The mound excavations consisted of a 21-m-long trench that was placed to bisect the mound from east to west. Beneath the mound, excavators uncovered the same midden found in village areas, and this was overlain by a building that Wauchope suggests was rectangular in plan. Above this the occupants of the site placed six strata (Wauchope 1966; Strata 3 through

8). While charcoal and midden deposits were found in two of these strata, the only clear occupational surface appears to be the final mound stratum (Wauchope 1966; Stratum 9). According to Wauchope (1939a:18), this was "a thick occupational deposit composed of charcoal, potsherds, and debris burned to a red color." The mound profile shows two possible postholes originating at this level, suggesting that the surface may have supported a building. On the basis of this information, it appears that the mound at Horseshoe Bend was built in one construction effort.

According to Wauchope, the premound midden and probably the two refuse pits date to the Etowah period. In the mound fill layers, Savannah and Etowah types appeared together in Strata 3 through 8, with Lamar ceramics being added to the mix after Stratum 8 was deposited. This suggests that the mound is either a Savannah or Lamar period construction. My counts from what remains of Wauchope's Horseshoe Bend collection (King 1996:180) indicate that the Etowah period ceramics date to the Late Etowah phase, while the Savannah collections include several Late Wilbanks diagnostics. The presence of stone slab burials, which occur only in the Early Wilbanks contexts at Etowah, suggests a possible Early Wilbanks occupation as well. In the Lamar ceramics, there are several examples of boldly incised sherds, narrow pinched rims, and pinched and punctated rims. These all appear as part of the Mayes phase of the early Lamar. There are also some sherds with fine incising and fairly wide rim folds, suggesting that there might also be a Brewster phase component at the site.

In the summer of 1995, I returned to Horseshoe Bend to conduct more testing and attempt to resolve the dating of the mound (King 1996:178–188). As part of this work, a small crew and I made a general surface collection, excavated 83 shovel tests at 20-m intervals over the heart of the site, and placed two 1-by-2-m test units in the vicinity of the mound. Since the time of Wauchope's visit the mound has been deflated and spread out by almost 60 years of plowing. As a result, it now exists as a low rise about 60 cm in height.

The two test units were placed on what appeared at the time to be the mound, near shovel tests with high sherd counts. Despite these efforts, it appears that Test Unit 1 actually was located on the very featheredge of the mound and therefore did not intercept much actual mound stratigraphy. Test Unit 2 was placed near the highest point of the mound remnant to ensure that it would intercept mound strata.

In that unit, the earliest deposit was a dark midden, beneath which was found a large, shallow, midden-filled basin (Feature 1) that is similar to Wauchope's refuse pits. Pottery recovered from Feature 1 and the premound midden confirm the Late Etowah assignment for the premound midden and associated refuse pits. Above the midden in Test Unit 2, there were a series of layers of sand, clay, and loam that represent mound fill. As I concluded from Wauchope's mound profile, the mound strata in Test Unit 2 appear to belong to a single construction stage. There are no occupational layers visible in mound strata, and no posts originate from surfaces within the mound. The ceramics from Test Unit 2 show that Wilbanks and Etowah pottery are found mixed throughout the mound fills, while Lamar diagnostics are quite scarce and appear only in the plow-disturbed uppermost stratum.

Unfortunately, Test Unit 2 produced no evidence for the occupational layer Wauchope encountered on the mound's summit (Stratum 9). I can only assume that it has been destroyed by plowing. Even if it has been destroyed, the diagnostics contained within that stratum should still be the most common on the mound summit. In Test Unit 2, Wilbanks sherds are the most common in the upper two strata. This, combined with the Late Wilbanks diagnostics present in Wauchope's mound excavations, suggests that the occupation of the mound summit, as well as the mound construction itself, dates to the Late Wilbanks phase.

3

A Political History of Etowah

The central focus of this book is to document and begin to explain the political changes that occurred in the Etowah River valley during the Mississippian period. Through the course of this period, the Etowah site grew to become the valley's largest and most complex political center. Given the site's clear importance in the history of the Etowah valley, this chapter is devoted to tracing the political history of the Etowah site. By political history, I mean the history of Etowah as a political center: When did it first emerge as a political center, how did that center evolve, and when was it abandoned?

THE ETOWAH SITE

The Etowah site is a large, multimound town located on the Etowah River in Bartow County, Georgia. There are six known mounds at the site, designated Mounds A through F (Figure 5). The largest of these, Mound A, stands over 21 m tall, has a prominent ramp projecting from its eastern side, and has a smaller terrace attached to its southern flank. Mounds B and C are each large, flat-topped pyramidal mounds measuring respectively 7 and 6 m tall. Of the two, only Mound C originally had a ramp, which also projected from its eastern flank. The smallest mounds at the site (D, E, and F) are rectangular to oblong platforms that each measure about 3 m high. To the south, the site is bordered by the Etowah River, but on all other sides it is surrounded by a series of borrow pits connected by a large ditch.

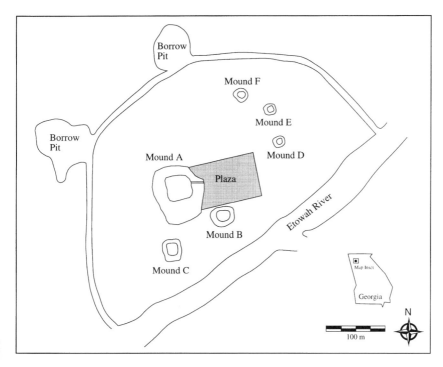

Figure 5. Plan map of the Etowah site.

This ditch encloses 21 ha and apparently extended to the river on both sides before it was partially filled for agricultural purposes.

Research conducted by professional archaeologists began at Etowah with the visit of John P. Rogan in 1883 and has continued intermittently spanning most decades of the twentieth century. For a thorough review of the excavation history of Etowah, see King (1996). Throughout those many years of excavation, all of the mounds at the site, with the exception of Mound F, have experienced some level of investigation (Kelly and Larson 1957; King 1995, 2001; Larson 1971a; Moorehead 1932; Thomas 1894). Only those areas between Mounds A, B, and C and to the east of Mounds A and B have been systematically tested, and extensive excavations also have been conducted west of Mound B and immediately east of Mound A. Non-mound areas away from the heart of the site have not been tested, although the area between the ditch and Mounds D, E, and F has been systematically surface collected.

Despite the lengthy history of investigations, the understanding of the Etowah site produced is far from perfect. Because the entire site has never been systematically tested, there are large portions about which nothing is known. In addition, the data available from the many years of excavation vary greatly with respect to quality, and these problems are compounded by the fact that many of the more recent seasons of work have not been analyzed sufficiently and published. The information presented here is an attempt to fill some of the gaps in our understanding of Etowah, but a great deal remains to be learned about the site. The reader is urged to keep this fact in mind when evaluating the arguments presented in the following sections.

THE EARLY ETOWAH PHASE: MODEST BEGINNINGS

The first Mississippian occupation of Etowah began during the Early Etowah phase, which also marks the presumed appearance of ranked social structures in the region (Hally and Langford 1988). Based on what is currently known about the site, it was not a very big or elaborate place at this time. Early Etowah phase materials appear to be restricted to an area along the river's edge between Mounds B and C, and no direct evidence has been found for Early Etowah phase mound construction stages. Only the outermost stages of Mound A have been investigated, however, so it remains possible that construction began on it during the Early Etowah phase. The great size of Mound A, both in absolute terms and relative to all other mounds built at the site, does suggest that it may have a longer construction history than any other mound at Etowah.

Whether social ranking was present at Etowah during this phase is difficult to determine with certainty. The Early Etowah mortuary record, which should shed some light on this subject, consists of a single burial. This burial, Kelly's Burial 21 (King 2001:40), was excavated into the side of a large, midden-filled pit under the outer flank of Mound B and contained the remains of an aged woman with no grave goods. It is possible that some of the graves recorded beneath Mound C also date to this phase, but this is difficult to determine because no systematic examination of the Mound C burials has been completed.

This general lack of mortuary data apparently is not uncommon for Early Mississippian sites in this area. Schroedl (1998) reports that no burials have been found in Hiwassee Island phase (A.D. 1000–1300) village or mound contexts in eastern Tennessee. Evidence suggests, however, that some of the burial mounds attributed to the Late Woodland Hamilton culture in eastern Tennessee actually date to the Hiwassee Island phase (Schroedl and Boyd 1991). Hamilton burial mounds are generally located away from habitation sites and often contain few temporally diagnostic artifacts such as pottery vessels. On the basis of the dates of some Hamilton mounds, Schroedl and Boyd (1991) suggest that, as was the case during the preceding Late Woodland period, the preferred mortuary treatment of Early Mississippian populations in eastern Tennessee was burial in mounds located away from habitation sites. Given the many other material similarities between Etowah and social groups living in eastern Tennessee (Hally and Langford 1988, and see below), it may be that a similar form of burial was preferred during the Early Etowah phase.

Cole's (1975) study of mortuary treatment in a series of Hamilton burial mounds from eastern Tennessee showed a generally egalitarian mortuary program, except that a small number of people were accompanied by small amounts of exotic materials, especially conch columellae. Cole (1975) found no correlation between the presence of exotics and age or sex categories, which is consistent with ascribed ranking. Because the mounds included in this study apparently date to both the Late Woodland and Early Mississippian periods, the inferences drawn may not be representative of the actual Late Woodland or Early Mississippian mortuary behavior. Regardless, the apparent use of single mortuary facilities for large portions of the social group, along with very modest differences in material possessions, is consistent with what might be expected of a corporately organized society.

Most of what we do know about the Early Etowah phase occupation of Etowah comes from the excavations conducted by Kelly adjacent to Mound B and Larson in the Mound C vicinity (Kelly and Larson 1957; King 2001; Larson 1971a). The earliest features in these areas were a series of large, midden-filled pits. Between 1954 and 1958, Kelly completely excavated four of these features, which he called saucers, on the west side of Mound B (Kelly and Larson 1957; King 2001:34–36). They ranged in size from 3 m to more than 10 m in diameter and from .61 to 2 m deep. Larson excavated at least five more, and these ranged from 1 m to more than 6 m in diameter. At least some of these features were described as consisting of two or more superimposed pits, while others apparently were individual holes dug into subsoil. Their fills consisted of alternating layers of midden and ash, and scattered throughout them were fired areas and concentrations of charred plant remains. At least in the case of Kelly's Saucer 3, the floor was uneven and contained deeper pits and pockets filled with midden. In addition, his Saucers 2 and 4 had short wall segments placed around portions of their periphery (Kelly and Larson 1957), which may have functioned as some type of screen (King 2001:36).

Field crews collected a wide variety of artifacts from the midden-filled pits, including animal bone, pottery, freshwater shell, botanical remains, tools made of bone and stone, chunkey stones, and mineral pigments like red and yellow ochre (Kelly and Larson 1957; King 2001:34–36). Bone and pottery were the most common artifacts recovered, and these were collected in vast quantities. According to the published account, deer and turtles were the most common species represented in the animal bone, while fish like catfish, drum, and gar or sturgeon also were present (Kelly and Larson 1957). Apparently, among the animal bone were pieces of human skulls and jaws that had been broken and burned in the same manner as the animal bone. The pottery recovered was described as consisting mainly of utilitarian wares, but painted and effigy vessels were also described. More recent analyses seem to confirm these general observations (Hally and Langford 1988; Hally and Rudolph 1986; King 2001). The published account also suggests that at least some of the vessels recovered were broken in place (Kelly and Larson 1957).

Kelly and Larson (1957) interpret these features as roasting pits for large-scale cooking and food consumption. While areas and whole strata within the pits were burned, their size and shape argue against their being cooking features. It seems more likely that they were refuse pits. The ash and sand layers may represent attempts to cover and/or burn exposed refuse, possibly to reduce the smell or attraction to scavengers. The pole screens found by Kelly may have somehow been related to these efforts. Their size and shape suggest that the features themselves were actually borrow pits excavated as sources of mound fill or house construction materials. The number and size of features excavated seem to argue that they were the source of mound fill rather than materials for building houses. Given their proximity to Mound A, these midden-filled pits may represent the best evidence for the construction of an Early Etowah phase stage of that mound.

In his work on the symbolism of mounds and mound construction, Knight (1986, 1989) has drawn several inferences that may be informative in this context. First, using linguistic and historical evidence, he has convincingly argued that to Southeastern natives the earthen platform mound symbolically represented the earth and that addition of a new stage was a symbolic burial of the earth. Further, he has argued that such earth renewals took place within the context of communally oriented rites of intensification that probably had the same associations with earth, fertility, and purification identified with the Green Corn ceremony of the Historic period. Finally, he (Knight 1989:285) has suggested that the use to which mound summits were put can be considered "analytically independent" of the symbolism of mounds and mound building. In other words, the earth/fertility symbolism associated with mounds and mound building as a communal act of burial and purification remained the same regardless of whether mound summits were used to support communal ritual buildings or a temple dedicated to the glory of the chiefly ancestors.

Kelly and Larson (1957) argue that the garbage found in the midden-filled pits represents the remains of large-scale feasting. The sheer quantities of animal bone and pottery seem to support this contention. The low occurrence of carnivore and rodent gnawing evident on the bone recovered indicates that these materials were buried rapidly, which is a pattern consistent with large-scale, rapid disposal events that should result from feasts (Wayne Boyko, personal communication 1999). What these midden-filled pits may represent, then, are the remains of feasting associated with the communal ritual of mound construction. Knight (2001) has summarized evidence indicating that feasting was an integral part of the construction and use of Middle and Late Woodland platform mounds, which he argues had the same symbolic associations as Mississippian platform mounds. Also, the feast was an important element of the Green Corn ceremony of the Historic period (Hudson 1976; Swanton 1946), which Knight (1989) argues was the historical transformation of prehistoric earth renewal rituals that included mound construction. In this light, it should not be surprising to find communal feasting and mound construction linked.

Hayden (2001) has recently presented a framework for identifying the general function of different kinds of feasts using the archaeological record. In addition to differences in the quantity and kinds of foods served, prestige goods are also likely to figure differently in different kinds of feasts. For example, the creation or destruction of prestige goods is likely to be relatively unimportant in feasts designed to promote the solidarity of social groups, and to figure somewhat more prominently in those feasts geared toward alliance formation. In contrast, prestige goods are likely to be most important in feasts that focus on power building through competition between leaders or the creation of debts through gift giving. Although a thorough examination of the pits' contents has not been completed, Kelly and Larson's (1957) observations suggest that few items that may have served as prestige goods (marine shell, copper, mica, exotic pottery, etc.) were recovered from the midden-filled pits. Therefore, the feasting that created those features may have been oriented more toward solidarity building or the forging of social alliances rather than power building through competition.

In addition to the midden-filled pits, Larson's crews recorded the remains of at least seven buildings in the Early Etowah phase contexts beneath Mound C (King 1996) (Figure 6). Unfortunately, comparatively little is known about Early Mississippian period architecture in northern Georgia. Just across the border in eastern Tennessee, however, a large sample of roughly contemporary (Hiwassee Island phase, A.D. 1000–1300) build-

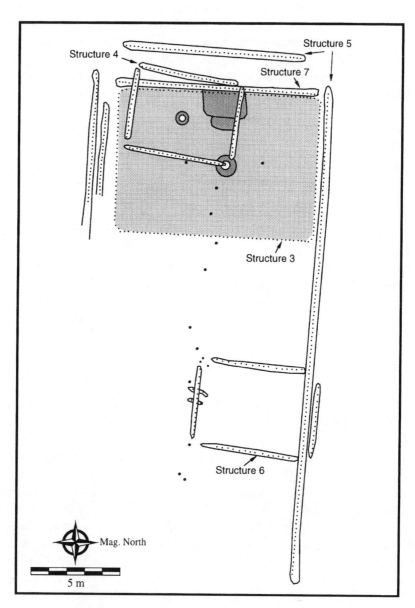

Figure 6. Early Etowah phase buildings beneath Mound C.

ings were excavated prior to the creation of the Chickamauga Reservoir in eastern Tennessee (Lewis 1995; Lewis and Kneberg 1946). The short distance separating the Chickamauga Basin and the Etowah valley, along with general similarities in material culture (Hally and Langford 1988), suggests a level of cultural affinity between the people living in the two areas. Therefore, the use of the Chickamauga Basin data to understand Early Etowah phase architecture at Etowah seems justified.

Of the buildings encountered by Larson's crew, Structure 3 was the most elaborate. It had a prepared clay floor covered with powdered red ochre, a rectangular, two-tiered clay platform in the center of its western wall, and a small clay step opposite this platform along the eastern wall. Similar Hiwassee Island phase buildings were recorded in the nearby Chickamauga Basin, and in some cases, for example, at Hixon (Neitzel and Jennings 1995) and Hiwassee Island (Lewis and Kneberg 1946), these buildings were found on mound summits. Clearly, the interior treatments and association with mounds suggest buildings like Structure 3 served some specialized purpose.

In the Chickamauga Basin, Lewis (1995) identified such buildings as community structures. No doubt this designation was based in part on the presence of elaborate interior furnishings, but it was also based on building size. Hiwassee Island phase domestic structures had between 22.5 and 54 m^2 of interior floor space, while buildings identified as community structures had between 72 and 180 m^2 of floor space (Lewis 1995:60–64). It seems that the more elaborate buildings were also designed to accommodate more people. Larson's Structure 3 had over 2.5 times the floor space (91 m^2) of contemporary domestic structures, indicating that it also may have had public functions.

Structures 5, 7, and several unidentified wall-trench segments represent even larger buildings constructed in the Mound C vicinity. Structure 5 was the most complete and consisted of a rectangular wall-trench outline with open corners and a series of paired interior support posts. What remained of Structure 7 suggests that it was similar in size and configuration, and it may be that the wall-trench segments uncovered on the northeast side of Mound C also represent similarly configured buildings. The massive size of these buildings (Structure 5 had a floor area of approximately 405 m^2) suggests that they too may have served a public function. In the Chickamauga Basin, large rectangular buildings were found beneath mounds at Hixon (Neitzel and Jennings 1995) and Hiwassee Island (Lewis and Kneberg 1946) and on mound summits at Davis (Cooper et al. 1995) and Sale Creek (Neitzel 1995). Clearly their association with mounds further reinforces their special nature.

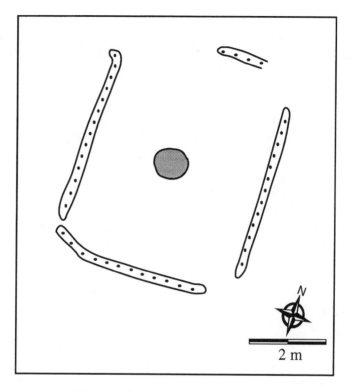

Figure 7. Plan map of Larson's Structure 8.

Unlike these other buildings, Structures 4, 6, and 8 (Figures 6 and 7) were similar in size and shape to residential buildings in the Chickamauga Basin (Lewis 1995:63–64). Each was a wall-trench building, rectangular in plan, with open corners, and none had an interior floor area greater than 40 m². Like many residential buildings, Structures 4 and 8 had a central clay hearth, while Structure 6 had a wall-trench entrance on its southern wall. In addition, Structure 8 had clearly identifiable domestic refuse on its floor that included broken pottery, animal bone, shell, charred wood, corn-cobs, and tools of chert, bone, and shell (Larson n.d.).

In terms of relative dating (Larson n.d.), it appears that the elaborate Structure 3 was the first building to be constructed in the area. The lack of evidence for burning suggests that it was dismantled or allowed to decay, and it was eventually covered by a layer of fill. Whether that fill was inten-tionally placed there or simply accumulated through time is unclear. Over the fill covering Structure 3, the Early Etowah inhabitants of Etowah built the first large, presumably public building, Structure 7. After that building was dismantled or fell into disuse, two residential buildings, Structures 4 and 6, were constructed. Finally, after those buildings fell into disuse or were dismantled, yet another large public building, Structure 5, was constructed in the area.

Unfortunately, existing documentation does not make clear the stratigraphic position of Structure 8 or the large wall-trench segments located to the north. It is tempting to suggest that Structure 8 was contemporary with the other residences and that the use of the area shifted from public to residential and back to public over time. It seems more likely, however, that some of the residences were contemporary with some of the public buildings. Although details about the relative chronology may be fuzzy, it is clear that several large and sometimes elaborate buildings were constructed in the Mound C vicinity. These no doubt hosted public functions that may have been attended by large groups of people. Interspersed among these special buildings were smaller structures that appear to be domestic residences. A similar combination of residential and nonresidential buildings was found in non-mound contexts at Hixon (Neitzel and Jennings 1995) and Hiwassee Island (Lewis and Kneberg 1946). The presence of ordinary dwellings among buildings with more specialized functions may suggest that access to those special buildings and the functions they hosted was open to all members of society.

Because of the way excavations proceeded at Etowah, it is difficult to know the full extent of the site or the arrangement of features on it. Intensive borrowing and feasting activities were conducted in the vicinity of Mounds B and C, and later a series of public and residential buildings were constructed beneath Mound C. Almost certainly, more of this occupation lies beneath Mound B and probably Mound A as well. Interestingly, Sears (1958b) found little Early Etowah phase material in his tests away from Mound B in the area between Mounds A, B, and C. This portion of the site had been damaged by flooding, no doubt on numerous occasions, but more recently in the 1880s and 1890s (Moorehead 1932), so it is possible that the relative absence of deposits is partially the result of natural factors. Sears did, however, find Late Etowah phase features in some of his tests in this area, suggesting that the earliest deposits might be expected to be preserved. If the area between Mounds A, B, and C was not intensively used, it may have actually served as a plaza during the Early Etowah phase. Schroedl (1998) and Lewis (1995) report that contemporary Hiwassee Island settlements in eastern Tennessee often contained an open plaza that was flanked by one or more public buildings, residences, and a palisade.

The available evidence presents at best a fuzzy picture of the structure of the Etowah site and the nature of its inhabitants' social organization during the Early Etowah phase. What seems to be most clear is that at this time Etowah was a small community complete with residences, community buildings, and possibly even a small mound and plaza. Although it is often assumed that institutionalized social ranking was present in the region at this time, mainly because it has been identified at sites like Macon Plateau, it is not clear that it was in fact present at Etowah. Contemporary evidence from nearby sites in eastern Tennessee, however, hints that some type of ranking system may have been in operation.

What seems to be clearer is that the Early Etowah phase archaeology gives the impression of a social group organized more around corporate rather than network principles. Few indications of external contacts were found, in terms of nonlocal materials of any kind, suggesting that such network interactions were not an important part of the social structure. The evidence of feasting, possibly in association with mound construction, suggests that solidarity-building activities may have been an integral part of Early Etowah phase Etowah society. The earth/fertility/purification symbolism associated with mounds and their construction depicts just the kinds of integrative themes that would be expected of a corporate strategy. In addition, the importance of communal activities is implied further by the creation of specialized facilities, in the form of large and elaborate buildings that appear to have been used for group functions. The proposition that Etowah's political economy was based in a corporate strategy is, as much as anything, supported by a lack of evidence for the association of wealth and prestige with individuals. Until the Early Etowah phase occupation of Etowah is explored and understood more fully, the corporate nature of the political economy must remain only a working hypothesis.

THE LATE ETOWAH PHASE: CONTINUITY

As is the case with the Early Etowah phase, the archaeology of Late Etowah phase Etowah presents a very limited picture of the structure of the Etowah site and the social group that inhabited it. On the basis of what has been excavated, it appears that the area occupied during the Late Etowah phase may have been more extensive than that used during the Early Etowah phase (Figure 8). That portion of the site between Mounds A, B, and C continued to be used, but occupation of the river terrace edge expanded east of Mound B (Sears 1958b) and west of Mound C (Wauchope 1966). Additionally, the occupation appears to have extended east and north of Mound A to the edge of the palisade ditch. Although it does not appear

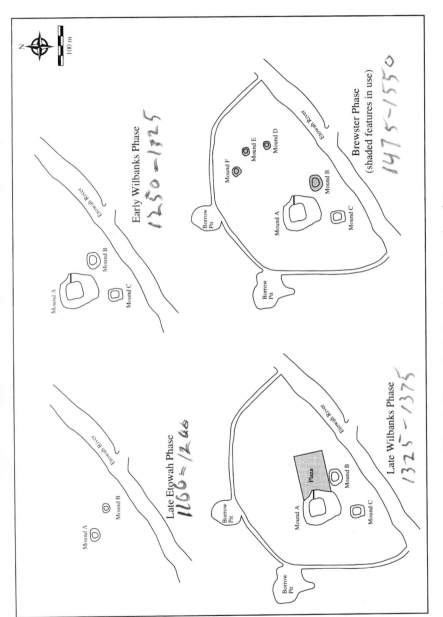

Figure 8. Changes in the Etowah site structure through time.

that the palisade was erected at this time, it is possible that the large borrow pits in this area were in use, because evidence has been found indicating that mound construction took place during the Late Etowah phase. Excavations at Mound B show that the first two stages of the mound were built at this time, creating a small platform no bigger than one-half the final size of Mound B (King 1995). It also is possible, although there is no evidence that can be used to evaluate this, that construction may have continued on Mound A.

Because of the size of the areas investigated at Etowah, it is difficult to determine how any of the locations occupied during the Late Etowah phase were actually used. Some evidence was found, however, suggesting that the Mound B vicinity may have served as a residential zone. Sears (1958b:8) uncovered portions of a rectangular wall-trench building containing a central hearth and the burial of an unaccompanied adult male on the northwest side of Mound B. This structure resembled the Early Etowah domestic buildings found beneath Mound C, suggesting that it too may have served as a residence. A portion of what may have been a similar building was recorded on the south side of Mound A, and it had an infant buried in the floor (Sears 1958b:41). Sears (1958b:47) also encountered the corner of another wall-trench structure approximately 30 m west of Mound B in the open area between Mounds B and C. Although the associated pottery sample is small, it may represent yet another Late Etowah residence in the Mound B vicinity. Interestingly, neither Sears (1958b) nor Larson (King 1996:81–87) found much indication that the Mound C vicinity, which was actively used during the Early Etowah, was used intensively during the Late Etowah phase.

Outside of these data, little else is available that can be used to determine whether ranking was a part of Late Etowah society and whether its social structure was organized around corporate or network principles. Currently, only a handful of Late Etowah burials are known from the site, the two mentioned above found in association with presumed residences and a third found intruding through the fill of Saucer 2 west of Mound B (King 2001:36–40). None of the three burials contained grave goods. This paucity of burials may indicate that, like Early Etowah phase mortuary practices, most Late Etowah people were buried in a single location possibly away from the rest of the site. Although available data are limited, it appears that few nonlocal goods or raw materials were present at the site, suggesting that external contacts may not have figured prominently in Late Etowah society. These data, thin as they are, may indicate that Late Etowah phase society was also structured around corporate principles. Only future archaeological research at Etowah can evaluate this hypothesis.

THE EARLY SAVANNAH PERIOD:
A PERIOD OF ABANDONMENT

When archaeologists first began working out the ceramic sequence of the Etowah valley, they noted a marked difference between pottery belonging to the Etowah period (Early and Late Etowah phases) and stratigraphically later ceramics assigned to the Savannah period (Early and Late Wilbanks phases). These differences were seen as so dramatic that many invoked an invasion of foreign people to explain them (Fairbanks 1950; Sears 1958a). More recently, excavations conducted in northern and central Georgia have recovered assemblages that appear to bridge the gap between Etowah and Savannah assemblages. Pottery collections from the Beaverdam Creek site (9EB85) on the middle Savannah (Rudolph and Hally 1985), Scull Shoals (9GE4) in the Oconee valley (Williams 1985), and Sandy Hammock (9PU10) on the Ocmulgee River (Stephenson et al. 1996) contain a mix of characteristics clearly showing that the Savannah pottery tradition developed from the preceding Etowah tradition. No such transitional assemblage has been identified at any of the sites currently recorded in the Etowah River valley (Hally and Langford 1988; Hally and Rudolph 1986; King 1997, 2001). Hally (Hally and Langford 1988:56; Hally and Rudolph 1986:53–57) has used these data to argue that the entire valley experienced a period of abandonment during the early part of the Savannah period (A.D. 1200–1250). Because no early Savannah period pottery assemblages have been found at Etowah (King 1996, 2001), this abandonment included the community located at the Etowah site.

THE EARLY WILBANKS PHASE:
THE QUICK RISE TO GREATNESS

Sometime during the Early Wilbanks phase, Etowah was reoccupied. This occupation marks the beginning of a period of unprecedented growth at the site (Figure 8). Site areas tested show that the Early Wilbanks occupation extended from the river terrace's edge northward to the palisade ditch, with the most intense occupations occurring to the east of Mound B, the west of Mound C, and the east of Mound A. In addition, the pace of mound construction increased considerably. Currently available evidence shows that the first three construction stages were built at Mound C (King 1996:110), at least two stages were built on Mound B (King 2001), and at least one stage was built on Mound A that included an impressive ramp and associated log-lined staircase (King 1995). Sears's (1958b:56) testing in the area between Mounds A, B, and C demonstrated that there was little if any occupation in that area postdating the Late Etowah phase, suggesting that this portion of the site functioned as a small plaza during the Early Wilbanks phase.

By the abandonment that followed the Late Etowah phase occupation, two stages of construction at Mound B had created a small platform whose exact size remains unknown. The northeastern corner of that platform was encountered near the outer edge of the current surface of Mound B at the center of its northern side (King 1995). This suggests that the Late Etowah platform covered no more than one-half the area of the final size of Mound B. During the Early Wilbanks phase, at least two stages were added to the mound, and evidence found on the northern side (King 1995) suggests that these construction efforts dramatically expanded Mound B to the north. Rogan (Thomas 1894) and Moorehead (1932) reported finding evidence that may indicate the presence of buildings on the summit of Mound B. Unfortunately, it currently is impossible to determine when these buildings were built or what they looked like.

Along the western periphery of Mound B, Kelly and his crew uncovered a large circular building (Structure 3, Figure 9) dating to the Early Wilbanks phase. This building was constructed on a prepared yellow clay surface that apparently was enclosed within a small compound adjacent to Mound B by a palisade wall set in a trench. Structure 3 measured approximately 12.8 m in diameter and was surrounded by a narrow trench and small embankment, both of which were probably created to protect the building from water coursing down the western slope of Mound B. Most of the posts associated with this building were found in a ring within a few meters of the encircling ditch and embankment, leaving the central portion devoid of posts. In that central area, crews recorded a fired area that probably served as a hearth, along with what appeared to be a small drainage ditch that originated at the hearth and continued westward out of the building. Both the overall post pattern and the presence of an interior drainage feature give the impression that the central portion of Structure 3 did not have a roof. The rather discontinuous distribution of posts within the building seems to indicate the presence of roof and bench supports, but the lack of any continuous outer wall. Therefore, Structure 3 may have been an open-walled, shedlike structure similar to the rectangular buildings associated with Historic period square grounds.

Stratigraphic evidence indicates that Structure 3 experienced three episodes of use, each terminated by the washing of sandy soil across the floor area. Details of the nearby mound stratigraphy suggest that those sands originated from mound surfaces that were exposed during periods of mound construction (King 2001:79). Therefore, with the addition of each

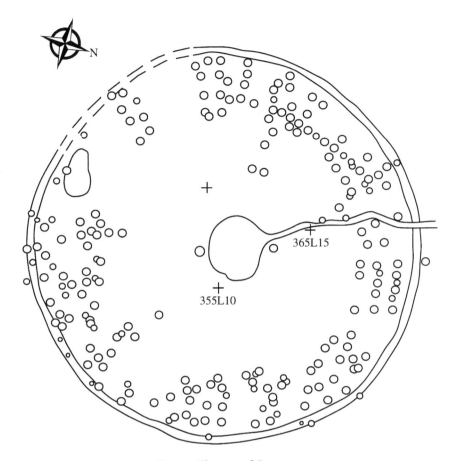

Figure 9. Plan map of Structure 3.

new stage, sand washed over the floor of Structure 3. If this building had open walls, then wash from the mound could have easily covered the floor. There are some indications, however, that Structure 3 may have been dismantled or destroyed with each successive construction stage. Associated with the last two uses of Structure 3 are charcoal-filled middens. While these may have been produced during the use of the building, it is also possible that they are the burned remains of Structure 3. In fact, it is possible that the destruction and burial of Structure 3 was part of the overall mound construction process. As I will discuss shortly, the prepared surface on which Structure 3 was built appears to be the beginnings of a small terrace actually connected to the summit of Mound B. Given this, it may be that Structure 3 warranted the same treatment as mound-top buildings.

The above discussion suggests that Structure 3 was something more than a residential building. Roughly contemporary Dallas phase domestic structures recorded in eastern Tennessee are rectangular, made of single-set post construction, and exhibit floor areas that average roughly one-third the floor area of Structure 3 (Lewis 1995:71–73). In fact, the large size of Structure 3 suggests that it was designed to accommodate a fairly large group of people. Unlike the public buildings present during the Early Etowah phase, however, Structure 3 was enclosed within a palisaded compound, indicating that the functions occurring within it were not open to all inhabitants of Etowah. Excavators reported finding scraps of copper in the middens associated with this building, suggesting that the activities taking place inside involved the manipulation of a material intimately associated with elite status in the Mississippian Southeast. Clearly, Structure 3 had special functions that appear to be associated with a restricted, and probably elite, segment of Etowah society. The possibility that it was destroyed, buried, and rebuilt with each new construction effort at Mound B further reinforces its very special nature.

Immediately to the south of Structure 3, outside of its palisade wall enclosure, Kelly's crew recorded the remains of at least two smaller, rectangular buildings (Structures 1 and 2) (King 2001:26–28). In terms of their size and shape, these buildings resemble the roughly contemporary Dallas phase domestic structures identified in the Chickamauga Basin of eastern Tennessee (Lewis 1995:71–73). Evidence also was found suggesting that at least two similar buildings were constructed to the west of Structures 1 and 3. The presence of these buildings indicates that some portion of this area also served as a residential zone, albeit probably only for individuals with specialized roles in Etowah society.

Across the small plaza west of Mound B, the Early Wilbanks construction boom brought about the building of the first three stages of Mound C (Figure 10). There is a striking degree of consistency in how each of these stages was constructed and used. After fills were placed to create each stage, their summits, flanks, and bases were used as repositories for graves, and in each case the mound and associated burials were surrounded by a wall-trench palisade. On the summit of Stage 1 Larson's crew recorded a small segment of a wall trench, suggesting that it may have supported a building. The summits of Stages 2 and 3 were entirely destroyed by the work of Moorehead (1932), but it remains possible that they also supported similar structures. Larson also found evidence suggesting that Stages 2 and 3 had small ramps projecting from their eastern sides, presumably supporting stairways to the mound summit. With the completion of Stage 3, Mound C stood approximately 4.5 to 5 m tall and was about 35 m in diameter.

Because of the confusion created by the excavation and recording tech-

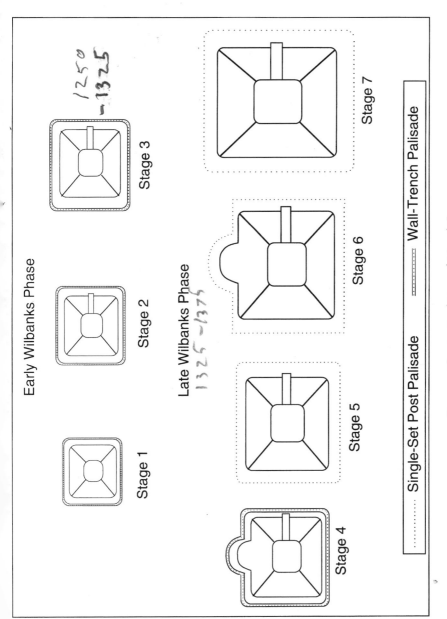

Early Wilbanks Phase

Stage 1

Stage 2

Stage 3

1250
~1325

Late Wilbanks Phase
1325 ~1375

Stage 4

Stage 5

Stage 6

Stage 7

.... Single-Set Post Palisade   ═════ Wall-Trench Palisade

Figure 10. Construction history of Mound C.

niques used by Rogan and Moorehead, it is not currently possible to associate definitively individual burials with a particular stage among the first
three construction stages of Mound C. Some observations can be made
about the burials that do appear to be associated with these stages, although
these are not based on any systematic examination of the Mound C mortuary program. First, the graves associated with the first three stages were
either simple pits or pits lined with limestone slabs. Also, not all graves in
these stages included grave goods, and, in those that did, shell beads and
sometimes shell gorgets were the most common items found. A small percentage of those graves contained clearly more elaborate items such as pottery vessels, flint blades, and headdresses with copper ornamentation (Figure 11). Most of these elaborate graves, which include many of the richest
burials recorded by Rogan (Thomas 1894) and Moorehead (1932), were
placed into the summits of the first three stages.

In his demographic study of the Mound C burial population, completed using age and sex distributions from Larson's excavated sample only,
Blakely (1995) found evidence that only selected individuals were buried
in the mound. Specifically, he found that, while present, children and adolescents were underrepresented, suggesting that only a small subset of all
children and adolescents were afforded burial in Mound C. In addition, the
probability of men being buried in Mound C increased with age, again
suggesting that people interred within the mound were selected by certain socially defined criteria. These same basic patterns were visible when
Blakely divided Larson's burials into two categories that included those
clearly associated with the last construction stages of the mound (final
mantle burials) and those associated with earlier stages (pre-final mantle
burials). My own analysis shows that the final mantle grouping is associated
with the Late Wilbanks stages of Mound C, while the pre-final mantle
burials should belong with the Early Wilbanks stages.

Clearly, during the Early Wilbanks phase, only a select subset of people
from Etowah were actually buried in Mound C. The presence of children
suggests that in some cases the criteria allowing burial in Mound C must
have been assigned at birth, while the fact that men increased their chances
of being buried in the mound with age suggests an element of achievement
also was involved in gaining access to burial in Mound C.

Outside of Mound C, only a few Early Wilbanks phase burials have
been identified, but the grave goods found within them stand in marked
contrast to those recovered from many of the Mound C burials. In the
Mound B vicinity, Kelly's crew excavated at least two Early Wilbanks
phase burials. One had no grave goods included, but had four limestone
slabs at its corners. The second was a simple pit containing an adult male

Figure 11. Embossed copper plate from Rogan's Burial a. From Philip Phillips and James A. Brown, Pre-Columbian Shell Engravings from the Craig Mound at Spiro, Oklahoma, *paperback, part I. Peabody Museum Press. Copyright 1978 by the President and Fellows of Harvard College. Used by permission.*

accompanied by a broad, side-notched projectile and a bone awl. Sears (1958b:106) uncovered another Early Wilbanks burial approximately 60 m east of Mound A's ramp, and it contained the remains of a single individual buried in a stone box grave with no grave goods. Although the comparative data are very thin, it seems that the people buried in Mound C had if not exclusive then greater access to elaborate burial furniture than people not buried in the mound. This inference is supported by Larson's characterization of Wilbanks burials he encountered during village area excavations. Of those village burials Larson (1971a:66) remarked: "Only rarely are these burials accompanied by grave goods. When such are present, they consist of either a stone celt or a pottery vessel with both objects being representative of types employed in a domestic context."

Many of the fabulous grave goods found in Early Wilbanks burials in Mound C were made using materials not available in the immediate vicinity of Etowah. For example, the shell used to make the beads and gorgets came from the Gulf Coast (Brown 1983), the chert used to make the "flint swords" was quarried in Tennessee (Larson 1971a), and the copper used to make the plates and other headdress elements probably also came from Tennessee (Goad 1980). In addition, many of these objects bore decoration executed in styles found widely distributed across the Southeast. For example, copper plates decorated in the same style as those recovered by Rogan have been found at sites distributed from Florida to Missouri (Phillips and Brown 1978). Therefore, it seems apparent that the same people afforded the right of burial in Mound C also had greater if not exclusive access to fancy goods that circulated widely throughout the region.

It has long been recognized that the fancy burial goods recovered from Mound C belong to a suite of ceremonial objects and symbolic themes shared widely across the Southeast during the Middle Mississippian period (A.D. 1250–1400). This set of objects and themes is known as the Southern Cult or Southeastern Ceremonial Complex (SECC) and is most often found in specialized mortuary settings similar to Mound C. In chiefdoms, in which elaborate materials often circulate widely, the most important element of society (the political and social leaders) has the greatest access to these items. In fact, it is very often the case that leaders manufacture and distribute these kinds of goods to meet certain political ends, thereby using them as prestige goods. Almost certainly, SECC goods, including those recovered from Mound C, were used in a similar fashion (Brown 1976; Welch 1996).

In light of the above discussions, available information about the mortuary record of Mound C indicates several important factors about Early Wilbanks phase society at Etowah. First, it seems apparent that institutionalized social ranking, both ascribed and achieved, was a part of Etowah's social structure. Further, the ranked structure was explicitly materialized through access to burial in Mound C as well as certain elaborate material goods like the SECC items. Finally, if those SECC items did in fact operate in some sense as prestige goods, then participation in external exchange networks may have been an integral part of leadership in Early Wilbanks society. Each of these elements is consistent with the operation of a network political economic strategy.

As might be expected, the construction boom that caused the enlargement of Mound B and the creation of Mound C did not leave Mound A unaltered. Currently available evidence shows that at least one stage of the ramp projecting from the east side of Mound A was built during the Early Wilbanks phase, and it is highly probable that this addition was part of a larger construction effort designed to enlarge the entire body of Mound A. Unfortunately, no excavations have investigated deeply enough into the mound to determine whether more than one stage was added during this phase. Since only one Late Wilbanks and no Brewster phase construction stages were subsequently added, it seems likely that a major portion of this enormous mound probably was built during the Early Wilbanks phase. On the face of the Early Wilbanks phase ramp, the inhabitants of Etowah built a staircase of packed clay and logs, which measured approximately 7 m wide (Figure 12). This impressive staircase no doubt added to the grandeur of Mound A.

One of the most noticeable features at Etowah is the ditch that once surrounded the site on three sides. Just inside of that ditch Larson (1972) recorded a portion of a palisade wall with bastions that, with the ditch, made up a formidable fortification complex. In those palisade excavations, Larson's crew found a thin deposit of Etowah period pottery and a much denser concentration of Wilbanks ceramics, including some Late Wilbanks diagnostics (King 1996:119–122). In some of the palisade postholes and the associated wall trench, Larson's crew recovered both Etowah and Wilbanks pottery, but no Late Wilbanks diagnostics. These data suggest that the palisade wall was erected sometime during the Wilbanks phases. The ditch links a series of large borrow pits, which I suggested previously first may have been used during the Late Etowah phase. Almost certainly, the ditch linking those borrow pits was used as a source of mound fill. Given the fact that mound construction continued into the Late Wilbanks phase, it may be that the ditch and palisade wall as a defensive complex was not completed until after the Early Wilbanks phase.

With the Early Wilbanks phase re-occupation of Etowah, the site and the social group inhabiting it took on a dramatically different look. Com-

Figure 12. Clay staircase on the face of Mound A's ramp. Photograph by A. King.

pared with that in the previous Late Etowah phase occupation, the size of the site area used increased markedly. In addition, there appears to have been an increased emphasis on monumental constructions, as major portions of Mounds A, B, and C were all built. Although it is difficult to determine how most areas of the site were used, it does seem clear that the area between Mounds B and C was converted to a small plaza that was flanked on three sides by specialized areas. To the north of this plaza stood the already massive Mound A. On its eastern side stood Mound B and the large public building, Structure 3, enclosed within a palisade wall, while on its western side the elite mortuary facility, Mound C, also stood enclosed within a palisade. The mortuary evidence contained within Mound C, although incompletely understood, demonstrates that social ranking was clearly a part of Early Wilbanks Etowah. Further, it indicates that specialized mortuary treatment, elaborate displays, and external connections were all intimately associated with persons of high status. Overall, there appears to be a shift from the corporate nature of the Etowah period society to a more exclusionary network approach to organizing the political economy during the Early Wilbanks phase.

THE LATE WILBANKS PHASE:
ENTRENCHMENT AND SUDDEN COLLAPSE

In most respects, the patterns established during the Early Wilbanks phase continued into the Late Wilbanks occupation at Etowah (Figure 8). Monumental construction continued unabated, and burial in Mound C and access to nonlocal, symbolically charged items remained the prerogatives of a selected subset of Etowah society. It also seems clear that the network orientation established during the Early Wilbanks phase continued into the Late Wilbanks.

During the Late Wilbanks phase occupation of Etowah, stages were added to Mounds A, B, and C. At Mound A, evidence from the summit indicates that a single construction stage was added during the Late Wilbanks phase. In addition, a small landing platform was built at the base of the ramp, covering the bottom 6 m of the staircase. At Mound B, available excavation data indicate that a single construction stage was added to this mound during the Late Wilbanks. Also, the inhabitants of the site extended the clay cap covering this stage out into the area to the west of the mound, creating a small terrace. This terrace was constructed over the final wash episode covering the floor of Structure 3. Instead of rebuilding Structure 3 for a fourth time, Etowah's inhabitants constructed a large rectangular building (Structure 4) on this new terrace.

This building measured approximately 7.6 by 12 m, was open at its south end, and, at least during part of its life, had its interior space divided by one or two partition walls. The presence of multiple lines of posts along each exterior wall indicates that Structure 4 was rebuilt on several occasions. Like the Early Wilbanks buildings constructed in the area, Structure 4 had a small embankment along its eastern wall, presumably to divert mound slope runoff. Kelly's field notes indicate that a hearth was located along the northern wall of Structure 4, and like Structure 3, it was associated with a small drainage feature. Those field notes also state that excavators found animal bone, cut mica, small chunkey stones, ceramic animal figurines, parts of a copper plate, and negative painted pottery on the floor of Structure 4.

Understanding the function of Structure 4 is difficult to do with available information. It is a large building and clearly larger than most contemporary domestic residences, even those located on mound tops. If Kelly's interpretation of the post pattern is correct, then Structure 4 may have had both open and private spaces, separated by partition walls. Given its location, it is possible that it hosted group functions just as Structure 3 had during the Early Wilbanks phase. If this is the case, then, in contrast to Structure 3, the partitioning of Structure 4 suggests that some activities were conducted in secret or were designed to include a smaller number of people. It is also possible the post pattern of Structure 4 represents an architectural arrangement similar to that found on several mound summits in Georgia and eastern Tennessee (Lewis and Kneberg 1946; Polhemus 1987; Smith 1994). At these sites, excavators found what appeared to be residential buildings adjacent to or attached to open-ended porchlike structures. It has been argued that these architectural features were designed to accommodate the public and private activities of important personages (Polhemus 1987; Smith 1994), and the same interpretation may hold for Structure 4. The presence of animal bone on the floor of the building is consistent with its use as a residence, while the recovery of materials intimately associated with elite status in the Southeast suggests some connection with important members of Etowah society.

The differences between Structures 3 and 4 suggest that the use of the area west of Mound B may have changed in some manner from the Early to Late Wilbanks phase. The large amount of open space in Structure 3, along with the lack of any partitioning walls, seems to indicate that it was designed to accommodate a gathering of people in an open or public setting. The fact that this building was enclosed within a palisaded compound indicates that access to those functions may have been restricted to a subset of Etowah society. If Structure 4 was also in some manner a public building, then the partitioning within it suggests that the functions it housed included a smaller number of people than Structure 3 was designed to accommodate. If Structure 4 was actually a residence with attached public space for an important person, then use of the area adjacent to Mound B was even further restricted to a smaller set of people. In either case, it appears that access to the Mound B vicinity became more restricted from the Early to Late Wilbanks phase.

Also during the Late Wilbanks phase, four additional construction stages were added to Mound C (Figure 10). The first of these (Stage 4) was built to cover three burials placed just outside the palisade encircling the mound (Figure 13). Included among those burials was Larson's Burial 57, which is notable not only for its unique location, but also for the fact that it was placed in a new form of grave—a log-lined tomb. Included with the single individual in Burial 57 were a shell gorget, eight conch-shell cups, five or six embossed copper plates, two copper celts, a pair of copper-covered ear disks, a copper bead, and numerous shell beads (Larson 1971a). Larson's field notes indicate that the individual was buried wearing a headdress composed of copper ornaments, a garment embroidered with pearls, a feather robe, and a collar of shell beads. This interment subsequently was covered with mound fill, creating a small rectangular terrace abutting the northern edge of Mound C, and the palisade wall ringing the mound was adjusted to accommodate the new addition. Subsequently, two more burials were placed to the north of Burial 57, each necessitating an adjustment to the palisade wall. The first of these was Burial 47, which contained the remains of a single individual, and it was followed by an unnumbered mass grave containing the poorly preserved remains of seven people (Larson 1971a). The small terrace eventually was enlarged to cover the two additional burials, completing the first Late Wilbanks stage at Mound C.

After the completion of Stage 4, the entire mound was surrounded by a cane wall set in a trench, which eventually was dismantled as part of the construction of Stage 5. Rather than being filled with soils washed from the mound surface, the trench for the cane wall was filled with Stage 5 construction materials. This prompted Larson to suggest in his field notes that the cane wall had been erected to serve as a short-term screen used only during construction of Stage 5. After construction was completed, the inhabitants of Etowah again used the flanks and base of Mound C as a repository for the dead. Both the mound and associated burials were once again surrounded by a single-set post palisade.

As they had done with the construction of Stage 4, the builders of Mound C placed another log-lined tomb (Burial 38) just to the north of the palisade around Stage 5. In this tomb were the remains of five indi-

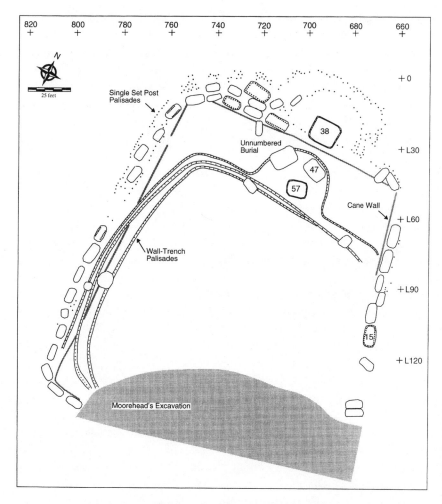

Figure 13. Final ring of Mound C burials. Adapted from Larson 1971a:60.

viduals, each accompanied by a copper celt and a pair of copper-covered ear disks. Four of the individuals were buried wearing elaborate head-dresses composed of small sheet-copper ornaments, hawk skins, and feath-ers (Larson 1971a). The fifth person apparently had no headdress, but was accompanied by a scalloped and engraved stone palette and a shell gorget. Burial 38 subsequently was covered with mound construction fill, creating yet another small terrace on the north side of Mound C. That same mound fill also was deposited along the flanks of the mound (Stage 6), effectively widening Mound C at its base but not increasing its height. As they had done with earlier construction stages, Etowah's inhabitants placed burials at the foot of this new stage and surrounded it with a palisade.

Eventually, the small terrace and the rest of the burials at the base of Mound C were again covered by a new construction effort (Stage 7), which brought Mound C to its final height of approximately 5.8 m. Once again it was surrounded by a palisade wall, made of single-set posts. As with earlier stages, the summits of Stages 5, 6, and 7 had been completely removed before Larson began his excavations, so it was unclear whether each supported a structure. In addition, it appears that the ramp on the eastern side of the mound was retained and probably augmented during these construction stages. With the completion of Stage 7, all construction and mortuary activities, with the exception of two burials to be discussed shortly, appear to have ceased at Mound C.

While the archaeology of Mound C shows some remarkable consistency from the Early to Late Wilbanks in terms of construction and use of the mound and surroundings, there are some noticeable differences in the two mortuary records. First, stone-lined tombs appear to be replaced by log-lined graves during the Late Wilbanks phase. Also, it appears that the practice of placing burials into the summit was abandoned after the Early Wilbanks phase, while the covering of particularly rich graves with small terraces on the north side of Mound C was adopted. Finally, it has been noted that the ring of burials associated with the Late Wilbanks stages (Figure 13) appears to be composed of discrete clusters (Brain and Phillips 1996; Larson 1971a, 1993). Brain and Phillips (1996) argue that these clusters represent individual mortuary events triggered by the death of important people. It may be just as reasonable to suggest that they represent burial plots within the Mound C complex designated for distinct subgroups of the larger Etowah society.

If these trends stand after a systematic examination of the Late Wilbanks mortuary record has been completed, then they may signal some interesting changes in Etowah society. For example, if truly absent during the Early Wilbanks phase, the discrete burial clusters of the Late Wilbanks may support the notion that individuals from a wider range of segments of Etowah's society (lineages, clans, etc.) gained access to both prestige goods and Mound C burial. If this was the case, then it may signal the loss of a monopoly over important sources of power on the part of Etowah's ruling subgroup. Whether these changes are real or not, the Late Wilbanks mortuary record of Mound C does seem to indicate that both ascribed and achieved social ranking were still in operation (see Blakely 1995; Larson 1971a). It also seems clear that access to nonlocal material, often adorned with elaborate and symbolically loaded decoration, remained primarily in the hands of those highly ranked people buried in Mound C.

At some point during the Late Wilbanks phase, a large plaza was constructed in the area east of Mound A. The previous use of this area is poorly understood, but the presence of midden deposits in some locations suggests that it may have been used for habitations or other functions involving the discard of refuse. Above these deposits, Sears (1958b:94–107) encountered a prepared clay surface made of basket-loaded clay. In the area closest to the base of Mound A's ramp, the surface may have been repaved after its original creation. In an excavation to the east of Mound B, Sears (1958b:84) found rock slabs abutting the edge of the plaza surface, which he interpreted to represent a rock wall constructed around the periphery of the plaza. Larson found a corner and two segments of a wall trench placed on the plaza surface during his investigation of the eastern end of the plaza. Those wall segments were fairly long (22 and 69 m), suggesting that they were probably part of some type of enclosure rather than walls to a building.

It seems likely that the palisade wall and associated ditch also were completed during the Late Wilbanks phase. Late nineteenth-century descriptions of the site written by Jones and Whittlesey (cited in Thomas 1894) indicate that the ditch began at the river's edge on the western side of the site, connected two very large borrow pits located on the northern side, and ended in another shallow borrow pit at the eastern edge of the site. It is probable that the ditch once surrounded the entire site, but portions of it had clearly been filled in to facilitate cultivation during the nineteenth century. Excavations conducted at the northern edge of the ditch indicated that a wall-trench palisade line had been constructed just inside the ditch (Larson 1972). Portions of a rectangular bastion also were recorded, suggesting that these were probably spaced at intervals along its entire periphery. From the depth that the posts were placed into the trench, Larson (1972) estimated that the palisade wall stood as high as 3.65 m. Excavators found daub in the vicinity of the palisade, indicating that its surface had been plastered with clay.

The creation of the palisade wall and ditch implies a concern for defense that apparently had not existed, at least to the same degree, during earlier occupations of the site. It may be that this concern was warranted, because excavation data suggest that the palisade wall burned. In his original 1962 excavations and in the more recent 1995 work, Larson's crews noted that many of the palisade posts were charred, and the daub recovered in the vicinity had clearly been fired. Additionally, no indications were found by

Figure 14. Marble statues from Larson's Burial 15. Photograph by A. King.

Larson that a second palisade wall was ever built, suggesting that the burning had ended the use life of Etowah's palisade and ditch complex.

It is surely no coincidence that Etowah was abandoned sometime during
the Late Wilbanks phase. Although it is possible that the destruction of the
palisade was an accident, the fact that it happened just prior to a period of
abandonment and was never rebuilt suggests that it was intentional and
somehow related to the abandonment of Etowah. Lemoyne's classic drawing of a Timucua attack, in which warriors shot flaming arrows into a town
from outside its palisade, suggests that fire was used as part of military at-
tacks during the late prehistoric Southeast. The de Soto expedition also
witnessed the use of fire as part of native warfare, as their palisaded en-
campment was attacked by the Chicaza (Hudson et al. 1989) and as
Guachoya's raiders burned the town of Anilco (Hudson 1997).

Late in the construction sequence, an interesting series of mortuary
events occurred that also may be related to the burning of Etowah's palisade. These events were initiated by the placement of a log-lined tomb
(Burial 15) at the base of Mound C's ramp. In this grave Larson's crew
found the famous male and female painted marble figures (Figure 14). Also
in Burial 15 were the disarticulated remains of four individuals, which had
been scattered across the floor along with shell beads, copper-covered ear
spools, antler projectiles, fragments of sheet copper ornaments, and stone

and clay pipe bowls. The marble figures were found one on top of the other and both had been broken, as if they had been dropped or carelessly tossed into the pit (Larson 1971a:65). In Larson's reconstruction of these events, a thin, midden-like smear of human bone and other objects (Burial 1) was deposited down the face of Mound C's ramp shortly after Burial 15 was completed. This deposit contained many of the same kinds of grave goods found in other Mound C burials, including a stone palette, shell beads, copper-covered ear disks, a pipe bowl fragment, antler projectile points, pieces of ceramic vessels, and whelk and oyster shell. Like Burial 15, this deposit contained the disarticulated remains of as many as four people.

This series of mortuary events calls to mind the hurried burial of Etowah's ruling chiefly lineage (Kelly and Larson 1957), followed by the sacking of Mound C's mortuary temple (Brain and Phillips 1996). It has been argued that statues recovered in mound contexts in the Southeast, including those from Etowah, represented the founders of ruling lineages (Brown 1976; Knight 1986; Waring 1968). Such figures may be similar to the stone statue reportedly kept in the temple at the Grand Village of the Natchez, which was apparently the remains of *The*—a supernatural being who descended from the Sun, taught the Natchez how to govern and live properly, and turned his body to stone before leaving the earth (Swanton 1922). The nature of Burial 15 suggests that the marble figures, and by extension the lineage they represented, were given a burial just like those provided to other members of Etowah's elite ranks. The jumbled state in which Burial 15's contents were found represents a departure from the more orderly and undisturbed appearance of most Mound C burials, suggesting that Burial 15 may have been completed under some duress. In some way, that duress may have been related to the events leading to the burning of Etowah's palisade.

If Etowah was invaded, then Larson's Burial 1 may have an important meaning. The de Soto chronicles contain several references to the desecration of enemy temples by invading armies (see Anderson 1994; DePratter 1991; Steinen 1992). Garcilaso de la Vega (Varner and Varner 1951), who is unfortunately widely considered to be the least reliable of the chroniclers, provided one of the most vivid of these descriptions. At least some of the events he described are corroborated by more reliable sources (for example, the sacking of Pacaha's temple noted in Elvas 1993:116–122), suggesting that, as other researchers have argued (Anderson 1994:80; DePratter 1991), ransacking an enemy's temple was one of the greatest insults an invader could perpetrate and was a primary goal of a military attack. From this perspective, the midden-like smear of human remains and sacred objects Larson recorded on the face of Mound C's ramp may have been the remaining contents of Etowah's mortuary temple that were tossed from the temple as it was ransacked by invaders.

THE EARLY LAMAR PERIOD:
A SECOND PERIOD OF ABANDONMENT

As Anderson (1994:81) has argued, such an attack on the center of a chiefdom may have been enough to bring about its eventual abandonment. Although it is not certain that military attack was the cause, available evidence suggests that Etowah was in fact abandoned during the Late Wilbanks phase. No Stamp Creek or Mayes phase materials have been recovered from the site, indicating that it remained abandoned until the Brewster phase.

THE BREWSTER PHASE:
REOCCUPATION OF AN ANCIENT CHIEFLY CAPITAL

When Etowah was reoccupied in the Brewster phase, it became a very different place than it had been a century before (Figure 8). Habitation areas were concentrated in the area east of Mounds A and B, overlying the Late Wilbanks plaza surface. Moorehead (1932) also found Brewster phase deposits to the west of Mound C, and Sears (1958b:58–59) excavated a domestic structure just off the southeastern corner of Mound B. Very little Brewster phase material was found by Sears (1958b) between Mounds B and C, however. Additionally, few Brewster phase sherds were recovered during the Mound C excavations, and these were all found on the outer surfaces of the mound. The investigations completed on the summit of Mound A also found few Brewster phase deposits, showing that Mound A probably was not extensively used or added to during this phase. At Mound B, however, dense Brewster phase deposits were recorded on the summit, as well as a postlike feature, suggesting that this surface in fact was used intensively (King 1995).

The only clear evidence for mound construction was collected by Larson during his 1965 excavations at Mound D. On the basis of stratigraphy and artifacts, it appears that Mound D was built in a single episode during the Brewster phase (King 1996:112–117). The stratigraphic information left behind by Rogan's excavation of Mound E, although not considered very reliable, suggests that it was built in two stages. Unfortunately, no artifact collections exist that can help date those stages. Given the relative proximity of Mounds E and F to Mound D, along with the high occurrence of Brewster phase sherds in surface collections conducted in the area, it seems probable that all three mounds were built during the Brewster phase. Unfortunately, it remains unclear exactly how these mounds were used.

Brewster phase burials were excavated by both Larson and Moorehead during their investigations of village areas at Etowah. Unfortunately, it is difficult in many cases to distinguish Brewster phase graves from those associated with earlier occupations. Humpf (1995) examined the burials excavated by Larson during his several seasons of work in the Brewster phase village. Humpf's results alone provide few insights, however, into the ranking system in place during the Brewster phase at Etowah. This is primarily because the sample of burials available to Humpf was small (35 burials) and their arrangement with respect to architectural features such as mounds or buildings remains poorly understood. Humpf was able to identify some sex-specific grave-goods associations, as well as recognize three adult burials (two male, one indeterminate) containing artifacts that Hatch (1974), on the basis of his study of the partially contemporary Dallas phase mortuary patterns, found to be closely associated with high status. Those items included conch-shell cups and minerals such as galena and graphite.

One of the most interesting elements of the Brewster phase occupation of Etowah is the evidence of a sixteenth-century Spanish presence at the site. According to the route of de Soto reconstructed by Hudson and colleagues (DePratter et al. 1985; Hudson 1997:220–224), de Soto and his army spent nine days, from August 21 to 30, 1540, at the Etowah site (known as the town of Itaba) awaiting a drop in the rain-swollen Etowah River. Evidence of that extended stay has been found in some abundance in the Brewster phase village. While excavating the Brewster village east of Mound A, Larson recovered an iron spike, a piece of chain mail, and an iron celt (Larson, personal communication 1995; Smith 1976). Larson's crews also found a portion of a sword hilt, similar to the hilt of the sword found at the King site, in those village excavations (Brain and Phillips 1996:173; Larson, personal communication 1995). Probably the most interesting of the European artifacts recovered by Larson are the two fragments of a European-style sandstone rotary quern. Each fragment was found on a different house floor in the Brewster phase village area (Brain and Phillips 1996:173).

Unfortunately, the archaeological evidence available from Etowah provides scant information about the orientation of the Brewster phase political economy. There are hints in the burial record that elevated status may have been symbolized by access to a restricted set of materials, including nonlocal items like marine shell, copper, and mineral pigments. If this was the case, then it is possible that the network approach, similar to the one applied during the Wilbanks phases, was still in use during the Brewster phase. A broader look at contemporary archaeological data from the region appears to support this inference. As expected if a network strategy was being applied, social ranking systems appeared to be well defined and individuals of the highest statuses were clearly distinguished through special treatment and access to certain nonlocal goods. For example, mortuary data from contemporary contexts in northern Georgia (Humpf 1995; Seckinger 1977) and eastern Tennessee (Hatch 1974; Polhemus 1987; Sullivan 1986) indicate that late Lamar period ranking systems in the region included both achieved and ascribed status positions and that the highest statuses were buried adjacent to or within mounds accompanied by specialized artifacts such as conch-shell cups, painted bottles, copper artifacts, and minerals like graphite and galena.

Data concerning mound-summit architecture may provide further support for the operation of a network strategy. Where a network strategy is applied, political leaders will be distinguished clearly from the rest of society and often will rely on some form of patrimonial rhetoric to reproduce their status positions. Throughout northwestern Georgia and eastern Tennessee, structures have been recorded on mound summits or adjacent terraces dating to the late Lamar period that are similar in form to, although often larger than, domestic buildings recorded in non-mound contexts (Hally 1994; Polhemus 1987). In many cases, mound summits contained multiple buildings that included small porches and complexes of what appear to be residential and public buildings. These data suggest that some segment of late Lamar society was set apart from the rest by residing on and using mound summits for other important functions. Sixteenth-century ethnohistoric data suggest that those people were the political and social leaders of late Lamar chiefdoms (see DePratter 1991). Those same ethnohistoric sources indicate that some mound summits also supported temples dedicated to the ancestors of chiefs. Such a specialized facility designed to glorify a particular ruling segment and its legitimate claim to political power represents an example of patrimonial rhetoric.

THE EARLY HISTORIC PERIOD:
THE FINAL ABANDONMENT

Sometime after 1550, Etowah was abandoned and never again saw substantial aboriginal occupation. According to Smith (1987, 1989, 2000), this occurred as the native inhabitants of the Etowah valley progressively moved downriver toward the Coosa River and Alabama. Presumably, these moves were in response to the social disruption caused by European diseases and the increasing European presence along the coast of Georgia and South Carolina.

4

The Rise and Fall of
Etowah Valley Chiefdoms

Armed with a clearer picture of the history of Etowah, I would like to turn to exploring how Etowah fits in the broader political history of the Etowah River valley. In this chapter, I will attempt to reconstruct the sequence of political changes experienced by the Etowah valley chiefdoms, using both settlement and ceramic data. As I outlined in the introduction, my attempt to understand political change will include an exploration of both political complexity and the nature of political economic strategies used by leaders in the valley.

In the first part of the chapter, I use information on the occupational histories of all mound centers located in the Etowah valley (Chapters 2 and 3), along with the spacing of those centers and evidence for hierarchies among them, to reconstruct changes in political complexity. As in the previous chapter, I will rely on information derived from mortuary data, architecture, and the presence of nonlocal goods to determine the emphasis of political economies. In the second half of this chapter, I will use changes in ceramic assemblages from political centers to evaluate a specific hypothesis concerning chiefdom development in the Etowah valley that was generated by the settlement data.

THE COURSE OF POLITICAL CHANGE
IN THE ETOWAH VALLEY

In identifying simple and complex chiefdoms in the Etowah River valley, I rely on Hally's (1993) work with the spacing of Mississippian political centers in northern Georgia. According to that research, simple chiefdoms can be recognized by the presence of a single-mound site separated from all others by at least 22 km and most likely by distances that exceed 32 km. Complex chiefdoms can be identified by the presence of two or more mound sites separated by 18 km or less, if they can be arranged hierarchically. I will also be aware that in some cases particularly large and powerful complex chiefdoms may have had administrative centers separated by distances as great as 22 km. The distances between mound sites are expressed as straight-line distances and have been taken from the extensive work of Hally (1993).

As Peebles and Kus (1977) have cautioned, in order for settlement hierarchies to represent actual functional hierarchies in a social system, they must not only reflect size but also function. Although none of the mound sites in the Etowah valley have been investigated extensively enough to understand all of their functions within administrative systems, the functions of the mounds themselves are, in most cases, fairly well understood. Therefore, in constructing hierarchies in mound sites, which presumably will reflect administrative hierarchies, I will look for the number of different functional types of mounds at individual sites.

Any effort to reconstruct political relationships using the spacing and timing of use of political centers will be limited by the present state of knowledge of those political centers. Archaeological investigation in the Etowah valley began early and has included several large survey projects (Caldwell 1957; Ledbetter et al. 1987; Southerlin 1993; Wauchope 1966). In addition, there is a fairly large and active population of collectors in the valley (Hally and Langford 1988). For these reasons, it seems likely that all substantial mound sites have been recorded. As discussed in Chapter 2, the cultural histories of some mound sites are poorly known, and in the case of Nixon (9FL162), site destruction has left little chance of rectifying that situation. Until more primary fieldwork can be done at existing mound sites and additional survey data can be collected, these problems can only be acknowledged.

Another factor that may limit the ability to reconstruct an accurate picture of political change is the recognizability of political centers. It is possible that newly established capitals, because of their relative age, possessed very small mounds. This would effectively limit the recognizability of new, emerging primary or secondary political centers. Given the tendency throughout northern Georgia for political centers to be abandoned and reused (see Hally 1996), the effects of this problem may be relatively minor. Again, until additional excavations can be conducted at a series of sites, the effects of this problem will remain unknown.

In addition, it may be that the earliest Mississippian chiefdom capitals in the region had no mounds at all. While Hally (1993, 1996) has argued convincingly that mounds were an integral part of chiefly authority structures, the possibility still remains that institutionalized ranking emerged in the Southeast before chiefs adopted the mound as a symbol of chiefly status. At the present, there are no mounds in northern Georgia that can be assigned unequivocally to the Late Woodland/Early Mississippian transition (Cobb and Garrow 1996). Therefore, the earliest polities in the valley may not be recognizable if chiefdoms are identified only by the presence of mound sites. Until the emergence of ranked societies can be more thoroughly investigated in northern Georgia, the presence or absence of mounds will remain the best use of current knowledge for recognizing the emergence of chiefdoms in the region.

The Early Etowah Phase (a.d. 1000–1100)

There is very little hard evidence indicating that chiefdoms had formed in the Etowah valley by the Early Etowah phase (Figure 15). There is no unequivocal evidence for the existence of any mounds in the valley, and, in fact, of all the investigated mound sites, only Etowah has a confirmed Early Etowah phase component. As I argued in the previous chapter, it is possible that construction had begun on Mound A at Etowah during this phase, although the mound has not been investigated extensively enough to evaluate this possibility. There is some indirect evidence, however, that mound construction may have been taking place. I have inferred this from the presence of at least nine large, basin-shaped features located just south of Mound A that appear to have been borrow pits. The number and size of these features indicate that the amount of fill derived was quite large, suggesting some type of large construction effort like mound building.

Additionally, very few mortuary data are available from the Early Etowah component at Etowah, so it is difficult to determine whether ranking was a part of its social structure. Data from the nearby Hiwassee Island phase of eastern Tennessee, however, hint that Early Etowah phase society may have been ranked. Schroedl and Boyd (1991) argue that communal mound burial probably was the preferred mortuary treatment during the Hiwassee Island phase. Cole's (1975) analysis of the mortuary patterns contained within those mounds suggests that, although material differences between burials were not great, there is some evidence in the form of grave goods suggesting that both ascribed and achieved social ranking may have been in existence.

The inferred mortuary patterns of the Hiwassee Island phase are consis-

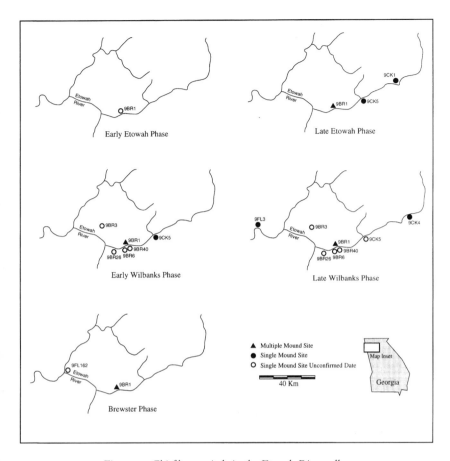

Figure 15. Chiefdom capitals in the Etowah River valley.

tent with the application of a corporate approach to organizing the political economy. Two separate lines of evidence suggest that this same corporate orientation was in use at Early Etowah phase Etowah. First, the borrow pits noted above appear to have been filled with refuse generated by feasting, suggesting that mound construction took place within the context of some communally oriented function. Further, following Hayden (2001), the lack of possible prestige goods in these middens indicates the feasts were aimed at corporate strategy themes like solidarity building or forging social alliances rather than competitive power building associated with network approaches. Additionally, several large and sometimes elaborate buildings were constructed at Etowah during the Early Etowah phase. Their size and the fact that access to them was not restricted in any way suggest that large portions of the Etowah community participated in important events, as might be expected within the context of a corporately organized political economy.

If Mound A at Etowah was in fact under construction during the Early Etowah phase and its social structure was similar to that inferred for the Hiwassee Island phase, then it is possible that the site served as the capital of a simple chiefdom. Given our incomplete understanding of Etowah at this time, it obviously is difficult to know with any degree of certainty how its society was structured and whether it was part of a larger chiefdom. There does seem to be a fairly clear orientation toward a corporate approach to mobilizing sources of social power, but again this inference requires further evaluation.

The Late Etowah Phase (A.D. 1100–1200)

In the Late Etowah phase, mound construction began at three sites in the valley (Figure 15). At Etowah the first two stages were built on Mound B and, although it has not been confirmed, construction may have begun at Mound A as well. Up the Etowah River at the Wilbanks site (9CK5), a possible earth-embanked building (what Sears [1958a] called an earth lodge) and subsequently a platform mound were constructed. Farther up the river, three stages of a single mound at the Long Swamp site (9CK1) were built.

As is the case with the Etowah site, there is comparatively little information available about the dominant political economic strategies in use during the Late Etowah phase at Long Swamp and Wilbanks. In part, this is no doubt because neither of the sites was completely excavated, but the overall consistency in the material patterns apparent at all three sites also seems to suggest a certain level of organizational and behavioral similarity. Just as at Etowah, very few mortuary data were recovered in the excavations conducted at Wilbanks and Long Swamp, possibly suggesting that the preferred burial treatment throughout the valley included interment away from habitation areas. Additionally, no nonlocal items that may have served as prestige goods were recovered in any contexts at Wilbanks and Long Swamp.

While these data are admittedly very thin, they do hint that the dominant political economic strategy applied, not just at Etowah but also throughout the Etowah valley, during the Late Etowah phase was organized around corporate rather than network principles. The purported earth lodge recorded by Sears (1958a) at Wilbanks may provide limited support for this assertion. Beneath the first stage of the Wilbanks mound, Sears recorded an arrangement of logs, rocks, and a low clay wall that he interpreted to be the remains of a large, earth-covered building. As discussed in Chapter 2, doubts have been expressed as to the nature of that building (Rudolph 1984) and even its very existence (Larson 1994). If some kind of building did in fact predate the Wilbanks mound (whether earth embanked or earth covered), then its large size (196 m^2) suggests that it may have been some type of community building designed to accommodate large groups, similar to the Early Etowah phase examples recorded at Etowah.

Based on Hally's spacing arguments, all three occupied centers appear to have been capitals of independent simple chiefdoms. The distance separating Etowah from Long Swamp (48.5 km) falls within the range expected if each was the capital of a separate chiefdom. Similarly, the distance between Long Swamp and Wilbanks (26.5 km), although somewhat less than expected given Hally's (1993) results, still exceeds the 18- to 22-km spacing anticipated if both were part of a single polity. Finally, Etowah and Wilbanks are separated by 22 km, which is a distance just at the margins of what would be expected of centers of a single polity. Given the small size of the centers and the relative youth of their polities, it seems likely that the distance separating these two centers was determined more by local ecology than political relationships. As Hally (1989) has noted, Wilbanks is located on the first substantial stretch of floodplain soils upriver from Etowah.

The Early Savannah Period (a.d. 1250–1300)

On the basis of what is currently understood about the pottery sequence of the Etowah valley, it appears that no mound sites were occupied during the early Savannah period. In fact, there is no convincing evidence that any sites in the valley were occupied (Hally and Langford 1988:62). As discussed in the previous chapter, this gap in the occupation is inferred from a discontinuity in ceramic decoration seen from the Late Etowah to the Early Wilbanks phase. The pottery is so different that Sears (1958a:183) originally suggested that ceramics of the Wilbanks phases represented an intrusion of foreign people into the region. More recent work by Hally and colleagues (Hally and Langford 1988:56; Rudolph and Hally 1985:261– 280) has demonstrated that Wilbanks types do in fact develop out of Etowah period pottery in other areas of Georgia. Given this, the gap in the ceramic sequence in the Etowah valley almost certainly represents a true gap in its occupational sequence.

The Early Wilbanks Phase (a.d. 1250–1325)

During the Early Wilbanks phase, the Etowah valley was reoccupied and new mound construction commenced (Figure 15). At Etowah, stages were added to Mounds A and B, and construction was initiated on the site's elite mortuary mound, Mound C. In the immediate vicinity of Etowah, there may have been as many as four additional single-mound sites established. There is ceramic evidence from stratified deposits showing that construction on the mounds at Two Run Creek (9BR3) and Free Bridge (9BR6) could have begun during the Early Wilbanks, and surface collections from Raccoon Creek (9BR26) and Conyers Farm (9BR40) suggest that mound construction may have taken place at these sites as well. Up the Etowah River into the Piedmont, mound construction resumed at the Wilbanks site.

As summarized in the previous chapter, archaeological evidence indicates that during the Early Wilbanks phase Etowah's leaders relied on a network political economic strategy. Most of the evidence supporting this contention comes from the mortuary record contained within Mound C. Elements of that strategy also may be represented weakly in the mortuary record of the Wilbanks site. Only four burials from Wilbanks have ever been excavated by professional archaeologists, and in those no grave goods were found (Wauchope 1966:281). Before Wauchope's visit and in the years between it and the flooding of Lake Allatoona, an unknown number of graves were exposed by floods and pilfered by treasure seekers (Sears 1958a:134; Wauchope 1966:281). One of those graves was reported to contain two monolithic axes. Another produced two carved stone ear spools engraved with a design that Phillips and Brown (1978) argue bears stylistic connections to the Spiro site in Oklahoma (Brown 1996). Reportedly, from another of those graves came a monolithic ax also bearing a carved design with stylistic connections to both Moundville and Spiro (Phillips and Brown 1978; Waring 1968). The fact that these items came from graves of individuals, rather than some more communal context, suggests that certain individuals had greater access to nonlocal goods that presumably served as conspicuous markers of elevated status.

The relative size of the Etowah site and the presence of both substructure mounds and a specialized mortuary facility establish it as the dominant center in the Etowah valley. The presence of as many as four single-mound centers within 15 km (9BR3, 9BR6, 9BR26, 9BR40) indicates that the polity dominated by Etowah was a complex chiefdom. Given the size and complexity of Etowah, not just compared with other Etowah valley centers, but compared with all other centers in northern Georgia, it may be reasonable to argue that Wilbanks, located 22 km from Etowah, was a fifth subsidiary center in this polity.

The possibility that Etowah's leaders may have been able to extend political authority to the Wilbanks site finds some support in the fact that construction began on Etowah's elite mortuary mound, Mound C, during the Early Wilbanks phase. As noted in the previous chapter, many of the burials removed from Mound C contained elaborate grave offerings, such as embossed copper plates, engraved shell gorgets, and flint swords, that are part of a suite of ceremonial objects and symbols known as the Southeastern Ceremonial Complex (SECC). It is generally accepted that these items moved throughout the region within exchange networks (Brown 1989; Brown et al. 1990), presumably linking individual political leaders and their centers. The sheer quantity of SECC goods recovered from Mound C suggests that Etowah's leaders were major participants in such exchange networks and that their political importance reached even beyond the Etowah valley.

THE LATE WILBANKS PHASE (A.D. 1325–1375)

During the Late Wilbanks phase, mound construction began or continued at as many as eight sites in the valley (Figure 15). At Etowah, stages were added to Mounds A, B, and C, with each reaching its maximum size. As in the previous phase, Mound C served as an elite mortuary facility in which were interred honored dead and status goods that suggest participation in external exchange networks. In addition, it is at this time that a raised plaza was constructed to the east of Mound A and the defensive ditch and palisade complex that surrounded the site was completed. Associated with this multiple-mound center were as many as four single-mound sites, all located within 15 km of Etowah. Evidence from Two Run Creek (9BR3) and Free Bridge (9BR6) shows that the mounds at these sites may have been added to during this phase, while surface collections from Raccoon Creek (9BR26) and Conyers Farm (9BR40) suggest that mound construction could have occurred at these sites as well. In addition, the Wilbanks site (9CK5), located 22 km from Etowah, may have been yet another subsidiary center in the polity.

Both up and down the river from Etowah's complex chiefdom, two more polities formed. These are represented by the single-mound sites of Horseshoe Bend (9CK4; 54.1 km from Etowah) and Plant Hammond (9FL3; 52.8 km from Etowah). Whether these polities also were under the political control, in some measure, of the Etowah site is unclear. On the basis of the amount of civic-ceremonial construction and the impressive displays in mortuary activities, it is during this phase, more so than in the Early Wilbanks phase, that the Etowah site reached its peak in terms of size and organizational complexity. In fact, it was larger and more complex than any other contemporary chiefly center in northern Georgia, southeastern Tennessee, and eastern Alabama. Also at this time, the greatest number of mound sites existed, occupying the greatest extent of the Etowah River valley. Given its apparent regional prominence, it is reasonable to suggest that Late Wilbanks phase Etowah was the capital of a paramount chiefdom whose authority stretched throughout the Etowah valley from Horseshoe Bend to Plant Hammond. As the Early Wilbanks Etowah-dominated complex chiefdom had been, this Late Wilbanks phase polity continued to be organized using a network political economic strategy.

THE STAMP CREEK AND MAYES PHASES (A.D. 1375–1475)

The abandonment of Etowah near the end of its Late Wilbanks occupation apparently coincided with the abandonment of all other political centers in the Etowah River valley. Although both Ledbetter et al. (1987) and Southerlin (1993) recorded early Lamar period sites in the valley, no evidence has been found indicating that mound sites or their mounds were actually used (Hally 1989; Hally and Rudolph 1986:7; King 1996) during the Stamp Creek and Mayes phases. On the basis of these data, chiefdoms may have disappeared from the Etowah valley for a century or more after the fall of Etowah.

THE BREWSTER AND BARNETT PHASES (A.D. 1475–1625)

By the sixteenth-century Brewster and Barnett phases chiefdoms again had appeared in the valley (Figure 15). As discussed in the previous chapter, these polities were likely also organized along network rather than corporate lines. At Etowah, Mound B was intensively used and at least one of the smaller mounds at the site (Mound D) was also constructed. In addition, at least a portion of the single mound at the Nixon site (9FL162), located 38 km downriver from Etowah, may have been constructed. The distance between Etowah and Nixon and the absence of additional mound centers within 18 km of either center indicate that both were capitals of separate simple chiefdoms.

IDENTIFYING PARAMOUNT CHIEFDOMS USING CERAMIC ASSEMBLAGE CHANGE

As I outlined in Chapter 1, it may not be possible to identify paramount chiefdoms, especially those organized around network principles, using the settlement data approach employed in the previous sections. As an alternative means, I will look to economic patterns. Regardless of the orientation of political economies, people, goods, and information were all drawn into chiefdom capitals as important ceremonies were celebrated, offerings were made to religious and political leaders, and preparations were made for warfare. As the political roles of individual capitals changed (i.e., from the capital of a simple chiefdom to the capital of a complex chiefdom), the direction and intensity of those flows also changed, and this should be reflected in material items like pottery. Therefore, as a way of testing the inference that a paramount chiefdom, with its capital at Etowah, emerged in the Etowah valley during the Late Wilbanks phase, I will examine changes in ceramic assemblages recovered from Etowah valley political centers.

CAUSES OF CERAMIC ASSEMBLAGE CHANGE

As Plog (1980) outlines, there are a variety of reasons that ceramic assemblages change. By comparing assemblages from functionally similar sites (mound sites) that are contemporary (the same phase), I intend to focus on causes of assemblage change that relate to the movement of goods, people, and information. One way that pottery assemblages of individual sites may be altered compositionally under these circumstances is through the introduction of pots made at other sites. In the Southeast, it is assumed that the majority of ceramic production took place at the household level (Hally 1983) and, in the absence of markets, that pottery moved between individuals or groups through reciprocal exchange networks among kin or up and down social hierarchies as offerings and redistributed goods. Although it may not have constituted tribute in Muller's (1997) use of the term, the ethnohistoric literature makes it clear that chiefs were entitled to collect labor and goods from subjugated groups (DePratter 1991; Dye 1990; Hally et al. 1990; Hudson 1990:52–125). In addition, Swanton (1946:737, 740) cites several examples in which pottery vessels were exchanged between Southeastern groups, and the archaeological literature of the Southeast is filled with evidence for the movement of ceramic vessels (Brown 1983; Kelly 1991; Steponaitis 1983).

Ceramic assemblages also may be altered through changes in decorative styles. Recent ethnographic studies have shown that style is a form of nonverbal communication that, through its visibility, relates information about social identity to individual participants in a social network (Wiessner 1983, 1984). Research concerned with style and communication has also shown that decorative styles placed on material items are manipulated actively and often are employed as part of a strategy to meet social ends (Earle 1990; Hodder 1977, 1981).

Although communication through style can be accomplished using a variety of different material items, it is clear that the physical size, life span, and contexts within which items are seen all will affect the kinds of social communication possible (Braun and Plog 1982). Pottery vessels are large enough to allow decorative aspects to be seen at relatively great distances, and they are durable but not so permanent that social messages cannot be updated periodically. Also, ceramics are used in a variety of contexts such as household serving and storage, performance of ritual, and public serving, and they can be used as exchange items or containers for exchanged commodities. Therefore, pottery has the potential to be a useful medium for social communication at several levels.

Under these circumstances, it is possible that individual producers or social groups might manipulate ceramic decorative style to further their own political ends. For example, it has been suggested that the type Ramey Incised was used by elites of the American Bottom as part of a strategy to maintain the social order. Pauketat and Emerson (1991) argue that these vessels were produced under the direction of elites and decorated with symbols that reinforced the importance of elites in the natural and supernatural worlds. According to Pauketat and Emerson (1991), Ramey Incised vessels were used and distributed during elite-sponsored rites of intensification, such as the Busk of the Historic period. In leaving the ceremony with these pots, supporting populations took home with them symbolic reminders of the important place of elites in their lives.

Another way that the composition of pottery assemblages may be altered is through the introduction of pottery producers. Historic accounts indicate that pottery in the Southeast was manufactured by women (Swanton 1946:549–555), and ethnohistoric data from the region show that alliances were often sealed by the exchange of wives (DePratter 1991; Dye 1990; Hudson 1976:276). Therefore, the introduction of a wife from a different community may have served to introduce new stylistic elements into local pottery assemblages. As Hodder (1977, 1981) argues, however, style is manipulated to meet social ends. Therefore, the circumstances under which a woman is brought to a political capital and the social environment in which she lives will affect her decision to maintain or alter her own ceramic decorative style.

EXPECTED ASSEMBLAGE CHANGES ASSOCIATED WITH POLITICAL CHANGE

With the movement of people, goods, and information to and from chiefdom capitals, I expect that assemblages associated with elite or public settings, as well as those of non-elites, would be affected. Elite/public assemblages will be impacted most by the introduction of new vessels as gifts and offerings are brought into political capitals, and possibly by the introduction of new stylistic information as wives are brought in from other areas to seal alliances. Because elaborate painted pots and effigy forms often appear as elite grave offerings in the Southeast, it might be expected that such vessels would comprise the majority of pottery introduced into elite/public assemblages. It seems just as likely, however, that utilitarian wares might also move through social hierarchies as containers for goods transported.

Non-elite pottery assemblages, both at the chiefdom capital and at outlying sites, are likely to change as individuals visit the capital to contribute labor for public works projects, attend ritual occasions, or bring offerings to important people. During these times, visitors would likely meet or even stay with kin or clan members. Historic descriptions of the multi-day Green Corn ceremony indicate that out-of-town attendees were commonly housed with clansmen (Hudson 1976:367). These encounters would have created the opportunity for pots, aspects of decoration, or even pottery producers to be exchanged.

Using the structure of chiefdoms, it is possible to derive expectations about how ceramic assemblages from political centers in simple, complex, and paramount chiefdoms will differ and how those assemblages will change with shifts in the political structure of the polity. In simple chiefdoms population levels are relatively low and there is only one political capital. In these polities, the vast majority of the goods, people, and information flowing to the capital will come from the immediate area (less than 18 km) and not from distant places. If there is no overarching political structure binding simple chiefdoms together, then the degree to which people, pots, and information are exchanged between polities is likely to be determined by distance. Under these conditions, ceramic assemblages from individual simple chiefdom capitals are likely to be relatively distinct and appear more distinct with greater distances.

Complex chiefdoms have greater supporting populations and are likely to be larger spatially than simple chiefdoms. As a result, goods, people, and information traveling to the primary capital will come from a larger area and from a wider array of social groups. The distance separating these social groups from the center, however, is still less than 18 to 22 km, making it likely that ceramic assemblages throughout the polity will be relatively similar. Because of this, the assemblage of the primary center is likely to be no more diverse than assemblages from secondary centers in the chiefdom.

In paramount chiefdoms, goods, people, and information will flow to the capital not only from the immediate surroundings, but also from centers located well beyond 22 km. Therefore, with the appearance of a paramount chiefdom, the ceramic assemblage of the paramount capital should become more diverse than assemblages from any other center in the polity.

This will occur as vessels, their makers, and ideas about how to decorate pots flow to the paramount capital from various subsidiary centers, each potentially with its own ceramic tradition.

At the same time, it is also possible that the ceramic assemblages from subsidiary political centers and the paramount capital will become more similar. This may happen for a variety of reasons. First, the ceramic assemblage of the paramount center may become more similar to those from subsidiary centers as pottery vessels and pottery makers move to the paramount capital as offerings and marriage partners, respectively. In addition, assemblages from the paramount capital and secondary centers may become more similar as actual vessels, pottery makers, and ideas about how to decorate pots are exchanged between non-elite residents of the paramount capital and visitors.

Also, individuals at subsidiary centers may adopt some aspects of ceramic styles commonly used at the paramount center as a way of identifying with that paramount center and the power it represents. A process similar to this seems to account for the appearance of Teotihuacan-style architecture, pottery, and iconography at Kaminaljuyu and throughout the Maya Lowlands during the Middle Classic Period (Demarest and Foias 1993:170–172). The appearance of locally produced copies of Cahokia-associated ceramic types like Ramey Incised and Powell Plain (Kelly 1991; Milner 1991) may also be explained by a desire to tap into the power and legitimacy of the Cahokia site.

With the establishment of a paramountcy, it is also possible that the assemblage of the paramount capital will become more diverse, but the assemblages from subsidiary centers will not change. The increasing diversity, as before, will result from the flow of ceramics and makers to the paramount capital from many sources. Individuals at subsidiary centers may choose not to adopt decorative aspects from the paramount center as a means of maintaining a distinct group identity in the face of an overarching political structure. As Hodder (1981) has argued, this kind of strategy is often used in circumstances in which economic or political tensions exist between social groups or segments.

MEASURING DIVERSITY AND SIMILARITY

In assessing ceramic assemblage change, I calculate measures of diversity and similarity for three sets of ceramic attributes: temper type, surface treatment, and decorative motifs (complicated stamped and incised). I have chosen these three attributes because they represent the three most readily recognizable and quantifiable aspects of variation in Mississippian ceramics of northern Georgia. Also, all three of these attributes vary in their frequency of occurrence across space and time in ways suggesting that they also serve as elements of stylistic variation (see Hally 1979, 1994; Hally and Langford 1988; Kelly 1972; Wauchope 1966).

To help identify changes in the diversity of ceramic assemblages, I use a measure of assemblage richness. The concept of diversity is composed of three distinct components: richness, evenness, and heterogeneity (Bobrowski and Ball 1989; Peet 1974). Richness refers to the number of classes present in a population, while evenness represents the absolute distribution of individuals across all classes. Heterogeneity measures the variability in the numbers of observations in each class and the abundance of individual classes using a single value. In assessing assemblage diversity, I am most interested in identifying increases or decreases in the number of surface treatments, temper types, and motifs present in an assemblage. Therefore, richness is the most appropriate component of diversity to be measured.

Concerning richness measures in ecology, Peet (1974:290) states that direct species counts, "while lacking theoretical elegance, provide one of the simplest, most practical, and most objective measures of species richness." Following this lead, I will calculate richness by counting the number of surface treatments, motifs, and temper types present in individual assemblages. Since these sets of attributes represent three potential avenues through which ceramic assemblages may vary, richness measures will be calculated for each and summed to produce a total richness index. Although individual richness scores will be discussed, the total richness index will be used to evaluate changes in ceramic assemblage diversity.

To measure similarities between ceramic assemblages, I use the Brainerd-Robinson coefficient (Brainerd 1951; Robinson 1951). This coefficient compares the percentage representation of each category in an assemblage from one region with the percentage representation of those categories in another region. The absolute value of the differences between regions (in each category) is summed, and that value is subtracted from 200 to produce the Brainerd-Robinson coefficient. A value of 200 represents maximum similarity between assemblages, while a value of zero represents maximum dissimilarity. As done for measures of diversity, surface treatments, temper types, and motifs all will be considered in assessing the similarity of Etowah valley ceramic assemblages. To do this, a Brainerd-Robinson coefficient will be calculated for each set of attributes. The overall pattern of changes in these individual coefficients will be used to determine whether assemblage similarity increased or decreased. Because percentages and not raw counts are used to calculate the Brainerd-Robinson coefficient, it is largely unaffected by sample size differences (as long as the samples are representative).

Table 2. Context and number of sherds used for ceramic assemblage analyses

		Surface			Motifs		
			Non-			Non-	
Site	Phase	Mound	Mound	Total	Mound	Mound	Total
9BR1	Early Etowah		825	825		104	104
	Late Etowah	309	541	850		95	95
	Early Wilbanks		827	827		97	97
	Late Wilbanks	209	651	860	28	68	96
	Brewster	518	291	809	49	27	76
9CK5	Early Wilbanks	548		548	90		90
9FL3	Late Wilbanks	508	385	893	12	11	23

THE DATA

Unfortunately, large and unbiased pottery collections are not available from all mound sites in the Etowah valley. No excavations have been conducted at Raccoon Creek (9BR26), and only small portions of the original collections recovered by Wauchope from Horseshoe Bend (9CK4), Long Swamp (9CK1), Two Run Creek (9BR3), Conyers Farm (9BR40), and Free Bridge (9BR6) currently exist. Also, the collection recently recovered from Horseshoe Bend is not large enough to be used in this analysis. Acceptable collections are only available from Etowah (9BR1), Wilbanks (9CK5), and Plant Hammond (9FL3). Even with this limited data set, it is still possible to use the expectations discussed above to evaluate the hypothesis that Etowah became the capital of a paramount chiefdom during the Late Wilbanks phase. To do this, I classified and tabulated the pottery collections summarized in Table 2. The raw sherd counts and contextual information concerning these collections can be found in King (1996:210–220, 299–304).

The ceramic samples chosen to represent assemblages from each of these sites consist, in most cases, of at least 600 sherds and approximately 100 sherds that contain motifs (Table 2). My own work with ceramics from the Etowah valley shows that a collection of about 300 sherds provides a representative sample of surface treatments and temper types and allows for accurate dating of contexts (King 2001). By doubling that figure, I intended to capture as wide a range of variation as possible, while keeping sherd sample sizes manageable. Because motif and sherd size can vary across time periods and contexts, I have also chosen to use a standard motif sample size of 100 for each assemblage.

The pottery collections included in site assemblages often consist of several excavation lots (see King 1996:299–304), and individual lots were chosen on the basis of the primary phase represented. Because political changes can cause changes in both elite and non-elite ceramic assemblages, I attempted to include lots from mound and non-mound contexts in site assemblages (Table 2). Mound contexts are generally associated with elite and public activities, while areas away from mounds are associated with domestic activities and the non-elite. Unfortunately, differing excavation strategies and densities of deposits investigated made it impossible in some cases to include pottery from both mound and non-mound contexts.

In examining changes in the diversity and similarity of ceramic assemblages of the Etowah valley, I intend to do three things. First, the changes in the diversity of the Etowah site assemblage will be examined during each phase of its occupation. Second, the diversity of the Etowah site assemblages will be compared with the diversity of assemblages from contemporary centers in the valley during the Early Wilbanks and Late Wilbanks phases. Finally, the similarity of the Etowah site assemblage and an assemblage from a contemporary center will be measured during the Early and Late Wilbanks phases.

As Table 2 shows, the ceramic sample that comprises the Early Wilbanks assemblage from the Wilbanks site (9CK5) is smaller than all other samples. Because of the relationship between sample size and diversity, the number of sherds that make up the Early Wilbanks assemblage from Etowah has been adjusted so that it is directly comparable with the Wilbanks site collection. This was done by removing the pottery from a single excavation lot (Lot #5841, see King 1996:302).

Similarly, Table 2 indicates that the motif sample from Plant Hammond (9FL3) is not as large as all other motif samples. To adjust for this problem, I have reduced the number of motifs in the Etowah site sample to match that from Plant Hammond (n = 23). This was done by taking 10 random samples of 23 sherds from the original 96 that were included in the Late Wilbanks motif assemblage from Etowah (see King 1996:214, table 6.3). The average number of different motifs from these samples was 6.5, and as a result one of the samples with six motifs was chosen at random to represent the reduced motif assemblage from Etowah.

Before changes in these measures can be interpreted as resulting from changes in the intensity of exchange of ceramic vessels or stylistic information, several other potential causes must be considered. First, it is critical that the ceramic samples used to represent the assemblages of individual political centers not be biased in any way that might affect diversity or similarity. Most, but not all, of the collections used here were recovered without the aid of screens. As a result, it is possible that some of the ceramic samples included here will not be comparable with others because of differences in recovery techniques. Unscreened samples should be biased toward larger sherds, but there should be no systematic bias selecting for or against specific ceramic types or surface treatments. For this reason, I do not expect that the differing recovery techniques will affect the comparability of these ceramic samples.

Also, ceramics from both mound and non–mound contexts are included in this analysis (Table 2). In most cases, the non–mound samples come from deposits located adjacent to mounds, and therefore also may represent the activities of elites. There is still the possibility that the activities carried out on mounds differ from those conducted adjacent to mounds, creating differences in the ceramic samples derived from those contexts. To minimize this problem, I have attempted to include roughly equal proportions of mound and non–mound ceramics in each assemblage. As Table 2 shows, however, this was not always possible and the differences in proportional representation of mound and non–mound sherds may affect the comparability of some assemblages.

Even when proportions of mound and non–mound sherds remain equal, it still may be possible that assemblages are not directly comparable. The exact range of activities carried out on and around mounds is poorly understood and probably varied from site to site. Most of the pottery samples used came from limited excavations, so usually it is not possible to determine the kinds of behaviors that produced the deposits investigated. Under these circumstances, it is difficult to know whether pottery from mound or non–mound contexts at one site can be considered comparable with pottery from similar contexts at a second site. Descriptions of each context from which pottery was taken to be included in site assemblages appear in King (1996:299–304).

In addition to biases introduced by the inclusion of pottery from different contexts, it is also well established that diversity (in this case richness) is positively correlated with sample size (Bobrowski and Ball 1989; Peet 1974). Therefore larger samples may appear more diverse or different from smaller samples simply because of the number of sherds they contain. To control for this problem, I have attempted to keep sherd samples roughly equal. As Table 2 shows, this was not achieved in all cases. This is most apparent in the cases of the number of sherds in the Early Wilbanks sample from the Wilbanks site and the number of motifs in the Late Wilbanks

Table 3. *Etowah site assemblage diversity through time*

Phase/Period	Early Etowah	Late Etowah	Early Savannah	Early Wilbanks	Late Wilbanks	Early Lamar	Brewster
Surface							
Treatment	7	7	—	9	10	—	7
Motifs	3	12	—	9	11	—	12
Temper	3	3	—	2	3	—	1
Total Richness	13	22	—	20	24	—	20

sample from Plant Hammond. Where necessary, sample sizes have been adjusted to make assemblages directly comparable.

Finally, when ceramic assemblages from different sites are compared, it
also must be clear that the ceramic assemblages being compared are contemporary. Because ceramic decorative styles and forms change over time,
the comparison of assemblages that are not strictly contemporary will indicate a divergence in assemblage characteristics that is due only to differences in time. In the Etowah valley, Mississippian phases range from 75 to
100 years in length, meaning that as much as 100 years could separate two
sites considered to be contemporary. Until new work is done to assess the
impact of this problem on the similarity and diversity measures presented
below, I will assume that the effects are negligible.

A LATE WILBANKS PHASE PARAMOUNT CHIEFDOM?

Using the settlement data, I suggested that Etowah became the capital of a
complex chiefdom during the Early Wilbanks phase and grew to become
a paramount chiefdom in the Late Wilbanks phase by incorporating polities centered at Plant Hammond (9FL3) and Horseshoe Bend (9CK4). If this
reconstruction is correct, then from the Early to Late Wilbanks phase the
Etowah site assemblage should increase in diversity and should become
more diverse than assemblages from subsidiary centers. Also, assemblages
from Etowah and subsidiary centers may become more similar during the
Late Wilbanks phase.

Table 3 contains the measures of richness for surface treatment, motifs,
and temper type for assemblages from each occupation of the Etowah site,
as well as a total richness index, which sums the individual measures. Given
the previous discussions, the emergence of a paramountcy during the Late
Wilbanks phase should bring about an increase in the diversity of the

Table 4. Diversity of Etowah and secondary center assemblages compared

Phase	Early Wilbanks		Late Wilbanks	
Sites	9BR1	9CK5	9BR1	9FL3
Surface Treatment	8	7	10	8
Motifs	9	9	6.5	5
Temper	2	2	3	3
Total Richness	*19*	*18*	*19.5*	*16*

Note: Motif richness in the Late Wilbanks assemblage from Etowah is the average richness of 10 random samples of 23 motifs drawn from the 96 motifs in the original assemblage (King 1996:214, table 6.3).

Etowah site assemblage. The actual assemblage changes presented in Table 3 show that the diversity of the Etowah site assemblage not only increases from the Early to Late Wilbanks phase, but also reaches its peak of diversity. Because the measure of richness used here is a simple index, it is not possible to determine whether this change is statistically significant. The fact that all three sets of attributes increase in richness from the Early to Late Wilbanks phase, however, argues that the difference is a real one.

As Table 4 shows, there is little difference in the richness of Early Wilbanks phase assemblages from the Etowah (9BR1) and Wilbanks (9CK5) sites. In fact, the only difference is created by the presence of one more surface treatment in the Etowah site assemblage. There is a greater difference between the Late Wilbanks phase assemblages from Etowah and Plant Hammond (9FL3), and it is created by the presence of a greater number of surface treatments and motifs in the Etowah site assemblage. The fact that the Etowah site assemblage is richer in two of the three ceramic attributes again suggests that the difference in the Late Wilbanks assemblages is real. Therefore, as expected, the Etowah site assemblage does become more diverse than assemblages from contemporary centers from the Early to Late Wilbanks phase.

Finally, Table 5 presents the similarity between assemblages from Etowah and those from contemporary mound centers using the Brainerd-Robinson similarity coefficient. For each category (surface treatment, motif, temper type), a similarity coefficient has been calculated. If a paramount chiefdom did exist in the Etowah valley during the Late Wilbanks phase, then it is possible that assemblages from Etowah and its secondary centers would become more similar.

From the Early to Late Wilbanks phase the similarity coefficients for

Table 5. *Similarity of assemblages from Etowah and a secondary center*

Phase/Period	Early Wilbanks	Late Wilbanks
Sites	9BR1 to 9CK5	9BR1 to 9FL3
Surface Treatment	163	170
Motifs	74	157
Temper	199	162

surface treatment increased slightly. In general, however, the high Brainerd-Robinson determinations suggest that the surface treatment assemblages from each phase are quite similar. The similarity of motif assemblages also increased, but in this case the change from a relatively low Brainerd-Robinson coefficient (74) to a fairly high coefficient (157) suggests a change from dissimilar to similar collections. The similarity of temper types actually decreased slightly, but the fairly high Brainerd-Robinson co-efficients suggest that the assemblages changed from nearly perfectly similar to quite similar. Overall then, the Early and Late Wilbanks phase assemblages remained similar in terms of surface treatment and temper types, but increased dramatically with respect to motifs. These results indicate that from the Early to Late Wilbanks phase, there was a slight increase in similarity in ceramic assemblages from Etowah and a contemporary center. Given the distance separating Plant Hammond from Etowah, this increase may be more pronounced than these data can show. Overall, the greater the distances separating sites, the more likely it is that their assemblages will contain more differences and be less similar. Despite this fact, the assemblage from Plant Hammond, which is 52.8 km from Etowah, is actually more similar to the Etowah assemblage than is the collection from Wilbanks, which is located only 22 km from Etowah.

OTHER POTENTIAL CAUSES OF CERAMIC ASSEMBLAGE CHANGE

Although I attribute the ceramic assemblage changes illustrated in Tables 3, 4, and 5 to the development of a paramount chiefdom in the Etowah valley, there are other factors that could have caused those observed changes. For example, logically it makes sense to suggest that the adoption of a network strategy for organizing political economies led to the increases in both similarity and diversity observed in the Etowah valley. Given the emphasis on external connections, a network strategy may bring ideas, pottery vessels, and even makers into political capitals from areas outside of the polity, causing an increase in pottery assemblage diversity. Following the same reasoning, increased contacts between political actors in different polities might also lead to increased similarities in the pottery assemblages of the two polities, as ideas, goods, and people moved between the polities.

Although I have not tested this directly, I expect that such extralocal connections had only a small impact on entire pottery assemblages from political capitals. Network political actors monopolize external connections, and the material and information gained from them, so their impacts on pottery assemblages are likely to be limited to collections recovered from a small number of elite or public settings. Also, the number of non-local vessels introduced into a political capital's assemblage is likely to be quite low, because materials flowing through external networks are likely to be limited to high-value and low-bulk prestige goods and ritual information.

Even if increases in external connections did significantly impact pottery assemblages, the adoption of a network strategy still does not satisfactorily explain the changes in assemblage diversity illustrated above. Since the network approach also was in use during the Early Wilbanks phase at Etowah, its adoption does not explain why the diversity of the Etowah site assemblage peaked in the Late Wilbanks phase. If leaders at Plant Hammond also relied on a network strategy, as it appears leaders at Wilbanks had done, then the application of a network strategy alone also cannot explain why the Etowah site assemblage was more diverse than the assemblage from Plant Hammond.

It is also possible that the Etowah site assemblage increased in diversity from the Early to Late Wilbanks phase because the Etowah site became the focal point for flows of goods, people, and information for reasons not related to the apparent political importance of the site. This might occur, for example, as the inhabitants of Etowah gained access to goods or materials not available in other parts of the valley, or as the town took on a new ritual significance that brought people and goods to the site. While this possibility has some degree of plausibility, it seems unlikely that Etowah would develop some economic, religious, or social significance outside of the political realm at the same time that the site reached its political peak. Given the timing, it seems more likely that Etowah would become a social, ritual, or economic focus *because* of its rising political importance. In fact, the imposition of an overarching political structure, such as the paramount chiefdom, is just the kind of change that should stimulate economic exchange and social contacts.

Finally, the Etowah site assemblage may have become more diverse because of population increases in the core area of the polity, rather than as a result of political change. In that area, population may have increased as immigrants, drawn by the success of the polity, settled in the area, or as fertility rates increased relative to those of other polities. In addition to bringing new pottery makers and ideas about how to decorate pots into the area, these changes may have led to alterations in the social relations between kin groups or social segments. Adjustments to the new social situation may have stimulated changes in ceramic styles, which may have led to increased assemblage diversity. In her analysis of Black on White ceramics in the Black Mesa region of northeastern Arizona, Hegmon (1986) argues that increased populations forced an alteration of the social networks in place in the region, and ceramic stylistic diversity increased as people manipulated styles to adapt to the changing social conditions.

As already discussed, there appears to be a gap in the occupation of the Etowah valley between the end of the Late Etowah phase (A.D. 1200) and the beginning of the Early Wilbanks phase (A.D. 1250) (Hally and Langford 1988; King 2001; Southerlin 1993). Since there were no inhabitants of the valley during the early Savannah period, the Early Wilbanks phase occupation represents a population increase. Whether populations continued to increase from the Early to Late Wilbanks phase is currently unknown, however, because surveys conducted in the area could not distinguish Early and Late Wilbanks phase occupations (because of small collections [Southerlin 1993] or because they predate the phase definitions [Hally and Langford 1988]). Therefore, increasing population in the core area of the Etowah polity cannot be ruled out as a potential cause of increasing assemblage diversity.

Interpreting Ceramic Assemblage Change in the Etowah Valley

As the preceding discussion illustrates, the actual changes in ceramic assemblages from Etowah valley political centers are consistent with those expected if a paramount chiefdom centered at Etowah appeared during the Late Wilbanks phase. Of the possible alternative causes discussed above, only changes in population levels cannot be dismissed on logical or empirical grounds as a potential cause of ceramic assemblage change. Therefore, until future research can further evaluate this approach and the inferences made based on it, I will tentatively suggest that the Etowah site served as the capital of a paramount chiefdom during the Late Wilbanks phase.

Unfortunately, this ceramic assemblage change approach cannot be used to help understand the overall extent of the Late Wilbanks phase Etowah-dominated polity. The similarity measure presented in Table 5 suggests that Etowah's authority may have stretched eastward to Plant Hammond, but a lack of data from Horseshoe Bend makes it impossible to determine whether that site was also part of the polity. The usefulness of this approach may become even more limited when areas outside of the Etowah valley are considered. This is because, all things considered, the greater the distance separating a subsidiary center and the paramount capital, the lower the intensity and frequency of contacts that are likely to take place between the two centers. As a result, fewer people and goods will travel those greater distances, and exchanges of people, information, and goods will take place less frequently. Additionally, the greater the distance between political centers, the greater the chances that the materials moving between them will be dominated by information and low-bulk/high-value commodities. Consequently, fewer pottery vessels might be expected to move over greater distances and political-center pottery assemblages will be less affected by changes in political structure.

A SUMMARY OF POLITICAL CHANGE
IN THE ETOWAH VALLEY

By examining the dating and spacing of political centers, and by constructing mound-site hierarchies, I have developed the following picture of changes in the organizational structure of Etowah valley chiefdoms. There is no clear evidence for the existence of chiefdoms in the valley during the Early Etowah phase, although it seems plausible to suggest that such social formations did in fact exist. Whatever their structure, it seems clear that Early Etowah phase societies were structured using corporate principles. Unequivocal evidence for mound construction appears in the valley during the Late Etowah phase, when Etowah, Wilbanks, and Long Swamp each served as capitals of independent, simple chiefdoms. Available evidence suggests that these polities also were organized following corporate principles.

By the early Savannah period these chiefdoms had collapsed, and the entire valley was abandoned. With the subsequent Early Wilbanks phase, Etowah emerged as the capital of a complex chiefdom with as many as five subsidiary centers within 22 km. In contrast to the Etowah period, the Early Wilbanks phase polity appears to have been formed using a network political economic strategy. With the continued application of a network strategy during the Late Wilbanks phase, the Etowah site reached its peak in size and complexity and may have become a paramount chiefdom, extending its authority over two simple chiefdoms located more than 50 km away. With the collapse of this polity, Etowah and the rest of the valley's political centers were abandoned and it appears that chiefdoms may have briefly left the valley. By the sixteenth century, two network-based simple chiefdoms had reappeared, with their capitals at Etowah and Nixon.

5

Understanding Etowah Valley
Political Change

In the previous chapters, I have attempted to reconstruct a sequence of political changes that occurred in the Etowah valley during the Mississippian period. My final purpose in this book is to begin to explore some of the potential causes of that sequence of political changes. In Chapter 1, I argued that most instances of political change are caused by the actions of political leaders and the reactions of their supporters, not by rarely occurring environmental disasters. Consequently, I see the nature of the political economic strategy applied by leaders, and the ramifications of that application, as an important starting point for understanding the causes of political change. I also argued that the Mississippian Southeast was an interconnected system, in which social groups and their leaders were linked to others in the wider region through exchange and political-military conflict. As a result, the implications of the decisions made by individual political actors reached beyond the individual polity to impact the wider region. Given this, in order to understand the causes of political change in the Etowah valley, it will be important to view those polities and their associated political economic strategies within the context of a larger regional system.

As in Chapter 4, I identify the appearance and disappearance of simple and complex chiefdoms throughout northern Georgia using the spacing between mound sites and apparent hierarchies in closely spaced centers. The data used for this, with some modifications, are based on Hally's (1993, 1996) work with the dating and spacing of mound sites in northern Georgia. My point here is not to identify every simple and complex chiefdom in northern Georgia, but to look at changes in the location or complexity of polities in valleys surrounding the Etowah River. To facilitate comparison with the Etowah valley in this discussion, I have divided the Mississippian period into spans of time that correspond to the Etowah valley phase sequence.

THE EARLY ETOWAH PERIOD (A.D. 1000–1100): THE EMERGENCE OF CHIEFDOMS

Although Mississippian forms of social organization may have developed earlier in other parts of the Southeast, the first evidence for the emergence of chiefdoms in northern Georgia is found at the Macon Plateau site (9BI1) located at the Fall Line in central Georgia (Figure 16). Currently available data show that the Mississippian occupation of Macon Plateau began around A.D. 900 (Hally and Williams 1994), earlier than at any other center in northern Georgia. Macon Plateau has always been something of an enigma in Georgia prehistory. Its material culture (pottery, architecture, burial practices) is clearly different from that of contemporary societies in central Georgia and does not appear to be related to the indigenous Late Woodland material cultures that preceded it. As a result, the intrusive or indigenous nature of Macon Plateau has long been debated (Schroedl 1994; Williams 1994). Unlike other early Etowah period mound centers in northern Georgia, Macon Plateau was a multiple-mound site. It also had a single-mound site (Brown's Mount, 9BI5) located close enough that Macon Plateau may have served as the capital of a complex chiefdom.

Sometime after A.D. 1000, while Macon Plateau was still an important center, chiefdoms may have made their first appearance in the Etowah River valley. As discussed previously, this is based on indirect evidence for construction on Etowah's Mound A. At about this same time, Sixtoe Field (9MU100) was occupied on the Coosawattee River. The location of these two centers clearly shows that each was the center of a simple chiefdom. Farther to the north in eastern Tennessee, the Hiwassee Island phase (A.D. 1000–1300) occupation began at Hiwassee Island.

On the basis of limited data, it appears that these earliest chiefdoms in Georgia may have had a corporate orientation to their political economies. Some of the strongest evidence for this corporate orientation comes from the earliest center in the region, Macon Plateau. Using data from the WPA-sponsored excavations conducted at the site, Hally and Williams (1994) show how the site grew to include as many as four separate subcommunities, each with its own set of civic and ceremonial facilities. Those facilities, at least during the first two periods of occupation, consisted of at least

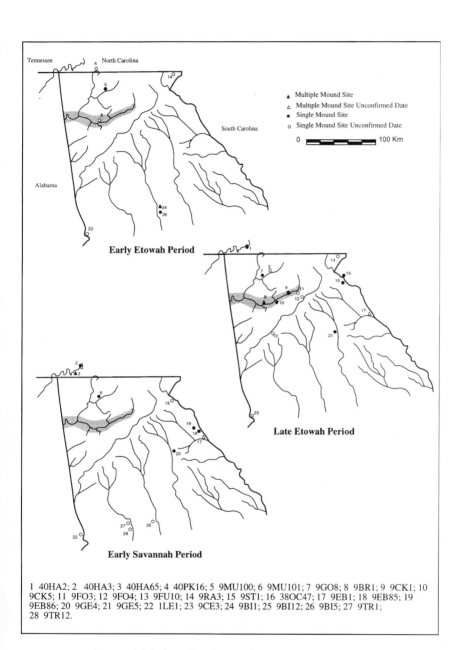

Legend (on map):

▲ Multiple Mound Site
△ Multiple Mound Site Unconfirmed Date
● Single Mound Site
○ Single Mound Site Unconfirmed Date

0 ▬▬▬▬▬▬ 100 Km

Early Etowah Period

Late Etowah Period

Early Savannah Period

1 40HA2; 2 40HA3; 3 40HA65; 4 40PK16; 5 9MU100; 6 9MU101; 7 9GO8; 8 9BR1; 9 9CK1; 10 9CK5; 11 9FO3; 12 9FO4; 13 9FU10; 14 9RA3; 15 9ST1; 16 38OC47; 17 9EB1; 18 9EB85; 19 9EB86; 20 9GE4; 21 9GE5; 22 1LE1; 23 9CE3; 24 9BI1; 25 9BI12; 26 9BI5; 27 9TR1; 28 9TR12.

Figure 16. Northern Georgia mound centers, A.D. *900–1300.*

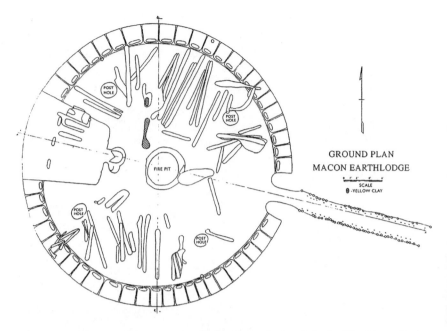

Figure 17. Plan map of the Macon Earthlodge. From Charles Fairbanks, The Macon Earthlodge, American Antiquity, 12. Copyright 1946 by the Society for American Archaeology. Used by permission.

one platform mound with summit architecture, a closely located earth-embanked structure, and possibly a plaza. The earth-embanked buildings were interpreted to be earth lodges by the original excavators (Fairbanks 1946; Kelly 1938), but have since been shown to represent buildings with earth banked against their outer walls (Hally and Williams 1994; Larson 1994).

The best example of the Macon Plateau earth lodges is Mound D-1 Lodge (Fairbanks 1946; Kelly 1938), also referred to as the Macon Earthlodge or Council Chamber (Figure 17), which stands today fully reconstructed at its original location. This was a circular building measuring 13 m in diameter with a long, covered entrance passage. A ring of molded seats with shallow basins in front of each was positioned on a clay bench that extended around the circumference of the building, and a circular fire basin was located in the middle of the floor. Opposite the entrance passage and extending from the bench out onto the building floor was a low clay platform in the shape of a bird's head. The similarity of this building to those described as council chambers of the Creek and Cherokee has shaped the interpretation of this structure as a meeting place for a decision-making body like the Historic period councils. Whether or not the "earth lodges" at Macon Plateau were used in the same fashion, their size and configuration suggest that they hosted events, presumably of civic and ritual importance, that were attended by a group of people. Such group involvement in decision making and ritual is consistent with a corporately organized social formation.

The presence of multiple subcommunities, each with its own set of roughly equivalent and spatially segregated civic and ceremonial facilities, may represent further support for the corporate orientation of Macon Plateau. This arrangement of subcommunities resembles Blitz's (1999) hypothetical center of a Mississippian confederacy, in which each subcommunity represents a basic political unit brought together by circumstances encouraging the fusion of previously independent polities. While it is clear that the number of subcommunities grew from one to as many as four throughout the occupation of Macon Plateau (Hally and Williams 1994), it is not clear whether this was the result of population growth, immigration, or the fissioning of a once closely united confederacy. As I argued in the first chapter, the fusing of simple chiefdoms to create a confederacy of roughly equal political units is most likely to occur only within the context of corporately oriented social systems. Network leaders make extensive use of material symbols, such as prestige goods and monuments, to reinforce their exclusive control over political decision making. Under these circumstances, it seems unlikely that network leaders would allow other, potentially competing, social segments to maintain civic and ceremonial facilities equal to their own.

The mortuary data recovered from Macon Plateau lend some additional, albeit thin, support to the corporate nature of its associated polity. Most of the information on mortuary treatment at Macon Plateau was recovered during the excavation of Mound C, also known as the Funeral Mound, and nearby village areas. A total of 83 burials were found in or associated with mound construction stages, another 19 were recorded beneath the mound, and five were found in village contexts near the mound (Powell 1994). In mound and submound contexts, both males and females were buried, as were people of all ages. The village burials were all adults of unknown sex. As Table 6 shows, grave goods occurred in roughly equal frequencies in burials from the mound, premound, and village areas, and, although the sample sizes are small, exotic grave goods were more commonly found in submound and village contexts than in the mound. The four richest graves were found in mound and submound contexts and the only non-marine-shell exotic grave goods (two small embossed copper ornaments) also came from a burial within the mound. Overall, however, the available evidence

Table 6. Distribution of grave goods in the Funeral Mound excavations

Context	N	Grave Goods (%)	Marine Shell (%)	Other Exotics (%)
Submound	19	21	21	0
Mound	83	16	8	1
Village	5	20	20	0

does not indicate that those afforded burial in the Funeral Mound had any greater access to nonlocal goods than those buried elsewhere.

While the Funeral Mound was clearly a specialized mortuary facility, the fact that nonlocal goods did not play an important part in defining statuses afforded burial within it is consistent with a corporately oriented political economy. Also consistent with a corporate orientation, there is no clear evidence that the nonlocal goods found in Funeral Mound burials were part of an international style. Blanton et al. (1996) indicate that the operation of a network strategy leads to the emergence of widely shared conventions in elite symbolism. To date, no evidence has been found supporting the existence throughout northern Georgia of widespread similarities in elite symbolism that would constitute an Early Mississippian international style.

By around A.D. 1000, the emerging chiefdoms centered at Etowah, Sixtoe Field, and Hiwassee Island (40MG31) also appear to have that same corporate orientation. At all three sites, architecture provides the primary data supporting this suggestion. At Etowah, a series of large buildings, a few containing interior platforms and partitions, were constructed in non-mound contexts during the Early Etowah phase. Buildings similar in size and configuration were constructed beneath and/or on the summits of Hiwassee Island phase mound stages at Hiwassee Island, Davis (40HA2), and Hixon (40HA3) in eastern Tennessee and on an Early Etowah phase summit at Sixtoe Field on the Coosawattee River. In his discussion of architecture in the Chickamauga Basin, Lewis (1995) identified these kinds of structures as community buildings, mainly on the basis of their size and association (in most cases) with mounds. Presumably like the Macon Plateau earth lodges, these community buildings would have hosted political and ritual functions attended by groups of people. Such group involvement in ritual and decision making is expected in corporately oriented chiefdoms.

Further indications of the corporate orientation of political economies may be provided by the large, midden-filled pits recorded at both Etowah and Sixtoe Field. Kelly recorded 17 midden-filled pits, like those encoun-tered at Etowah, in Early Etowah phase contexts adjacent to the Sixtoe Field mound. Like those recorded at Etowah, the Sixtoe Field features were filled with large quantities of pottery and animal bone, along with ash, charcoal, and fire-cracked rock. Kelly et al. (1965) make it clear that the midden-filled pits at Sixtoe Field were borrow pits for mound construction that were subsequently filled with midden. Their edges were clearly de-fined and no soil had washed into the pits, as if they had been filled shortly after being excavated. As I argued in Chapter 4, the midden in these pits may have derived from communal feasting that occurred as part of mound construction. As a ritual designed to purify the earth, mound construction may have been one of the rites of intensification that served to reinforce the solidarity of corporately organized chiefdoms.

At Hiwassee Island, mound-summit community buildings appeared in pairs on all but the last two mound summits. This suggests a duality to Hiwassee Island's organization not unlike the moieties recorded among the Historic period Creek and Cherokee. Moieties unite distinct corporate groups, often through an ideology that links them in complementary social roles. These are just the kinds of ideological constructs that leaders in cor-porately organized societies emphasize as a means of reinforcing social soli-darity. As Knight (1990) has argued, moieties often include elements of hierarchy that can be emphasized or de-emphasized depending on the na-ture of the social formation. Given this, it is possible for a moiety system to be manipulated to fit the needs of network leaders as well. If the paired buildings on the Hiwassee Island mound do represent facilities of different moieties, then their apparent equivalence (in terms of size, location, and elaborateness) suggests that any ranking inherent in the system may have been de-emphasized to promote social solidarity.

Unfortunately, with the exception of Macon Plateau, none of these early chiefdom centers have produced a great deal of mortuary data. No burials have been associated with Hiwassee Island phase contexts in eastern Tennessee (Lewis and Kneberg 1946; Schroedl and Boyd 1991), and very few have been recorded in Early Etowah phase contexts from Etowah and Sixtoe Field. Those that have been recorded at Etowah and Sixtoe Field contained no grave goods. Schroedl and Boyd (1991) argue, mainly on the basis of radiocarbon dates, that most Hiwassee Island phase people were buried in accretional burial mounds located away from substructure mound and village sites. Cole's (1975) study of demography and mortuary treatment associated with these burial mounds, which included both Late Woodland and Mississippian sites, suggests that these were communal facilities with few indications of social ranking. A small number of people were buried with exotic materials, particularly conch columellae, but nonlocal goods were not correlated with any age or sex group. Such a group-oriented mortuary program in which ranking is not clearly marked by access to nonlocal goods is to be expected of corporately oriented chiefdoms.

If my arguments concerning the organization of early Etowah period political economies in Georgia and southeastern Tennessee are correct, then they have interesting implications for understanding the context within which social ranking emerged in this region. It has long been popular to see ranking, especially in the Southeast, as a product of competitive interactions created by increasing populations and sedentism spurred by the adoption of corn horticulture. Little (1999) argues that Etowah's rise to prominence and the appearance of ranking in the Etowah River valley occurred within a similar context. According to this argument, increasing reliance on corn horticulture engendered competition between Late Woodland groups living in northwestern Georgia and northeastern Alabama. Out of this competition arose Etowah and its leaders as they subjugated other nearby populations and created institutionalized social ranking. The evidence Little presents for the incidence of warfare and the growing importance of corn during the Late Woodland period is solid. The orientation of the earliest Mississippian political economies in this area suggests, however, that ranking emerged not out of exclusionary actions like warfare and political domination, but rather through inclusive approaches stressing social solidarity.

As Little notes, warfare hinders horticultural economies, so there may have been a great interest on the part of Late Woodland social groups in finding an end to armed hostilities. Under these circumstances, inclusive ideologies like those associated with corporate political economies may have been quite effective at bringing those competing social groups together. The mutual nonaggression pact that created the League of the Iroquois, with its ideology of "spreading the great tree of peace," was just such a corporate solution to endemic warfare.

The earliest deposits at both Etowah and Sixtoe Field contain evidence potentially indicating that a similar approach was used in northwestern Georgia. At both sites, some of the earliest evidence of human activity includes borrow pits filled with large quantities of food remains and broken pottery. Using the data from Etowah, I argued that these features were filled with the refuse generated by the large-scale preparation and consumption of food, or feasting. Citing Knight's (2001) work with mounds,

I further argued that this feasting took place as part of mound construction, which was a communal rite of intensification organized around the themes of world renewal and fertility. Following Hayden's (2001) framework, the absence of prestige goods from these feasting contexts indicates that the purpose of the feasting was solidarity building or the forging of social alliances rather than power building through competition.

Given this evidence, it seems likely that the Early Mississippian chiefdoms in northwestern Georgia were formed as alliances were forged between once hostile subgroups and were maintained through action for the common good. Mound construction would have been one of many ways people were brought together to meet important and commonly held goals like ensuring fertility and purifying the earth and its inhabitants. Similar to what was observed among Historic period groups, ranking may have been expressed in these early chiefdoms in corporate-group rather than individual terms. For example, clans, phratries, or moieties may have been ranked with respect to one another. The details of the ranking system were probably determined by such things as relationships between the mythical founders of those corporate groups or the length of time corporate groups had lived in the area. The relatively thin data available in northern Georgia suggest that any existing ranking was subsumed to the ideal of society as a corporate whole.

THE LATE ETOWAH PERIOD (A.D. 1100–1200): THE SPREAD OF MISSISSIPPIAN CHIEFDOMS

After about A.D. 1100, chiefdoms developed throughout northern Georgia, with most political centers being located in the Ridge and Valley and Piedmont portions of the state (Figure 16). At this time the Etowah River valley was inhabited by three simple chiefdoms, and possible complex chiefdoms may have emerged on the Coosawattee and upper Savannah rivers. Some part of the occupations of the Hiwassee Island (40MG31) and Davis (40HA2) sites may have continued into this period as well.

The data concerning the orientation of political economies throughout the region are more equivocal and difficult to interpret. As already discussed, there are almost no mortuary data from Etowah, Wilbanks (9CK5), or Long Swamp (9CK1) in the Etowah River valley. Although this may indicate that some form of communal mound burial remained the preferred form of mortuary treatment, it is difficult to know this with any certainty. The presence of a large, earth-embanked building beneath the Wilbanks mound, large enough to accommodate group-oriented decision making and ritual, may stand as one of the few reasonably compelling pieces of evidence for a continuation of a corporate orientation to regional political economies.

Mound-summit architecture at Long Swamp, however, presents a somewhat different picture. On the two stages of that mound dated to the Late Etowah phase, Wauchope (1966) recorded Houses 3 and 4. Only House 3 was described in any detail, and it was recorded as a circular building with single-set posts that measured 6.8 m in diameter. It had a puddled clay hearth at its center, the floor was covered with a rich midden, and a shallow ditch encircled the exterior wall. Unlike the structure beneath the Wilbanks mound, this building is only somewhat larger than contemporary examples of domestic architecture and on the small end of the distribution of community buildings in the Chickamauga Basin. It also lacks the interior furnishings commonly found in community buildings like those at Hiwassee Island. The fact that it was made of single-set posts, rather than in a wall trench like most late Etowah period residential architecture, may indicate its special nature. The presence of a rich midden might indicate large-scale food consumption, but without the original excavated data (which is now largely gone; see King 1996), this is merely a supposition.

Data from outside the Etowah River valley are not much more informative. At least some portion of the mounds at Hiwassee Island and Davis in the Tennessee valley also may have been built during the late Etowah period. As I argued above, the inferred mortuary program and nature of mound-summit architecture may indicate a corporate orientation for the political economies of these sites.

The only other fairly extensive data from late Etowah period mound centers were recovered on the upper Savannah River at Tugalo (9ST1; Caldwell 1956) and Chauga (38OC47; Kelly and Neitzel 1961). Unfortunately, the chronological placement of the earliest stages at these mounds is problematic. At both sites, the early contexts have been assigned to the Jarrett phase, which, on the basis of similarities in the use of stamped motifs, has been dated to sometime between A.D. 1100 and 1200 (Anderson 1994; Hally and Rudolph 1986; Rudolph and Hally 1985). There is information from each of the sites indicating that at least some of the Jarrett phase construction stages actually date to the early or even late Savannah period. Until large collections of pottery can be examined in stratigraphic sequence from these sites, it can only be acknowledged that some unknown part of the mounds originally assigned to the Jarrett phase may have been built later in the Savannah period.

At both Tugalo and Chauga, the first several construction stages were assigned to the Jarrett phase on the basis of associated pottery. On the summits of these stages, excavators recorded square buildings ranging from 7 to 8 m on a side. The three structures recorded at Tugalo had single-set post walls with earth embankments, while the one building from Chauga had walls set in a trench. Like the summit building from Long Swamp, the Tugalo and Chauga structures are somewhat larger than most contemporary residences, but are smaller than most Hiwassee Island phase community buildings. Also, all lack the interior furnishings often found in community buildings in the Chickamauga Basin. As at Long Swamp, the fact that the structures located on the Tugalo mound are architecturally different from contemporary residential architecture may indicate that they served nonresidential functions.

Mortuary data from these sites do little to clarify our understanding of late Etowah political economies. The burials originally associated with the Jarrett phase stages at Chauga are clearly later in time, probably dating to the early Savannah period. At Tugalo, 11 burials were recorded just outside the palisade enclosing one of the last Jarrett phase stages. None of these contained grave goods. While this is consistent with a group-oriented political economy, the size of the sample creates little confidence in its representativeness.

Taken together, architectural and mortuary data provide few concrete clues as to the orientation of late Etowah period political economies. Buildings larger than, and often architecturally different from, residential structures continued to be placed on mound summits. This may indicate a continued group orientation to important ritual and decision-making events. Compared with the Mound D-1 Lodge at Macon Plateau or the community buildings at Hiwassee Island, however, it is not as clear that the late Etowah period summit buildings, especially those in northern Georgia, actually served as public structures. Mortuary data are quite sparse, so interpretations of mortuary treatments are based on small samples and circumstantial arguments. What is available clearly shows that elaborate displays using nonlocal prestige goods did not figure prominently in late Etowah political economies.

The most interesting political development to occur during the late Etowah period is the apparent spread of Mississippian chiefdoms throughout the Etowah River valley and other parts of northern Georgia. In the Etowah valley, it seems most likely that this was the result of population growth and the movement of people to suitable locations in the valley. The increase in the number of sites from the Early to Late Etowah phase apparent in available survey data (Hally and Langford 1988; Southerlin 1993) and the clear development of Late Etowah phase material culture from that of the Early Etowah phase seem to support this inference. Whether the appearance of chiefdoms in the upper Savannah and Oconee drainages is somehow related to the initial development of chiefdoms in the Ridge and Valley is open to debate.

During the early Etowah period, non-Mississippian social groups occupied both the Oconee and upper Savannah rivers. On the Oconee, these people are associated with the Vining phase (Elliott and Wynn 1991; Meyers et al. 1999), while along the upper Savannah they are associated with pottery complexes containing Connestee Simple Stamped and plain and brushed wares (Anderson 1996). Sometime before A.D. 1100, an Armor phase village was established along the upper reaches of the Oconee River at one of the largest expanses of floodplain soil in the drainage (Williams and Shapiro 1996). In terms of both house form and pottery decoration, Armour phase material culture is very similar to that of the Early Etowah phase in the Etowah River valley and dramatically different from Vining phase material culture. Along the upper Savannah, essentially Late Woodland material culture and lifeways remained until Tugalo, Chauga, and other Jarrett phase sites were established after A.D. 1100. Again, in terms of pottery decoration and architecture, the Jarrett phase is much more similar to Mississippian material culture in the Ridge and Valley than to that associated with indigenous Late Woodland groups.

Hodder (1977, 1981), among others, has taken pains to show that material culture does not perfectly correlate with social groups or ethnic identities. In fact, it is clear that people can and do manipulate material culture to meet social ends. Given this, it is possible that Late Woodland groups living in the Oconee and upper Savannah valleys abandoned their traditional way of life and adopted pottery decoration, house styles, and subsistence systems associated with Mississippian societies in other river valleys of northern Georgia. In this instance, however, I can think of no convincing social or ecological reasons for such a change. Although we may conceive of Mississippian subsistence systems as more productive than Late Woodland mixed foraging and horticulture, there is no reason to assume that indigenous people in these areas saw it the same way or even had any reason to be concerned with increasing subsistence productivity. Similarly, we may think of Mississippian ranked social systems as something non-ranked social groups, or at least subgroups within them, would aspire to. Rather than being quick to adopt ranking, most egalitarian social groups exposed to it tend to resist such changes.

Kopytoff's (1986) model of the Internal African Frontier provides a more intuitive and parsimonious explanation for the "spread" of Mississippian material culture in northern Georgia. Using oral history and ethnographic examples, he demonstrates how the disgruntled, the adventurous, and the expelled move with their followers to the spatial frontiers of established polities. Sometimes this results in the establishment of new polities, as more followers are lured away from the home polity and possibly others in the area. In other cases the separation from the original polity is only temporary. As Kopytoff shows, those setting off for the frontier take with them a version of the political culture of their home polity and apply that ideal in the creation of new social formations. The result, as seen in sub-Saharan Africa, is striking similarities in social formations across a wide area.

Although the New Archaeology may have taught many of us to distrust migration as an explanation for observed social changes, history and ethnographic data show that the movement of people has always been a real force in social change. It seems likely that the appearance of Mississippian chiefdoms in the Oconee and upper Savannah valleys may have been, at least in part, brought about by the inevitable movement of people to the frontiers of the older chiefdoms located in northwestern Georgia. As in sub-Saharan Africa, those frontiers often were occupied, creating the potential for hostilities, the dislocation of indigenous inhabitants, peaceful co-existence, or even assimilation. In the Oconee valley, where detailed information is emerging about the Vining phase, there is evidence for some level of co-existence, increased hostilities, the sharing of material cultures, and the eventual dislocation or assimilation of Vining populations.

THE EARLY SAVANNAH PERIOD (A.D. 1200–1300): THE FALL AND RISE OF THE ETOWAH VALLEY POLITIES

By the early Savannah period the Etowah valley polities had collapsed and chiefdoms had begun to emerge in the central and south-central parts of Georgia (Figure 16). To the north, Sixtoe Field was replaced by Bell Field as the capital of a simple chiefdom on the Coosawattee, and the multiple-mound Citico site (40HA65) was established in southeastern Tennessee as a seat of chiefly power. With these changes comes evidence that the orientation of chiefdom political economies across the region was shifting toward the individual-centered network approach. The archaeological records of two early Savannah period mound sites, Beaverdam Creek (9EB85) and Bell Field (9MU101), exemplify that process.

At Beaverdam Creek, a small single-mound center located on a tributary of the Savannah River in the Piedmont of Georgia, salvage excavations recorded two premound buildings, four mound construction stages, and 46 human burials (Rudolph and Hally 1985). The architectural sequence associated with the mound shows a shift from earth-embanked buildings beneath the mound, which Rudolph (1985) has called "earth lodges," to wall-trench and single-set post buildings placed on the mound's summit.

The two premound buildings (Structures A1 and A2), which were constructed sequentially in the same location, were square (7.5 and 6.2 m on a side) and made of single-set post walls with clay banked along their outer periphery. Because of the presence of clay embankments, these buildings were identified as earth lodges. Rudolph (1985) has suggested that these were important community buildings that, like Historic period council houses, may have hosted functions that were at times open to many segments of society. If true, this would indicate a corporate orientation to the political economy of Beaverdam Creek.

The relatively small size (no larger than contemporary domestic buildings) of the Beaverdam Creek earth lodges and their lack of distinctive interior furnishings (benches, platforms, etc.) may argue against their use as community buildings. There is evidence indicating, however, that earth-embanked structures, regardless of size, may have served important public functions. In terms of architectural detail, they are different from residential architecture in possessing the characteristic banking of soil against outer walls. Also, there is a marked tendency for earth-embanked buildings to be associated with mounds. In many instances (Wilbanks, Long Swamp, Tugalo, Bell Field, and Beaverdam Creek), these buildings precede the first stage of mound construction, implying that they served some specialized purpose later replaced by mound-summit buildings. The fact that the Beaverdam Creek earth lodges were not segregated from residential zones by palisades or large spaces might indicate that access to these special buildings was not restricted. This also would be consistent with a group-oriented political economy. The small size of these presumed public buildings might indicate that the group participating in important ritual and decision making was smaller and more restricted than during the Etowah periods.

The second of the earth lodges also was intentionally destroyed, and the area within its embankment was filled to create a platform. As many as two buildings may have been placed on this summit, and fragments of wall-trench buildings were noted on the summits of Stages 3 and 4 as well. Although information on these buildings is thin, they apparently differed from the earth lodges in some respects. First, the size of the fragments recorded suggests that these mound-summit buildings were smaller than the earth lodges in overall size. Also, they were architecturally different. Three of the recorded fragments had walls set in trenches rather than single-set posts and none were associated with substantial embankments.

Rudolph (1985) argues that the replacement of earth lodges with mound-summit buildings at Beaverdam Creek signals a restriction in access to public buildings and the functions they hosted. The smaller size of the mound-summit buildings does seem to suggest a restriction in access to public space, while the architectural changes may also signal a shift in function, possibly from public meeting space to residence. Such a change in the use of public space might signal a shift from a corporate to network emphasis in the political economy.

The mortuary data recovered from Beaverdam Creek provide similar hints at shifts in the political economy. Of the 46 burials recorded, nine came from village deposits away from the mound, another five derived from the occupation below the mound and earth lodges, and 14 were assigned to one of the earth lodges or mound stages. In general, grave goods are comparatively rare, only a very few individuals had more goods or more elaborate collections of goods than all others, and only one individual was found with a particularly rich set of materials that included shell and copper items. The presence of burials away from the mound shows that only a subset of Beaverdam Creek society was afforded burial within the mound. The higher incidence of grave goods in mound burials suggests that those graves may have included people of a higher rank than those buried in non-mound areas. Apparently, that elevated rank could be inherited, because not only adults but also children were buried in the Beaverdam Creek mound.

As at Macon Plateau, nonlocal prestige goods, while clearly present, do not seem to have played an important role in symbolizing individual status. Shell beads and other small shell ornaments (buttons, ear pins), whose raw material source was most likely the Gulf Coast (Brown 1983), were present both in mound/earth lodge contexts and in those predating the mound and earth lodges. The only nonlocal goods found only in the mound or earth lodges were three shell gorgets, a shell cup, and several copper items. These were restricted to the graves of three individuals, and only one of those (Burial 2) had something other than marine shell as a nonlocal grave good. While looting may have significantly biased this sample, the data available suggest a ranked social structure in which nonlocally acquired goods did not play a significant role in defining social ranks. This is consistent with a group-oriented political economy.

Although nonlocal goods, other than small marine shell ornaments, are not common in Beaverdam Creek burials, the ones present suggest the beginnings of an international style. As Blanton et al. (1996) describe, the operation of a network political economy is likely to cause the development of widespread similarities in elite symbolism, usually represented in nonlocal prestige goods, that serves as a regional marker of elite status.

These international styles develop within the context of prestige-goods exchange networks. Marine shell, made into beads and other small ornaments, had been part of mortuary treatments throughout the Southeast since the Archaic period. The appearance of engraved shell gorgets bearing styles from distant places and copper artifact forms (embossed plates, ear spools, celts) found fairly widely throughout the region in presumed elite contexts may mark the emergence of elite-moderated exchange networks.

One of the gorgets interred with Burial 48 at Beaverdam Creek is decorated in the Bennett style (Phillips and Brown 1978:183). The home of the Bennett style most likely is eastern Tennessee, but examples have been found as far away as Spiro in Oklahoma (Phillips and Brown 1978). The other two gorgets found at the site are poorly preserved, making it difficult to identify their decorative styles. Copper-covered celts and ear spools like those found at Beaverdam Creek have been recovered in early and late Savannah period contexts throughout Tennessee, Alabama, and Georgia. These goods may indicate the appearance of international standards of elite dress and the sharing of decorative styles across exchange networks. If so, this may mark a shift from corporate to network political economies.

A similar record is represented at the Bell Field site, an early Savannah period mound site located on the Coosawattee River (Kelly 1972). At Bell Field, salvage excavations recorded three superimposed building levels of premound "earth lodges," followed by as many as six mound construction stages supporting interconnected complexes of mound-summit buildings. While those mound-summit buildings were different architecturally from the earth lodges, being rectangular to square, possessing single-set posts, and lacking the earth embankments, they were no smaller in size. In addition, some of the mound-summit buildings contained interior features like benches and small platforms reminiscent of the Hiwassee Island phase public buildings of the Etowah period. Unlike at Beaverdam Creek, the only evidence for a restriction in access to public space at Bell Field is in the placement of presumed public buildings on mound summits.

The mortuary record from Bell Field, although poorly described, is in many respects similar to that of Beaverdam Creek. While people were buried both in and away from the mound, those buried near the mound had a greater incidence of grave goods. Only a small number of mound burials, however, had impressive collections of burial offerings. The two most impressive were found with Burials 10 and 13, each of which intruded into the preserved architecture from upper stages removed by plowing and flooding. Burial 10 was an adult male interred with a "copper headdress," a pearl necklace, a copper ear spool, a large *Busycon* shell, and a negative painted dog effigy vessel. Burial 13 included two individuals tentatively identified as adolescents, and they were buried with a sandstone human figure pipe, a 12-inch flint blade, red ochre, three galena cubes, three projectiles, a sawfish jaw fragment, a Fortune Noded vessel, and a vessel with four opposed human face adornos (two skeletal and two in the flesh).

Again, many of the goods found in these two graves also have been found in elite burials from contemporary contexts throughout the region, suggesting they are part of an emerging international style propagated by the widespread application of network political economic strategies. For example, headdresses containing decorative elements made of embossed copper and mica cutouts have been recorded from Lake Jackson in Florida to the Dallas area of eastern Tennessee. Large flint blades have a similar distribution, while Hatch (1976a) has shown that mineral pigments like red ochre and galena were integral elements of eastern Tennessee mortuary programs.

It would seem, then, that during the early Savannah period political economies across northern Georgia and adjoining areas were being transformed from group-oriented to individual-centered approaches. Whether these changes were related in any way to the abandonment of the Etowah valley after A.D. 1200 is open to question. Perhaps supporting populations were drawn away from the Etowah valley polities by the impressive, charismatic, and supernaturally charged leaders emerging at centers like Bell Field, Beaverdam Creek, Scull Shoals (9GE4), and Citico (40HA65). It is also possible that the corporate polities of the Etowah valley fissioned (*sensu* Blitz 1999), as leaders of constituent subgroups adopted new competitive and exclusionary ideologies and struck out to establish independent polities.

Given the emerging importance of nonlocal goods as a means to aggrandize and legitimize political leaders, perhaps competition over access to flows of such goods played a role in the demise of the Etowah valley polities. On the basis of distributions of elite items and important raw materials, Brown (1983; Brown et al. 1990) has suggested that one of the corridors through which status goods traveled during the Middle Mississippian period (early and late Savannah periods) extended from peninsular Florida through Georgia and into the Ridge and Valley, where it bent westward to the Nashville Basin, the Memphis area, the Arkansas valley, and eventually the Plains. One possible route that materials could follow from the Gulf Coast through Georgia and into the Ridge and Valley of Tennessee is up the Apalachicola and Chattahoochee rivers, across a small part of the Piedmont into the Ridge and Valley of Georgia and northward into Tennessee (Figure 18).

It is generally accepted that items associated with the Southeastern

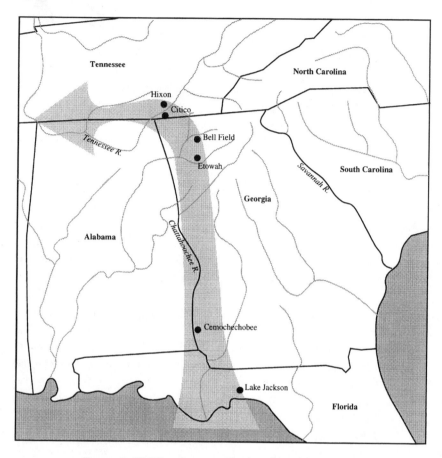

Figure 18. SECC exchange corridor through northern Georgia.

Ceremonial Complex (SECC) became widely distributed throughout the Southeast after about A.D. 1200 (Brown 1976; Muller 1989). Not long after that the Citico site in southeastern Tennessee was first occupied and became a major participant in the exchange of SECC items (Hatch 1976b). The emergence of an exchange corridor that connected Florida with the Tennessee valley, along with the rise of Citico as an important site along that route, may have made the Etowah and Coosawattee valleys strategic, but redundant, locations through which materials could pass between the Chattahoochee River and the Ridge and Valley province. This may have engendered competition between polities in the Etowah and Coosawattee valleys for access to flows of goods, ultimately leading to political collapse on the Etowah River.

With the dissolution of the Etowah valley chiefdoms, Bell Field would have become the major link between the Tennessee valley to the north and the Chattahoochee valley to the south. Because of its strategic location, Bell Field may have been incorporated into a large polity controlled by elites at Citico (see King 1996:237–241), and it may even be possible that such an alignment played a role in the collapse of the Etowah valley polities. Whether this political affiliation led to the competition posited above is not clear. Late Etowah phase deposits have not been explored in great depth at Etowah or the other Etowah valley political centers. Investigations conducted to date, however, have discovered little evidence suggesting that armed conflict brought an end to the occupation of valley centers.

It also remains possible that the collapse of the Etowah valley polities had little to do with shifts in the orientation of political economies and much more to do with the interplay between population and ecology. Some combination of increasing population levels and decreasing productivity of the landscape may have created imbalances that ultimately brought an end to those chiefdoms. Such imbalances need not have created Malthusian catastrophes. Instead they may have brought about the steady erosion of confidence in existing social structures, as Anderson (1994) describes for the abandonment of the Savannah River valley. Ranked social structures may have fallen apart as dissatisfied followers deserted chiefs who failed in their duty to maintain the proper balance between the real and supernatural worlds. Additional settlement studies and efforts to reconstruct environmental histories of northern Georgia are needed to more clearly define the role that population and ecology played in the demise of the Etowah period polities of the Etowah valley.

Whatever the ultimate cause of the collapse of the Etowah valley polities, chiefdoms did not stay away from the valley for very long. People returned to Etowah sometime after A.D. 1250, and the site experienced a florescence. Large amounts of labor were devoted to mound building, as Mounds A and B were significantly enlarged, and construction began on Mound C. Etowah's leaders also took on a major role in the regional exchange of SECC goods, as evidenced by the large numbers of such goods placed in Early Wilbanks graves at Mound C. Along with Etowah, as many as five single-mound centers were established near Etowah, indicating that the site became the capital of a complex chiefdom.

Given the importance of network approaches to organizing chiefdoms of this period, the same factors that may have brought the Etowah valley polities to an end a half century earlier may have prompted people to return. By establishing a new polity in the Etowah valley, network political actors positioned themselves to take advantage of an established network through which important raw materials and finished SECC goods traveled.

Etowah's rapid rise to regional importance attests to the success of that strategy.

THE LATE SAVANNAH PERIOD (A.D. 1300–1375): CONCENTRATION OF POWER

By the late Savannah period, Etowah had become a large and impressive center whose political influence may have extended throughout the Etowah valley, and even beyond, making it the likely capital of a paramount chiefdom. Given the size of Etowah's monumental constructions, the number of subsidiary centers in its polity, and the large quantities of SECC goods interred in its elite contexts, it seems clear that Etowah was the dominant seat of power in northern Georgia. At this same time, occupation of Bell Field may have continued, while Citico remained an important center on the upper Tennessee River (Figure 19).

Throughout the rest of northern Georgia, there appears to be a trend toward increasing concentration of political authority in fewer and larger polities. During the late Savannah period the number of multiple-mound sites in northern Georgia increased, while the total number of mound sites outside of the Etowah River valley actually decreased. In addition, some of the areas that were newly occupied by Mississippian chiefdoms during the early Savannah period lost their political centers, possibly as people were drawn to more established and powerful polities like those on the Oconee and Savannah rivers. These changes no doubt reflect the reorientation of chiefdom political economies as network strategies came into use across northern Georgia and beyond.

Evidence for the widespread use of network-type strategies abounds in the archaeological record of northern Georgia at this time. Not only at Etowah, but also at sites like Nacoochee (9WH3) on the upper Chattahoochee, Chauga (38OC47) on the upper Savannah, Hollywood (9RI1) at the Fall Line along the Savannah, and Shinholser (9BL1) on the Oconee River, elites were buried with nonlocal goods and supernaturally charged symbols. As at Etowah, these goods were buried in individual graves, indicating that they were important sources of power to individual leaders. Also, it seems apparent that the goods and symbols of the SECC functioned as an international style during the Middle Mississippian period. Not only certain elements of elite costumes, such as copper celts and headdresses with copper decorations, but also particular decorative styles became widely distributed across the region. For example, Hightower style gorgets have been found in Middle Mississippian contexts throughout eastern Tennessee, northeastern Alabama, and northern Georgia, and as far away

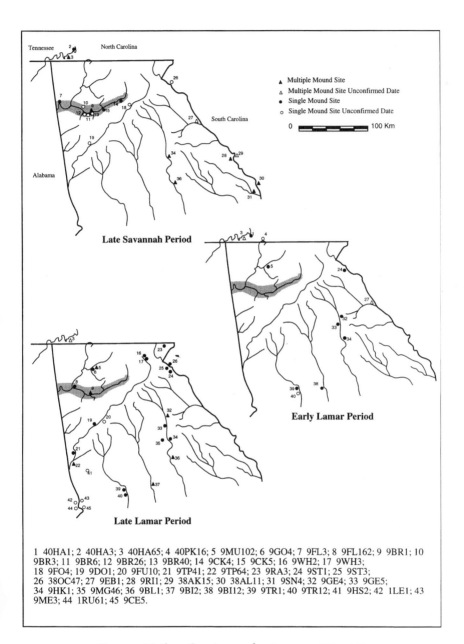

Figure 19. Northern Georgia mound centers, A.D. 1300–1550.

128   *Chapter 5*

as Oklahoma. Similarly, copper plates executed in the same style were found across large parts of the Southeast, including throughout Georgia and in parts of Florida and Alabama (Phillips and Brown 1978).

In addition to the exotic and symbolically charged SECC goods, Middle Mississippian leaders also appear to have used warfare and mound construction to justify and maintain their individual positions of power. During this period, some of the largest and most elaborate mound centers reached their peak (Anderson 1994:136), illustrating the widespread emphasis on monumental constructions. Additionally, the importance of the conduct and ideology of warfare is reflected by the widespread use of warfare-related symbols in the SECC and the common occurrence of palisaded villages and violence-related trauma in skeletal series of the Middle Mississippian period (Larson 1972; Milner 1999).

Taken together, these data sketch out some of the elements of a network strategy that was widely applied during the Middle Mississippian period. At the base of the strategy was the manipulation of externally acquired SECC goods, which were displayed and distributed in ways that reproduced the political position of individual leaders. Through display, as part of a costume or uniform in many cases, individual leaders connected themselves with supernatural beings and forces and demonstrated possession of important qualities, like military prowess (Earle 1990; Helms 1994; Larson 1989; Scarry 1996; Welch 1996; Wobst 1977). It also seems apparent that certain kinds of SECC goods may have been given by leaders as gifts to valued supporters to maintain their loyalty, as well as being exchanged in the wider region to create and maintain alliances and exchange relationships.

Middle Mississippian chiefs used the labor drawn to them to create another kind of aggrandizing display—mounds. The building and use of platform mounds allowed Mississippian chiefs to conspicuously display their social importance and supernatural connections in a variety of ways. As Knight (1989) has argued, Mississippian mounds may have been symbols representing the earth. Manipulating the earth, by placing a residence on it, conducting ritual from it, or being buried within it, clearly demonstrated a chief's power and importance. Similarly, sponsoring the construction of a new mound stage, which Knight (1981, 1986, 1989) argues was an earth-purification ritual, further reinforced that a chief had the supernatural connections to manipulate the purity of the earth and by extension the people living on it.

The labor accessed by Middle Mississippian chiefs also was used to conduct warfare, providing leaders other opportunities to reinforce their local and regional political positions (Dye 1995; Steinen 1992). By defeating ri-

val polities, leaders could gain or maintain political independence or dominate other groups in the region. Such successes would have had the added
benefits of reinforcing the social solidarity of the home polity and the personal military abilities of its leader.

The widespread application of strategies that focused on individuals
who took pains to exclude others from sources of power had two important consequences. First, it likely created impressive leaders who may have
been able to lure followers away from weaker chiefs. Also, those strategies,
because of their exclusionary nature, created competition for access to
sources of power and leadership positions. Under these circumstances,
competition for access to labor (followers) and prestige items may have led
to a concentration of authority in fewer and larger polities, as smaller and
weaker ones were incorporated into larger chiefdoms and ineffectual leaders were abandoned in favor of powerful chiefs. The result during the late
Savannah period in northern Georgia was the creation of larger, but fewer,
polities on the landscape. Seen from this perspective, the dramatic rise of
Etowah is a local outcome of larger regional processes spurred by the adoption of network strategies.

THE END OF THE LATE SAVANNAH PERIOD: COLLAPSE

Sometime before the end of the late Savannah period, the large and impressive polities occupying the northern Georgia landscape collapsed. This
collapse included the Etowah-dominated polity, as well as the large centers
on the middle Savannah and Oconee rivers. At the same time, the once
far-reaching exchange networks that distributed SECC goods across the
Southeast became more regionalized and the goods moving within them
became less elaborate.

While it seems quite likely that changes occurring over such a large
area probably had a variety of interrelated causes, the application of network strategies was undoubtedly an important factor. Blanton et al. (1996)
argue that network polities have a tendency to become embroiled in local
and regional political competition, and, as a result, are likely to be unstable.
The exclusionary tactics of network leaders can engender local factional
competition, as rival claimants to leadership positions attempt to usurp
monopolized sources of power. At the same time, network polities may be
involved in political competition at the regional level, as network participants compete with one another for control over flows of goods, people,
and information. Under these circumstances, leaders may be unseated or
polities even destroyed by local factionalism or attempts by other leaders in
the region to cut them out of interaction networks. At Etowah, there is

evidence suggesting that its demise was caused by military attack. While the other polities in northern Georgia may not have fallen to invading armies, it is possible that their collapse was due in part to the competitive political atmosphere created by the widespread use of network strategies.

In network-type strategies, the political fortunes of individual leaders and their associated polities are directly impacted by access to interaction networks that provide prestige goods, esoteric knowledge, and other important sources of power. The operation of these networks links polities and leaders across space, creating interconnectedness and even interdependency. As already discussed, indirect evidence for that interconnectedness in northern Georgia can be seen in the distribution of certain elite artifact forms and decorative styles. In this kind of a system, the demise of one or a few important network participants could have an adverse impact on the entire system. The breakdown of interaction networks eventually may have caused an erosion of confidence in individual leaders as they lost consistent and predictable access to important sources of power. The large size and potentially diverse ethnic composition of the late Savannah polities may have made them particularly unstable political formations. Under these circumstances, the loss of power sources and the factionalism encouraged by exclusionary network tactics might have led to the fragmenting of those polities. Throughout the interconnected system, these kinds of changes may have started a chain reaction ultimately altering the political landscape of northern Georgia.

Another factor potentially contributing to the collapse of the late Savannah polities is related to what Knight (1986, 1997) has called the communalization of chiefly symbolism. According to Knight (1986), after the Middle Mississippian period, across the Southeast, symbols that had been reserved exclusively for elite use became available to a wider range of Mississippian society. The loss of exclusive use of symbolically loaded goods like those of the SECC could have undermined the power base of late Savannah chiefs, leading to an erosion of their legitimacy and ultimately the fragmentation of their large polities.

This communalization might have been an unintended result of elite strategies aimed at maintaining social control. Knight (1997) suggests this may have happened at the Moundville site during the Moundville III phase. At that time, most of the site's resident population abandoned Moundville and dispersed into the surrounding region (Knight and Steponaitis 1998). According to Knight (1997), the pottery type Moundville Engraved, variety Hemphill, with its elaborate symbolism, was produced under elite control and dispersed to those outlying populations. As Pauketat and Emerson (1991) argue for Ramey Incised at Cahokia, Knight suggests that the symbols on the engraved pots carried messages reinforcing the elite world-view, and their intentional distribution was part of an elite strategy designed to keep increasingly removed supporters tied into Moundville's ranked social structure. The result was to remove important supernatural symbols from the exclusive control of elites.

The same result may have come from intentional efforts on the part of other actors or subgroups to break the monopoly network leaders maintained over supernatural symbolism. Such efforts may have come from common people, rebelling against the strict ranking systems that justified the individual power of network leaders. It also may have come from leading members of other subgroups seeking to grab political control from entrenched decision makers—or at least a share of it.

Finally, imbalances between population levels and the natural environment and subsistence systems also may have contributed to the collapse of the late Savannah chiefdoms. As noted above, during the late Savannah period there were fewer political centers on the landscape than during previous periods. If this was the case, then larger populations may have been concentrated around a smaller number of chiefdom capitals, leading to the overexploitation of local environments and eventually declining productivity. The resulting subsistence stress may have caused the large, late Savannah polities to fission, as subgroups relocated to more productive areas. The demise of individual centers as a result of these factors could have brought about or spurred the breaking apart of Middle Mississippian interaction networks and the ultimate fragmentation of late Savannah chiefdoms across northern Georgia.

In the Etowah valley, there is some evidence suggesting that the dominant center was attacked and ultimately abandoned. If this turns out to be the case, then competition over labor and flows of goods and information engendered by network strategies seems the likely cause. As with the other large late Savannah polities, the Etowah-dominated polity, because of its size and social composition, was no doubt prone to internal factionalism as well. To what degree the polity may have been weakened by internal strife is unclear. Additionally, subsistence stress caused by population levels out of balance with local resources may have been yet another factor making the Etowah-dominated polity vulnerable to attack.

THE EARLY LAMAR PERIOD (A.D. 1375–1475): DISPERSAL AND DECENTRALIZATION

Whatever the ultimate causes for this collapse, by the early Lamar period political centers again had disappeared from the Etowah valley and the

Citico-dominated polity may have been in decline as well. At the same time, the Little Egypt site (9MU102) located on the Coosawattee River was first occupied (Figure 19). Single-mound sites were again occupied at the Fall Line on the Flint and Ocmulgee rivers, and the number of mound sites increased in the Oconee valley. Overall, however, there is a decrease in the number of known mound sites in the region, and no complex chiefdoms have been identified. These changes suggest that political power may have become more decentralized at this time.

Because of a lack of good data, it is difficult to understand all of the changes that took place in chiefdom political economies from the late Savannah to early Lamar period. Many people have observed the general trend across the Southeast toward less elaborate grave goods and a regionalization of once far-reaching exchange networks (Anderson 1994; Brown 1985; Milner 1990; Morse and Morse 1983; Muller 1989). In the archaeological record of northern Georgia, once widely distributed artifact forms and styles like copper celts, Greater Braden style copper plates, and Hightower style gorgets do not occur in early Lamar contexts. These appear to be replaced by gorget and mask styles with fairly tight geographic distributions (Brain and Phillips 1996).

Whether these changes signal a return to more corporate forms of organization remains difficult to determine. Knight (1990) has argued that, in historic times and probably also in prehistory, Southeastern native societies were composed of sets of corporate groups that were internally egalitarian but ranked with respect to one another. That ranking structure could be emphasized or de-emphasized, creating more or less hierarchically organized social formations. Almost certainly the corporate groups that dominated Early Mississippian political structures of northern Georgia did not disappear during the Middle Mississippian period. Instead, it is likely that their social importance was de-emphasized by prevailing individual-centered elite ideologies. As Knight's argument suggests, the social power of corporate groups no doubt lay just below the surface of those social structures molded by network strategies.

The political collapse at the end of the late Savannah period may have provided an opportunity for corporate groups to reassert their power. The social fragmentation and dispersal caused by the collapse of the late Savannah polities likely facilitated that shift, because corporate ideologies are more effective at uniting disparate social groups into single polities (Blanton et al. 1996). The result may have been a period in which chiefdom organization shifted more toward the group-oriented corporate approach.

While this scenario is speculative, there are small amounts of data suggesting that in some areas corporate ideologies may have taken hold. One possible example comes from the Dallas site (40HA1) in eastern Tennessee. According to Sullivan (2001), the Dallas site had two Mississippian occupations: one contemporary with the Hixon site (40HA3) and a second dating to the fifteenth century. That later occupation is associated with all construction stages of the Dallas mound as well as a palisaded village. As part of this occupation, the site's inhabitants built three structures identified by Nash et al. (1995) as community buildings. Each was larger than all but one of the site's residential buildings and they were architecturally different from those residences. Like the community buildings of the Etowah and early Savannah periods, these structures had earth embankments against their outer walls and special interior features such as clay benches. One of the community buildings lay beneath the first construction stage of the mound, while a second was positioned on the first summit. The final three summits had been destroyed by plowing, so it is impossible to know whether they supported similar buildings. The third community building was recorded in the village area away from the mound.

The presence of these community buildings, especially those positioned on the summit of the mound, suggests that important ritual and political activities involved groups of people, as might be expected of a group-oriented chiefdom. The mortuary data from Dallas are consistent with this possibility. While the mound served as a specialized mortuary facility, there are few differences between mound and non-mound burial populations when it comes to the number or kind of burial goods interred. About the same percentage of mound and non-mound burials contained grave goods, and the same range of goods was found in each area. Those grave goods were limited mainly to pottery vessels and shell beads, with a smaller number of shell gorgets and masks. As might be expected of a corporately oriented polity, nonlocal goods do not appear to have been important markers of individual status or important sources of individual power.

In northwestern Georgia, the fall of Etowah appears to have set in motion a series of historical events that eventually led to the formation of the Coosa paramount chiefdom described by de Soto (King 1999). Apparently, not long after the fall of Etowah, mound construction began at the Little Egypt site (9MU102) on the Coosawattee. Historically, it is known that Little Egypt became the capital of the Coosa chiefdom during the late Lamar period and held sway over polities in both the Etowah and upper Tennessee valleys (Hally et al. 1990; Hudson et al. 1985). Little Egypt's rise to prominence was likely facilitated by the collapse of the Etowah paramountcy and the decline of the Citico-dominated polity. Therefore, in northern Georgia the early Lamar appears to represent a period when the locus of regional power was in the process of shifting toward the Coosawattee and away from the Etowah and upper Tennessee valleys.

THE LATE LAMAR PERIOD (A.D. 1450–1550): PEER-POLITIES AND PARAMOUNTCIES

The decentralization and dispersal of the early Lamar eventually created a late Lamar landscape in which political centers were abundant and fairly evenly distributed (Figure 19). Compared with earlier periods, there were more mound sites, multiple-mound sites, and complex chiefdoms across northern Georgia. In addition, political centers were located in almost every large drainage in the region. Apparently, the political units dispersed by the late Savannah collapse had reestablished themselves as separate polities occupying distinct territories by the late Lamar period.

The late Lamar period marks the coming of the first European explorers to the interior Southeast, and the descriptions they left behind have provided a wealth of information about native Southeastern societies. Those Spanish explorers described a landscape dominated by large paramount chiefdoms, whose territories sometimes extended several hundred kilometers and whose polities incorporated multiple simple and complex chiefdoms. As the Spanish described them, those paramount chiefdoms were highly integrated political units whose all-powerful leaders controlled vast amounts of surplus labor and produce. In reality, those paramountcies were likely loose confederations of chiefdoms assembled through some combination of alliance, military might, and threat of force, and the political control exerted by their leaders, especially over distant groups, was fairly limited (Hally et al. 1990; King 1999).

The Spaniards also describe a landscape that was fraught with political and military competition. Paramount chiefs were constantly competing with neighboring paramounts for positions of regional dominance. While short-term advantage was sometimes achieved over neighbors, those political relations appear to have been difficult to maintain over the long term. The result was a landscape dominated by a series of peer-polities. Even the dominance hierarchies within paramountcies were difficult to maintain over the long term, as evidenced by the fact that the Spanish describe instances in which subject polities attempted to break free of the paramount structure.

The political situation described by the Spaniards fits what might be expected of a region in which polities were structured using network principles. In fact, I have argued elsewhere that chiefs applied just those kinds of strategies across northern Georgia during the late Lamar period (King 1999). My arguments are based on several factors. First, as expected of network systems, the Spanish chronicles describe a well-defined ranking system in which leaders were singled out through special treatment, such as being transported on elaborately decorated litters (Biedma 1993:230; Ranjel 1993:278, 284), living in residences that were larger than all others (Elvas 1993:75), having their residences placed on mounds or in close association to mounds (Biedma 1993:239; Elvas 1993:95), and wearing distinctive and elaborate clothing. Also, unlike the relative anonymity expected of corporate leaders, sixteenth-century paramounts were conspicuously conceived of as individually important leaders. The most explicit acknowledgment of the importance of individuals as leaders is found in the naming of paramounts and their polities. All paramount chiefs encountered by de Soto shared their name with the polity over which they ruled. This practice seemingly equated the political body with the person of the paramount. Finally, there is some evidence for widespread conventions both in treatment of paramounts (Hally and Smith 1992) and in their dress and paraphernalia (King 1999), suggesting the existence of an international style.

Archaeological data from northern Georgia (see also Chapter 3) provide further evidence for the clearly defined ranking systems and aggrandizement of individual leaders expected in network polities. Late Lamar mortuary data suggest that clearly defined ranking systems existed, wherein the people of highest status were buried adjacent to or within mounds accompanied by specialized artifacts such as conch-shell cups, painted bottles, copper artifacts, and minerals like graphite and galena (Hatch 1974; Humpf 1995; Polhemus 1987; Seckinger 1977; Sullivan 1986). Additionally, architecture recorded on mound summits indicates that political leaders were set apart from the rest of society by residing on and conducting important public functions from mound summits (DePratter 1991).

Just like during the Middle Mississippian period, participation in external social networks provided late Lamar chiefs with important sources of power. The most relevant source of power, however, was no longer the supernaturally charged set of SECC goods. In the highly competitive atmosphere of the sixteenth century, the most relevant way for a chief to demonstrate his or her veracity was by successfully competing with other leaders in the region. Under these circumstances, links were created between leaders as they sought to establish alliances, intimidate competitors, or force competitors into submission. As Anderson (1994:137) has argued, chiefly legitimizing strategies changed after the Savannah period, with appeals to the supernatural world giving way to "more secular measures, including the overt use of force." While scarce and symbolically loaded items also moved through these networks and were used to meet chiefly political ends (Dye 1995), the archaeological record suggests they were not as important as in the Savannah period.

The shift in emphasis from nonlocal symbols to political competition apparent in late Lamar network strategies may be related in some way to the apparent communalization of chiefly symbols. By the late Lamar period, marine-shell gorgets, which were once more closely associated with elites, are commonly found in non-elite contexts. Similarly, smaller and less elaborate versions of the chert blades found in elite contexts at sites like Etowah and Hixon appear in a variety of burial contexts during the late Lamar. Also, once-exclusive symbolic objects appear in non-elite contexts in altered forms, such as the monolithic ax effigy pipe found in a Mouse Creek phase burial at the Rymer site in eastern Tennessee (Fairbanks and Neitzel 1995:484). If the communalization of once-exclusive symbols did occur after the late Savannah period, then late Lamar network strategies had to be formulated without the aid of supernatural symbolism. To compensate for the absence of an important source of legitimation, network actors reoriented ideological structures to emphasize political competition, creating the competitive political landscape encountered by de Soto.

During the late Lamar period, Etowah was reoccupied and became the multiple-mound center of a simple chiefdom. Another simple chiefdom, centered at Nixon, also was established at this time. The return of these polities to the Etowah valley is part of the same process of social dispersal followed by landscape in-filling that occurred across northern Georgia. By the time Etowah had reemerged on the political scene, however, the center of power in the region had clearly shifted to the Little Egypt site, the capital of the Coosa paramount chiefdom, whose territory stretched from the French Broad in eastern Tennessee through the Ridge and Valley to the Lower Tallapoosa in eastern Alabama (Hally 1994; Hally et al. 1990). At that time Etowah, known to de Soto as the town of Itaba, was a subject town in that paramountcy (Figure 20). Despite its former greatness, Etowah's network leaders appeared too late on the political scene to challenge the legitimacy Little Egypt's leaders had been establishing for almost a century. In the end, Etowah became a subject town in the larger Coosa paramountcy (King 1999).

The early European explorations of the first half of the sixteenth century gave way to an increasing European presence and efforts to missionize Southeastern native people and colonize the Southeastern landscape. The introduction of European diseases and European economic agendas tore apart the fabric of native Southeastern societies and fundamentally altered

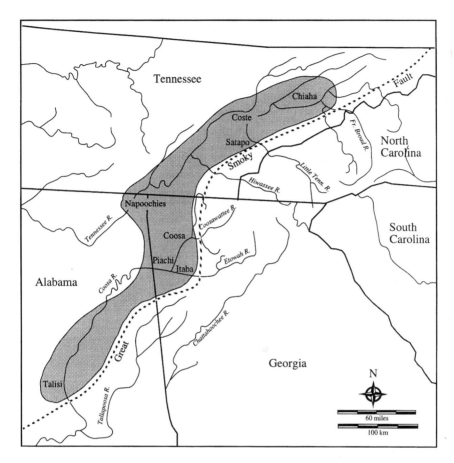

Figure 20. The Paramount Chiefdom of Coosa. Adapted from Hudson et al. 1985:733.

the native political and social landscape. Although the scale and pace of social disruption varied across the Southeast (Knight 1994), processes set into action by the coming of Europeans ultimately created the Historic period native confederacies like the Creek and Cherokee.

Historic descriptions make it clear that those new native polities were organized along corporate lines, in which clans and other important subgroups shared decision-making power within the context of councils. Social ranking did not disappear, but it was reoriented and subsumed to the egalitarian ethic of the clan and moiety system. Given that inclusive corporate ideologies are better suited for uniting disparate social groups, it should not be surprising that the social disruption caused by the European presence forced such a shift in political economies.

These changes brought about an end to Mississippian chiefdoms in northern Georgia. In northwestern Georgia, according to Smith (1987, 1989, 2000), populations, decimated by disease, coalesced and moved down the Coosa drainage into Alabama and ultimately became part of the Creek Confederacy. Before the close of the sixteenth century the Etowah site was abandoned one last time and chiefdoms disappeared from the Etowah River valley.

6

Summary and Future Directions

In this volume, I have attempted to reconstruct a sequence of political changes and offer some possible explanations for the changes observed. In exploring political change, I have separated political complexity from the nature of the political economy designed to support particular social formations. My contention is that these are two separate elements of political organization that can vary independently. By exploring them separately it is possible to get a much richer picture of Mississippian political variation. In attempting to explain political change in the Etowah valley, I contend that social factors, rather than ecological processes, are the more likely to bring about instances of social change. Further, I have argued that the Mississippian Southeast was an interconnected system, so that social changes occurring in the wider region were important causal factors of local-level change. As a result, I have taken an explicitly regional perspective on understanding political change in the Etowah valley.

My approach to reconstructing political change is not without its methodological limitations and potential biases. In Chapter 1, I acknowledged those problems and offered some justification for continuing with the research despite them. Ultimately, however, they do have the potential to introduce inaccuracies into the inferences I have made. As the Mississippian record of the Etowah valley is examined from other perspectives and in the pursuit of other research objectives, I have confidence that the shortcomings of this research will be corrected.

A SUMMARY OF ETOWAH VALLEY POLITICAL CHANGE

Although not the earliest, Etowah may have been one of the few political centers to emerge in northern Georgia during the Early Mississippian period. At this time, available data suggest that most social groups organized their political economies along corporate lines. Although there is no direct evidence for social ranking in the Etowah valley, indirect evidence from the larger region hints that it was a part of Early Mississippian societies in the area. The corporate orientation of Early Mississippian societies suggests that the formation of ranked societies in northern Georgia was accomplished not through exclusive and competitive means like warfare. Instead, social ranking appears to have developed within inclusive ideological frameworks that stressed social solidarity.

From the early to late Etowah period two additional chiefdoms appeared in the Etowah valley. This mirrors a broader trend of the spread of Mississippian material culture and presumably the chiefdom form of organization, as more mound centers appeared throughout the Piedmont and even some on the Coastal Plain of Georgia. It seems highly probable that this spread occurred following a process similar to Kopytoff's (1986) Internal African Frontier, in which social segments split from established polities and formed new ones on more sparsely settled frontiers. The scanty evidence available suggests that late Etowah period political economies maintained a corporate orientation.

By the beginning of the early Savannah period, the Etowah valley polities had collapsed and the river valley was devoid of Mississippian populations. Somewhat more abundant archaeological evidence suggests that the orientation of political economies had shifted from group-oriented corporate approaches to individual-centered network strategies. This is especially apparent in the beginnings of an international style in elite symbolism. By creating a competitive political landscape and emphasizing external social networks, this shift may have been in part to blame for the demise of the Etowah valley polities. Those polities occupied a strategic location along a corridor through which important raw materials and SECC goods traveled, making them a potential target for other network leaders in the region looking to monopolize those flows. It is also possible that supporting populations in the Etowah valley were lured away by impressive, supernaturally charged, powerful leaders emerging in the surrounding region. At the present, it also is not possible to rule out the possibility that the Etowah valley collapse was the result of some manner of subsistence stress caused by population increases or concentrations in circumscribed areas.

Near the end of the early Savannah period, Etowah was reoccupied and became the impressive capital of a complex chiefdom. The creation of an elite mortuary facility and the association of elite individuals with the supernaturally charged SECC goods show not only that social ranking was a part of Etowah's social structure, but also that nonlocal goods played an important role in defining elite status. The quantities of SECC goods recovered from Early Wilbanks burials in Etowah's Mound C also clearly show that the site was an important participant in the exchange of SECC goods throughout the region. With the reoccupation of Etowah, its leaders clearly had adopted network strategies for justifying the chiefdom's social structure. Given the importance placed on external social networks throughout the region, it seems likely that the reoccupation of Etowah was attempted in part to take advantage of the site's strategic location along an SECC goods exchange corridor through which materials moved between the Gulf Coast of Florida and the Tennessee valley and beyond.

By the late Savannah period, Etowah had become an impressive, fortified capital of a paramount chiefdom. Its influence extended at least throughout the Etowah valley and possibly beyond to adjacent valleys. It seems apparent that Etowah's rise to greatness during the Early and Late Wilbanks phases was part of a larger trend across northern Georgia. Network political leaders employed a strategy emphasizing the manipulation of supernatural symbols (SECC goods), mound construction, and warfare to justify exclusive political control and access to surplus production. Supporting populations that were once more widely dispersed across the landscape gravitated to a limited set of large and impressive political centers, effectively concentrating populations and political control.

That concentration of power and population was not to last. By the early Lamar period the Etowah-dominated polity had collapsed and many other large centers in northern Georgia also went into decline. It seems likely that the causes of this widespread collapse had their roots in the nature of network strategies. Because of the exclusionary tactics inherent in network strategies, they encourage competition, both within and between polities. Competition between polities in the region may have brought about the demise of the Etowah site. Across the rest of northern Georgia, similar competitive processes, whether between social segments within polities or between polities on the broader landscape, resulted in the weakening or collapse of individual polities. In an interconnected system of polities like that of northern Georgia, the collapse of one or two important links in that system could have led ultimately to the decline of the entire system.

During the early Lamar period, the large late Savannah polities were replaced by a smaller number of more widely dispersed mound sites, suggesting that with the collapse of the large polities, political control became more decentralized across the region. In northwestern Georgia, this created something of a power vacuum, which ultimately was filled by the Little Egypt site. Evidence concerning the orientation of political economies is generally scarce across the region, although there is some information suggesting a possible shift back to corporate approaches, at least in some areas. The corporate approach, with its inclusive ideology, would have been more effective at bringing together the various social segments dispersed by the late Savannah collapse.

By the late Lamar period, Etowah was reoccupied and was the capital of a simple chiefdom. Historical information indicates that rather than returning to its role as the seat of regional power, Etowah became a subject town in the Coosa paramount chiefdom. Across the rest of northern Georgia, the dispersal of the early Lamar resulted in a political landscape fairly well packed with political centers. If political economies had shifted from network to corporate during the early Lamar, they changed again by the late Lamar. Historical descriptions left by Spanish explorers and archaeological data suggest political leaders again relied on some form of a network approach for organizing their polities. Instead of an emphasis on the exchange of supernaturally charged goods, these new network strategies focused on competition between polities and leaders. The application of these strategies created a highly competitive political landscape, in which leaders continually competed with their neighbors to establish or break free from political domination.

Out of this competition arose paramount chiefdoms like those described by de Soto. Unlike the late Savannah paramountcies, which seem to have grown from the center out, late Lamar paramount chiefs imposed their political will on a landscape already filled with polities through alliance, attack, and threat of force. These polities were in all likelihood weakly integrated, and, because of the exclusive tactics on which they were based, also were relatively unstable and short-lived. Forming a paramount chiefdom took time and the efforts of individual chiefs who had earned reputations as great warriors and strong allies. By the time Etowah was reoccupied, leaders at Little Egypt had been in the process of consolidating power for over a century. As latecomers on the political scene, Etowah's leaders were destined to become the dominated rather than the dominators.

Within a few decades of de Soto's entrada, the increasing European presence led to the ultimate demise of Mississippian chiefdoms across northern Georgia. Out of the remnants of those chiefdoms formed confederacies of formerly independent social groups known to history as the Cherokees and Creeks. With these changes came yet another shift in the orientation of native political economies, from the individual-centered network to the group-oriented corporate approach. Corporate ideologies, with their inclusive nature, no doubt were perfectly suited for bringing together populations reduced and dislocated by European diseases and economic interests.

FUTURE CONSIDERATIONS

This volume is not intended to be and should not be the final word on the Etowah site and Mississippian chiefdoms of the Etowah River valley. Both the issues I raise in it and the limitations of the approach I have used beg for additional work. Many of the questions I raise, as well as many other important issues, can be addressed through analysis of existing collections, whose research potential I have barely tapped. Many more can be examined through well-planned and targeted excavations at Etowah, along with additional settlement survey and site testing away from Etowah.

Without question the data set in the greatest need of additional analysis comes from the excavations conducted at Mound C. These data contain an incredible wealth of information about the production and consumption of native art objects (SECC goods), mortuary practices, elite symbolism, Mississippian ranking structures, and exchange networks. As repatriation consultation continues, the real possibility looms that portions of these collections will be removed from public access. These data need to be analyzed and documented thoroughly so that current and future researchers can learn from them. From a moral and legal standpoint, this cannot be done outside of consultation with the Native American descendants of Etowah's inhabitants—the Creek Indians.

While my own research agenda focuses on continued work with the Etowah site, particularly Mound C and the systematic testing of the site, there is a great deal of room for collaborators. Some of the most productive research projects involve collaborative efforts that crosscut disciplines and universities. One needs to look no further than Moundville in Alabama and the long-term research initiated by Chris Peebles to understand the potential of such projects. The Mississippian record of Etowah and the Etowah River valley is rich enough to support a similar effort.

As a prehistoric archaeologist of European descent, it is clear to me that the object of my research is someone else's history. The work presented in this book was done without the aid or input of Native Americans. The descendants of Etowah's inhabitants still live, practice their culture, and have a history. The perspectives and knowledge of those people can only improve the inferences we as archaeologists make. More than just a question of improving our understanding of the past, native participation is about acknowledging the fact that native rights and wishes have been ignored by previous generations of archaeologists. We simply cannot conduct our research in that way anymore. As the impacts of NAGPRA have taken their course and my awareness has been raised, it is now clear to me that any new research at Etowah must include native participation as a routine part of the process.

Appendix: Radiocarbon Dating
the Occupations at Etowah

Table 7 presents the phase sequence for the Etowah site. The sequence itself is based on fairly detailed analyses of pottery samples recovered from stratigraphic excavations at the site (see Hally and Langford 1988; King 1996, 2001). Its placement in time, however, is based on a relatively small number of radiocarbon dates from sites across northern Georgia (Hally and Langford 1988). Only a subset of those dates were run on samples from Etowah site contexts. In fact, the only dates obtained on Etowah samples were those run by Larson using materials recovered during his Mound C excavations (Crane and Griffin 1959, 1962). Because these dates were run so early in the history of the radiocarbon dating method, they have very wide standard deviations and are difficult to interpret. As a result, there is a general lack of radiocarbon dates from the Etowah site that can be used to confirm directly the dating of its occupations inferred from regional data.

Recently (see King 2001), new dates have been obtained for Etowah site contexts. In the following sections, I use these newly run dates, along with the older ones, to evaluate prevailing ideas about the dating of Etowah's occupations. All dates have been corrected and calibrated using the software package CALIB 4.3 (Stuiver and Reimer 1993). So far, my attempts to date Etowah site contexts have focused on the Etowah and Savannah period components at the site. The Lamar period Brewster phase occupation has been placed in time fairly well using information gleaned from ethnohistoric accounts and the known manufacture dates of Spanish materials found in Brewster phase contexts (Hally and Langford 1988; Hally et al. 1990; Smith 1976).

ETOWAH PERIOD CONTEXTS

The most intensive investigation of Etowah period deposits occurred with the excavations conducted by Kelly west of Mound B (King 2001) and to a lesser extent with the work conducted by Sears (1958b) between Mounds

Table 7. Etowah site phase sequence

Date (A.D.)	Period	Regional Period Designation	Phase
1475–1550	Late Mississippian	Lamar	Brewster
1375–1475	Late Mississippian	Lamar	Unoccupied
1325–1375	Middle Mississippian	Savannah	Late Wilbanks
1250–1325	Middle Mississippian	Savannah	Early Wilbanks
1200–1250	Middle Mississippian	Savannah	Unoccupied
1100–1200	Early Mississippian	Etowah	Late Etowah
1000–1100	Early Mississippian	Etowah	Early Etowah

B and C and Larson (1971a) beneath Mound C. In my analysis of pottery collections from these contexts (King 1996:81, 2001:41–46), I confirmed that the earliest deposits in these areas are the large midden-filled pits (Kelly's saucers) recorded adjacent to Mound B and beneath Mound C. Diagnostic pottery indicates that these features date to the Early Etowah phase. Across much of the area between Mounds B and C a well-defined midden was deposited over the saucers, which belongs to the Late Etowah phase on the basis of diagnostic pottery collections.

Table 8 presents the results of radiocarbon dating performed on soot removed from sherds recovered in Kelly's Saucers 1 through 4 as well as the Late Etowah midden above them. Although pottery assemblages from the saucers belong to the Early Etowah phase, I found evidence of localized mixing of Late Etowah deposits with the earlier saucer fills (King 2001:46). As a result, in choosing my samples to date, I attempted to pick sherds from excavation lots near the bottom and top of each saucer. Unfortunately, this was not always possible.

As might be expected when dealing with large and complicated features like the saucers, the dates returned are anything but neat and tidy. In general, the dates from Saucer 1 fit well with the expected dating of Early Etowah phase pottery. The date from Saucer 2, however, is much later and actually falls at the outer end of the expected Late Etowah phase date range. Since the pottery assemblage from this feature was like that recovered from Saucer 1, I suspect that this is the result of mixing or problems understanding Kelly's excavation and provenience system.

As I have discussed elsewhere (King 2001:13), the records remaining from Kelly's 1950s excavations at Mound B are incomplete and often difficult to interpret clearly. The provenience information on the Saucer 2

Table 8. Radiocarbon dates from Etowah period contexts

Lab Number	Provenience	Material	C-14 yrs B.P.	STD	Correction	Intercept (Cal) A.D.	1 STD	2 STD
Beta-144161	Saucer 1	Soot	980	40	−24.3	1023	1002–1148	983–1158
Beta-145489	Saucer 1	Soot	980	40	−23.7	1021	999–1034	980–1157
Beta-144162	Saucer 2	Soot	830	40	−25	1218	1165–1260	1069–1280
Beta-144164	Saucer 3	Soot	820	40	−25.6	1223, 1231, 1238	1195–1275	1161–1283
Beta-145491	Saucer 3	Soot	860	40	−22.8	1161	1041–1211	1025–1239
Beta-144163	Saucer 4	Soot	830	40	−24.1	1214	1162–1253	1044–1277
Beta-145490	Saucer 4	Soot	1050	40	−23.2	982	899–1015	889–1022
Beta-144811	300R200★	Soot	820	50	−25	1221	1165–1275	1058–1285

★Excavation Lot 358, recovered by Sears (1958a).

lot that I dated consisted of a label on a bag reading "Level 3 and below." Without knowing the thickness of the levels in this case, it is difficult to tell how deep in the feature these sherds were found. Also, given that Kelly's crew clearly had some difficulty in distinguishing the Late Etowah midden from the saucer fills stratigraphically, it is possible that this sample actually derives from a Late Etowah context or at least one containing both Early and Late Etowah diagnostics. The sherd from which the sample was drawn was of the type Etowah Complicated Stamped and had a ladder-base diamond motif stamped on it. Unfortunately, this sherd could have been found in either an Early or Late Etowah phase assemblage.

The dates from Saucer 3 are just as messy. One of the samples (Beta-145491) was recovered at the floor of the feature and it produced a date that falls somewhere in the range of the end of the Early Etowah phase and the beginning of the Late Etowah phase. The second date (Beta-144164) falls beyond the range proposed for the Late Etowah and comes closer to what might be expected from an early Savannah period context. The assemblage from this lot contained what looked to be Early Etowah pottery, but the sherd containing soot was Etowah Complicated Stamped without a recognizable motif. The provenience was labeled as "Saucer 3, 4th 12 inch level." Again, it is difficult to tell where in the stratigraphic column the excavators began assigning collections to Saucer 3, so it is possible that the sherd could have come from a Late Etowah context.

Unfortunately, the dates from Saucer 4 are even more perplexing. One of the samples (Beta-144163), which according to provenience information was recovered near the floor of the feature, returned a date near the outer end of the Late Etowah date range. The sample (Beta-145490) that provenience information identifies as coming from near the top of the feature produced a very early Early Etowah phase date. I can only guess that either localized mixing of the feature fill or confusion about proveniences accounts for these results.

The final date in Table 8 derives from a sample removed from a sherd recovered from a Late Etowah context east of Mound A. This was recovered by Sears (1958a) during his testing project that preceded Kelly's excavations at Mound B. Although the date is somewhat later than expected given the presumed date range for the Late Etowah phase, it still conforms to the general conception of the Etowah period sequence.

If we ignore provenience for a moment, there is a pattern in these dates. Radiocarbon dates are essentially means derived from samples taken from a larger population. As a result, they can be manipulated using simple statistics to identify statistically significant groupings. Using the chi square test (95% confidence level) included in the CALIB 4.3 radiocarbon date

—

Table 9. Statistically significant date groupings

Lab Number	Provenience	−1 STD	Intercept (Cal) A.D.	+1 STD
Beta-145490	Saucer 4	899	982	1015
Beta-145489	Saucer 1	999	1021	1034
Beta-144161	Saucer 1	1002	1023	1148
	Average	997	1017	1022
Beta-145491	Saucer 3	1141	1161	1211
Beta-144163	Saucer 4	1165	1218	1253
Beta-144162	Saucer 2	1162	1214	1260
Beta-144164	Saucer 2	1195	1231	1275
Beta-144811	Late Etowah Midden	1165	1221	1275
	Average	1189	1215	1221

calibration software package, the dates in Table 8 can be divided into two statistically different sets that represent estimates of two different population means. Since the two sets are statistically significantly different, the dates within each can be averaged.

Table 9 presents those two groups of dates, along with their averages, arranged in chronological order. In general, these two groups of dates, and their averages, fit well with the expected dating of Early and Late Etowah contexts, except that the later grouping of dates has an average somewhat later than anticipated. Overall, despite the apparent problems created by mixing of deposits and working with collections that are half a century old, the dates from the saucers and overlying midden support reasonably well the existing chronological placement of the Early Etowah phase between A.D. 1000 and 1100 and the Late Etowah phase between A.D. 1100 and 1200.

SAVANNAH PERIOD CONTEXTS

Table 10 presents the calibrated results of four radiocarbon dates recently obtained on material associated with Early and Late Wilbanks phase pottery collections. The first date in the series was obtained on soot removed from the surface of an Early Wilbanks sherd. It was recovered from a midden associated with a rectangular building (Structure 1) excavated by Kelly west of Mound B (King 2001:26–28).

Table 10. Radiocarbon dates from Wilbanks contexts

Lab Code	Provenience	Material	C-14 yrs B.P.	STD	Correction	Intercept (Cal) A.D.	1 STD	2 STD
Beta-145488	Structure 1	Soot	1540	50	−24.4	536	430–597	410–637
Beta-67942	F 64A	Charred Corn	480	70	−9.3	1282	1244–1299	1164–1395
Beta-67943	F 64A	Wood Charcoal	680	70	−252.5★	1296	1276–1393	1214–1418
Beta-67944	F 64B	Charred Corn	340	50	−11.6	1403	1322–1422	1298–1439
Average	F 64A&B					1304, 1367, 1384	1297–1395	1286–1405

★Estimated correction factor from Stuiver and Polach 1977.

The remaining three dates were obtained from samples recovered from two features (Features 64A and 64B) excavated by Kelly on a small platform, called the Orange Layer, adjacent to Mound B. These features contained very dense concentrations of charred botanicals, especially corncobs (see Bonhage-Freund 1994 for a complete species list). My analysis of pottery from Kelly's excavations indicates that his Orange Layer was positioned in the middle of the Wilbanks deposits next to Mound B. Beneath the Orange Layer only Early Wilbanks phase pottery was recovered, while the middens found on and above it contained only Late Wilbanks phase pottery. Logically, Features 64A and 64B were probably made sometime during the Late Wilbanks phase, and possibly near the beginning of the phase.

The date obtained from the Early Wilbanks sherd is clearly much too early and may have been contaminated with older carbon either while still in the archaeological record or while part of the curated collection. The three dates from the Late Wilbanks context return results that span the late thirteenth through early fifteenth century. According to the chi square test included in the CALIB 4.3 package, the dates from Features 64A and 64B can be treated, with a 95% confidence level, as samples taken from the same population. Therefore, they can be averaged to create a more accurate estimate of the true date, which falls within the middle of the fourteenth century.

As discussed elsewhere (King 1997, 2001:74), I use these dates to place the Late Wilbanks phase between approximately A.D. 1325 and A.D. 1375. Keeping in mind the absence of any evidence for an early Savannah period occupation at Etowah or in the Etowah valley (Hally and Langford 1988; King 1996, 2001; Southerlin 1993), I suggest that the Early Wilbanks phase dates between approximately A.D. 1250 and 1325.

THE MOUND C RADIOCARBON SERIES

With these more recently obtained dates in mind, I would like to turn to a consideration of the dates obtained by Larson from his Mound C excavations (Table 11). These dates are important because they serve not only to place the Wilbanks phases and Mound C in time, but also to date the creation and use of the SECC goods buried in Mound C. Originally, Larson (1971a) suggested that Mound C was constructed during the Late Etowah and Wilbanks phases. On the basis of my analysis of pottery vessels from Mound C burials and pottery sherds from the Mound C stratigraphic excavations, I have suggested that the entire mound was built during the Early and Late Wilbanks phases (King 1996:99–105)—a result that is cor-

Table 11. *Mound C radiocarbon series*

Lab Code	Provenience	Material yrs	C-14 yrs B.P.	STD	Correction[a]	Intercept (Cal) A.D.	1 STD	2 STD
M-402	Burial 38	Wood	725	200	−20±2	1225, 1226, 1243	1020–1392	781–1469
M-542	Burial 57	Wood	910	200	−20±2	1023	783–1260	654–1397
M-543[b]	Burial 57	Shell Beads	500	250	0±2	1438	1261–1662	1005–1950
M-1060	Mantle 2	Charred Vegetal	225	150	−10±2	1437	1315–1634	1265–1947
M-1061	Burial 155	Charcoal	670	200	−25±2.5	1297	1164–1437	982–1648
M-1062	Burial 164	Charred Wood	450	200	−25±2.5	1441	1300–1654	1192–1953
M-1064	Feature 19	Charcoal	850	150	−25±2.5	1212	1020–1292	889–1410
Average[c]	Mound C	Mixed				1324, 1350, 1389	1293–1416	1266–1444

[a]Correction factors estimated using Stuiver and Polach 1977.
[b]Reservoir correction factor −520 from Stuiver and Braziunas 1993.
[c]Average of corrected dates, calibrated using mixed marine and atmospheric data set, assuming 16.7% marine carbon with a reservoir correction factor −5±20 from Stuiver and Braziunas 1993.

roborated by Brain and Phillips's (1996) examination of Mound C mortuary vessels.

With that phase assignment seemingly fairly well in place, the debate has turned to the dating of the Wilbanks phases. Using arguments based on artifact styles, Brain and Phillips (1996) and Larson (1993) have suggested that the Wilbanks phases date to the fifteenth century or even later. The Mound B radiocarbon dates presented above, along with a great deal of cross dating from other sites in the Southeast, argue for a Middle Mississippian date for those phases, Mound C, and the SECC.

At first glance, it appears that the Mound C radiocarbon series (Table 11) has little to offer in the way of information about the dating of Mound C. Because the dates were obtained early in the history of the radiocarbon dating method, their standard deviations effectively span the entire Mississippian period. However, by paying some attention to context and correcting, calibrating, and averaging those dates it is possible to narrow that range down to a more interpretable level.

Beginning with a consideration of context, one of the seven dates (M-1064) can be excluded for my purposes here because it was not run on a sample from Mound C. Feature 19 was a large midden-filled pit not unlike Kelly's saucers, which was recorded by Larson beneath Mound C. Pottery collections from the feature show that it dates to the Early Etowah phase (King 1996:280). Although I cannot explain the later than expected result, it is clear that this feature predates the building of Mound C and can be excluded from any further efforts to date the mound.

On the basis of my reconstruction of the history of Mound C (King 1996), the rest of the dates in the Mound C series were run on samples from Late Wilbanks phase contexts. When the relative stratigraphic position of the features dated is compared with the dates returned, it becomes apparent that there is little internal integrity to those dates. For example, Burial 57 is the earliest of the contexts and it returned some of the earliest and latest dates. Similarly, Burials 38, 155, and 164 are all roughly contemporary, but the dates from two of the three are over a hundred years earlier than the remaining one.

Given these problems, it may be best to consider these dates as a series drawn from the same general context and ignore the details of their relative placement in Mound C. When this series is tested for statistically significant differences among the dates (chi square test, 95% confidence level), none are found. This indicates that all of the dates can be treated as probabilistic estimates of the same population parameter, and therefore can be averaged to produce a more precise estimate of that parameter. When calibrated, that average returns a result that falls in the middle of the thirteenth century and overlaps nicely with the date range of the Wilbanks phases determined by the more recent Mound B dates.

Although the total number of dates is comparatively small, the consistency between the Mound B and Mound C series clearly presents a strong argument for placing the Wilbanks phase and the construction of Mound C in the period from A.D. 1250 to 1375. As noted above, this is consistent with the current dating of the Middle Mississippian period and the SECC across the rest of the Southeast.

References Cited

Anderson, D. G.

1990 Stability and Change in Chiefdom-Level Societies: An Examination of Mississippian Political Evolution in the South Atlantic Slope. In *Lamar Archaeology: Mississippian Chiefdoms in the Deep South,* edited by M. Williams and G. Shapiro, pp. 187–213. University of Alabama Press, Tuscaloosa.

1994 *The Savannah River Chiefdoms: Political Change in the Late Prehistoric Southeast.* University of Alabama Press, Tuscaloosa.

1996 Indian Pottery of the Carolinas. Council of South Carolina Professional Archaeologists. Manuscript on file, South Carolina Department of Archives and History, Columbia.

Baden, W.

1987 A Dynamic Model of Stability and Change in Mississippian Agricultural Systems. Unpublished Ph.D. dissertation, Department of Anthropology, University of Tennessee, Knoxville.

Biedma, L. H.

1993 Relation of the Island of Florida by Luys Hernandez de Biedma. Now Newly Set Forth by the Gentleman of Elvas. In *The De Soto Chronicles: The Expedition of Hernando de Soto to North America in 1539–43,* vol. 1, edited by L. A. Clayton, V. J. Knight, and E. C. Moore, pp. 221–246. University of Alabama Press, Tuscaloosa.

Blakely, R. L.

1995 Social Organization at Etowah: A Reconsideration of Paleodemographic and Paleonutritional Evidence. *Southeastern Archaeology* 14(1): 46–59.

Blanton, R. E., G. M. Feinman, S. A. Kowalewski, and P. N. Peregrine

1996 A Dual-Processual Theory for the Evolution of Mesoamerican Civilization. *Current Anthropology* 37(1): 1–14.

Blitz, J. H.

1993 *Ancient Chiefdoms of the Tombigbee.* University of Alabama Press, Tuscaloosa.

1999   Mississippian Chiefdoms and the Fission-Fusion Process. *American Antiquity* 64(4): 577–592.

Bobrowski, P. T., and B. F. Ball

1989   The Theory and Mechanics of Ecological Diversity in Archaeology. In *Quantifying Diversity in Archaeology,* edited by R. Leonard and G. Jones, pp. 4–12. Cambridge University Press, Cambridge.

Bonhage-Freund, M. T.

1994   The Etowah Site: A Paleoethnobotanical Analysis of Wilbanks Phase Corn-Cob Features. Paper presented at the 59th annual meeting of the Society for American Archaeology, Anaheim.

Brain, J. P., and P. Phillips

1996   *Shell Gorgets: Styles of the Late Prehistoric and Protohistoric Southeast.* Peabody Museum Press, Cambridge, Massachusetts.

Brainerd, G. W.

1951   The Place of Chronological Ordering in Archaeological Analysis. *American Antiquity* 16:301–313.

Braun, D., and S. Plog

1982   Evolution of "Tribal" Social Networks: Theory and Prehistoric North American Evidence. *American Antiquity* 47:504–524.

Brown, J. A.

1976   The Southern Cult Reconsidered. *Midcontinental Journal of Archaeology* 1(2): 115–135.

1983   Spiro Exchange Connections Revealed by Sources of Imported Raw Materials. In *Southeastern Natives and Their Pasts: A Collection of Papers Honoring Dr. Robert E. Bell,* edited by D. G. Wyckoff and J. L. Holman, pp. 129–162. Studies in Oklahoma's Past No. 11. Oklahoma Archeological Survey, Norman.

1985   The Mississippian Period. In *Ancient Art of the American Woodland Indians,* edited by D. Brose, J. A. Brown, and D. W. Penny, pp. 92–145. Harry N. Abrams, New York.

1989   On Style Divisions of the Southeastern Ceremonial Complex: A Revisionist Perspective. In *The Southeastern Ceremonial Complex: Artifacts and Analysis,* edited by P. Galloway, pp. 183–204. University of Nebraska Press, Lincoln.

1996   *The Spiro Ceremonial Center: The Archaeology of Arkansas Valley Caddoan Culture in Eastern Oklahoma.* Memoirs of the Museum of Anthropology, University of Michigan, No. 29. University of Michigan, Ann Arbor.

Brown, J. A., R. A. Kerber, and H. D. Winters

1990   Trade and the Evolution of Exchange Relations at the Beginning of the Mississippian Period. In *The Mississippian Emergence,* edited by B. Smith, pp. 251–280. Smithsonian Institution Press, Washington, D.C.

Brumfiel, E. M., and T. K. Earle

1987   Specialisation, Exchange, and Complex Societies. In *Specialisation, Exchange, and Social Complexity,* edited by E. M. Brumfiel and T. K. Earle, pp. 1–9. Cambridge University Press, Cambridge.

Brumfiel, E. M., and J. W. Fox (editors)

1994   *Factional Competition and Political Development in the New World.* Cambridge University Press, Cambridge.

Cable, J. S., L. H. Raymer, and C. L. Abrams

1994   *Archaeological Excavations at the Lake Acworth Site (9CO45): A Palisaded Mississippian Village in the Upper Piedmont of Northwest Georgia.* New South Associates Technical Report 117. New South Associates, Stone Mountain, Georgia.

Caldwell, J. R.

1956   Progress Report on Excavation at Tugalo (9ST1-Georgia). Manuscript on file, Department of Anthropology, University of Georgia, Athens.

1957   Survey and Excavations in the Allatoona Reservoir, Northern Georgia. Manuscript on file, Department of Anthropology, University of Georgia, Athens.

Chamblee, J. F., T. Neuman, and B. Pavao

1998   Archaeological Salvage of the Plant Hammond Site. *Early Georgia* 26:1–116.

Chase-Dunn, C., and T. Hall

1991   Conceptualizing Core/Periphery Hierarchies for Comparative Study. In *Core/Periphery Relations in Pre-Capitalist Worlds,* edited by C. Chase-Dunn and T. Hall, pp. 5–44. Westview, Boulder.

1993   Comparing World-Systems: Concepts and Working Hypotheses. *Social Forces* 71:851–886.

Clark, W. Z., and A. C. Zisa

1976   *Physiographic Map of Georgia.* The Geologic and Water Resources Division of the Georgia Department of Natural Resources, Atlanta.

Cobb, C., and P. Garrow

1996   Woodstock Culture and the Question of Mississippian Emergence. *American Antiquity* 61:21–38.

Cole, P. E.

1975   A Synthesis and Interpretation of the Hamilton Mortuary Pattern in East Tennessee. Unpublished Master's thesis, Department of Anthropology, University of Tennessee, Knoxville.

Cooper, P. L., J. D. Jennings, and C. H. Nash

1995   The Davis Site. In *The Prehistory of the Chickamauga Basin in Tennessee,*

Volume II, edited by L. P. Sullivan, pp. 419–440. University of Tennessee Press, Knoxville.

Crane, H. R., and J. B. Griffin

1959   University of Michigan Radiocarbon Dates, IV. *Radiocarbon* 1:173–198.

1962   University of Michigan Radiocarbon Dates, VIII. *Radiocarbon* 3:105–125.

Creamer, W., and J. Haas

1985   Tribe versus Chiefdom in Lower Central America. *American Antiquity* 50:738–754.

D'Altroy, T. N., and T. K. Earle

1985   Staple Finance, Wealth Finance, and Storage in Inka Political Economy. *Current Anthropology* 26:187–206.

Demarest, A. A., and A. E. Foias

1993   Mesoamerican Horizons and the Cultural Transformations of Maya Civilizations. In *Latin American Horizons,* edited by D. Rice, pp. 147–192. Dumbarton Oaks, Washington, D.C.

DePratter, C. B.

1991   *Late Prehistoric and Early Historic Chiefdoms in the Southeastern United States.* Garland Publishing, New York.

DePratter, C. B., C. M. Hudson, and M. T. Smith

1985   The Hernando de Soto Expedition: From Chiaha to Mabila. In *Alabama and The Borderlands: From Prehistory to Statehood,* edited by R. Badger and L. Clayton, pp. 108–211. University of Alabama Press, Tuscaloosa.

Dye, D. H.

1990   Warfare in the Sixteenth-Century Southeast: The De Soto Expedition in the Interior. In *Columbian Consequences,* vol. 2, edited by D. H. Thomas, pp. 211–222. Smithsonian Institution Press, Washington, D.C.

1995   Feasting with the Enemy: Mississippian Warfare and Prestige-Goods Circulation. In *Native American Interactions: Multiscalar Analyses and Interpretations in the Eastern Woodlands,* edited by M. Nassaney and K. Sassaman, pp. 289–316. University of Tennessee Press, Knoxville.

Earle, T. K.

1973   *Control Hierarchies in the Traditional Economy Halelea District, Kaua'i, Hawaii.* Ph.D. dissertation, Department of Anthropology, University of Michigan, Ann Arbor.

1978   *Economic and Social Organization of a Complex Chiefdom: The Halelea District, Kaua'i, Hawaii.* Anthropological Papers 63, Museum of Anthropology, University of Michigan. Ann Arbor.

1987   Chiefdoms in Archaeological and Ethnohistorical Perspective. *Annual Review of Anthropology* 16:279–308.

1990   Style and Iconography as Legitimation in Complex Chiefdoms. In

The Uses of Style in Archaeology, edited by M. Conkey and C. Hastorf, pp. 73–81. Cambridge University Press, Cambridge.

1991   The Evolution of Chiefdoms. In *Chiefdoms: Power, Economy, and Ideology,* edited by T. K. Earle, pp. 1–15. Cambridge University Press, Cambridge.

Elliott, D. T., and J. T. Wynn

1991   The Vining Revival: A Late Simple Stamped Phase in the Central Georgia Piedmont. *Early Georgia* 19:1–18.

Elvas, Fidalgo de

1993   True Relations of the Hardships Suffered by Governor Hernando de Soto & Certain Portuguese Gentlemen during the Discovery of the Province of Florida. Now Newly Set Forth by the Gentleman of Elvas. In *The De Soto Chronicles: The Expedition of Hernando de Soto to North America in 1539–43,* vol. 1, edited by L. A. Clayton, V. J. Knight, and E. C. Moore, pp. 19–219. University of Alabama Press, Tuscaloosa.

Fairbanks, C. H.

1946   The Macon Earthlodge. *American Antiquity* 12(2): 94–108.

1950   A Preliminary Segregation of Etowah, Savannah, and Lamar. *American Antiquity* 16(2): 142–151.

Fairbanks, C. H., and S. Neitzel

1995   The Rymer Site. In *The Prehistory of the Chickamauga Basin in Tennessee, Volume II,* edited by L. P. Sullivan, pp. 467–497. University of Tennessee Press, Knoxville.

Feinman, G. M., and J. Neitzel

1984   Too Many Types: An Overview of Sedentary Prestate Societies in the Americas. In *Advances in Archaeological Method and Theory,* vol. 7, edited by M. B. Schiffer. Academic Press, New York.

Garrow, P. M., and M. T. Smith

1973   *The King Site (9FL-5) Excavations April, 1971 through August 1973: Collected Papers.* Dennis Hodge's Office Supply Company, Rome.

Goad, S. I.

1979   *Chert Resources in Georgia, Archaeological and Geological Perspectives.* Report No. 21, University of Georgia, Laboratory of Archaeology Series. Athens.

1980   Chemical Analysis of Native Copper Artifacts from the Southeastern United States. *Current Anthropology* 21:270–271.

Goldman, I.

1970   *Ancient Polynesian Society.* University of Chicago Press, Chicago.

Gramsci, A.

1971   *Selections from Prison Notebooks of Antonio Gramsci.* Translated by Q. Hoare and G. N. Smith. International Publishers, New York.

Griffin, J. B.

1985   Changing Concepts of the Prehistoric Mississippian Cultures of the Eastern United States. In *Alabama and the Borderlands: From Prehistory to Statehood,* edited by R. Badger and L. A. Clayton, pp. 40–63. University of Alabama Press, Tuscaloosa.

Hall, T., and C. Chase-Dunn

1996   Comparing World-Systems: Concepts and Hypotheses. In *Pre-Columbian World Systems,* edited by P. N. Peregrine and G. M. Feinman, pp. 11–26. Monographs in World Archaeology No. 26. Prehistory Press, Madison.

Hally, D. J.

1979   *Archaeological Investigations at the Little Egypt Site (9MU102), Murray County, Georgia, 1969 Season.* Report No. 18, University of Georgia, Laboratory of Archaeology Series. Athens.

1983   The Interpretive Potential of Pottery from Domestic Contexts. *Midcontinental Journal of Archaeology* 8(2): 163–196.

1989   The Cultural and Ecological Context of the Etowah Site. Paper presented at the annual meeting of the Southeastern Archaeological Conference, Tampa, Florida.

1993   The Territorial Size of Mississippian Chiefdoms. In *Archaeology of Eastern North America, Papers in Honor of Stephen Williams,* edited by J. B. Stoltman, pp. 143–168. Archaeological Report No. 25. Mississippi Department of Archives and History, Jackson.

1994   An Overview of Lamar Culture. In *Ocmulgee Archaeology, 1936–1986,* edited by D. J. Hally, pp. 144–174. University of Georgia Press, Athens.

1996   Platform Mound Construction and the Instability of Mississippian Chiefdoms. In *Political Structure and Change in the Prehistoric Southeastern United States,* edited by J. F. Scarry, pp. 92–127. University Press of Florida, Gainesville.

Hally, D. J., P. M. Garrow, and W. Trotti

1975   A Preliminary Analysis of the King Site Settlement Plan. *Southeastern Archaeological Conference Bulletin* 18:55–62.

Hally, D. J., and H. Kelly

1998   The Nature of Mississippian Towns in Georgia. In *Mississippian Towns and Sacred Spaces: Searching for an Architectural Grammar,* edited by R. B. Lewis and C. Stout, pp. 49–63. University of Alabama Press, Tuscaloosa.

Hally, D. J., and J. B. Langford, Jr.

1988   *Mississippi Period Archaeology of the Georgia Valley and Ridge Province.* Report No. 25, University of Georgia, Laboratory of Archaeology Series. Athens.

Hally, D. J., and J. Rudolph
  1986   *Mississippian Period Archaeology of the Georgia Piedmont.* Report No. 24, University of Georgia, Laboratory of Archaeology Series. Athens.
Hally, D. J., and M. T. Smith
  1992   Chiefly Behavior: Evidence from Sixteenth Century Spanish Accounts. In *Lords of the Southeast: Social Inequality and the Native Elites of Southeastern North America,* edited by A. Barker and T. Pauketat, pp. 99–110. Archeological Papers of the American Anthropological Association, No. 3. Arlington, Virginia.
Hally, D. J., M. T. Smith, and J. B. Langford, Jr.
  1990   The Archaeological Reality of De Soto's Chiefdom of Coosa. In *Columbian Consequences,* edited by D. H. Thomas, pp. 121–138. Smithsonian Institution Press, Washington, D.C.
Hally, D. J., and M. Williams
  1994   Macon Plateau Site Community Pattern. In *Ocmulgee Archaeology, 1936–1986,* edited by D. J. Hally, pp. 84–95. University of Georgia Press, Athens.
Hammond, N.
  1979   Locational Models and the Site of Lubaatun, A Classic Maya Centre. In *Models in Archaeology,* edited by D. L. Clarke. Methuen, London.
Hatch, J. W.
  1974   Social Dimensions of Dallas Mortuary Patterns. Unpublished Master's thesis, Department of Anthropology, Pennsylvania State University, University Park.
  1976a Status in Death: Principles of Ranking in Dallas Culture Mortuary Remains. Unpublished Ph.D. dissertation, Department of Anthropology, Pennsylvania State University, University Park.
  1976b The Citico Site (40HA65): A Synthesis. *Tennessee Anthropologist* 1(2): 75–103.
Hayden, B.
  2001   Fabulous Feasts: A Prolegomenon to the Importance of Feasting. In *Feasts: Archaeological and Ethnographic Perspectives on Food, Politics, and Power,* edited by M. Dietler and B. Hayden, pp. 23–64. Smithsonian Institution Press, Washington, D.C.
Hegmon, M.
  1986   Information Exchange and Integration in Black Mesa, Arizona, AD 931–1150. In *Spatial Organization and Exchange: Archaeological Survey on Northern Black Mesa,* edited by S. Plog, pp. 256–281. Southern Illinois University Press, Carbondale.
Helms, M. W.
  1979   *Ancient Panama: Chiefs in Search of Power.* University of Texas Press, Austin.

1994   Chiefdom Rivalries, Control, and External Contacts in Lower Central America. In *Factional Competition and Political Development in the New World,* edited by E. M. Brumfiel and J. W. Fox, pp. 55–60. Cambridge University Press, Cambridge.

Hodder, I.

1977   The Distribution of Material Culture Items in the Baringo District, W. Kenya. *Man* 12:239–269.

1981   Society, Economy and Culture: An Ethnographic Case Study Amongst the Lozi. In *Pattern of the Past: Essays in Honor of David Clarke,* edited by I. Hodder, G. Isaac, and N. Hammond, pp. 67–96. Cambridge University Press, Cambridge.

Hudson, C. M.

1976   *The Southeastern Indians.* University of Tennessee Press, Knoxville.

1990   *The Juan Pardo Expeditions: Explorations of the Carolinas and Tennessee, 1566–1568.* Smithsonian Institution Press, Washington, D.C.

1997   *Knights of Spain, Warriors of the Sun: Hernando de Soto and the South's Ancient Chiefdoms.* University of Georgia Press, Athens.

Hudson, C. M., M. T. Smith, and C. B. DePratter

1989   The Hernando de Soto Expedition: From Mabila to the Mississippi River. In *Towns and Temples along the Mississippi,* edited by D. H. Dye and C. A. Cox, pp. 175–201. University of Alabama Press, Tuscaloosa.

Hudson, C. M., M. T. Smith, D. J. Hally, R. Polhemus, and C. B. DePratter

1985   Coosa: A Chiefdom in the Sixteenth Century United States. *American Antiquity* 50:723–737.

Humpf, D. A.

1995   Coosa: Biocultural Studies of a Sixteenth Century Southeastern Chiefdom. Unpublished Ph.D. dissertation, Department of Anthropology, Pennsylvania State University, University Park.

Johnson, A. W., and T. K. Earle

1987   *The Evolution of Human Societies, from Foraging Group to Agrarian State.* Stanford University Press, Stanford.

Johnson, G. A.

1982   Organizational Structure and Scalar Stress. In *Theory and Explanation in Archaeology,* edited by C. Renfrew, M. Rowlands, and B. Seagraves, pp. 389–421. Academic Press, New York.

1987   The Changing Organization of Uruk Administration on the Susiana Plain. In *The Archaeology of Western Iran,* edited by F. Hole, pp. 107–155. Smithsonian Institution Press, Washington, D.C.

Jones, C. C.

1873   *Antiquities of the Southern Indians, Particularly of the Georgia Tribes.* D. Appleton, New York.

Kelly, A. R.
  1938   *A Preliminary Report on the Archaeological Explorations at Macon, Georgia.* Bulletin 119. Bureau of American Ethnology, Washington, D.C.
  1972   The 1970–1972 Field Seasons at Bell Field Mound, Carter's Dam. Report submitted to the USDI, National Park Service, Atlanta, Georgia.
Kelly, A. R., and L. H. Larson
  1957   Explorations at the Etowah Indian Mounds near Cartersville, Georgia: Seasons 1954, 1955, 1956. *Archaeology* 10(1): 39–48.
Kelly, A. R., and R. S. Neitzel
  1961   *The Chauga Site in Oconee County, South Carolina.* Report No. 3, University of Georgia, Laboratory of Archaeology Series. Athens.
Kelly, A. R., F. T. Schnell, D. F. Smith, and A. L. Schlosser
  1965   Explorations in the Sixtoe Field, Carter's Dam, Murray County, Georgia: Seasons 1962, 1963, 1964. Report submitted to the USDI, National Park Service, Atlanta, Georgia.
Kelly, J. E.
  1991   The Evidence for Prehistoric Exchange and Its Implications for the Development of Cahokia. In *New Perspectives on Cahokia: Views from the Periphery,* edited by J. B. Stoltman, pp. 65–92. Monographs in New World Prehistory, No. 2. Prehistory Press, Madison, Wisconsin.
Kelly, P.
  1988   The Architecture of the King Site. Unpublished Master's thesis, Department of Anthropology, University of Georgia, Athens.
King, A.
  1995   Steps to the Past: 1994 Archaeological Excavations at Mounds A and B, the Etowah Site (9BR1), Bartow County, Georgia. Georgia Department of Natural Resources, Atlanta.
  1996   Tracing Organizational Change in Mississippian Chiefdoms of the Etowah River Valley, Georgia. Unpublished Ph.D. dissertation, Department of Anthropology, Pennsylvania State University, University Park.
  1997   A New Perspective on the Mississippian Ceramic Sequence of the Etowah River Valley. *Early Georgia* 24(2): 36–61.
  1999   De Soto's Itaba and the Nature of Sixteenth Century Paramount Chiefdoms. *Southeastern Archaeology* 18(2): 110–123.
  2001   *Excavations at Mound B, Etowah: 1954–1958.* Report No. 37, University of Georgia, Laboratory of Archaeology Series. Athens.
King, A., and J. A. Freer
  1995   The Mississippian Southeast: A World Systems Perspective. In *Native American Interactions: Multiscalar Analyses and Interpretations in the Eastern*

Woodlands, edited by M. Nassaney and K. Sassaman, pp. 266–288. University of Tennessee Press, Knoxville.

King, A., and R. J. Ledbetter
  1992 Upland Mississippian Occupation in the Allatoona Area. *Early Georgia* 20(2): 19–32.

Kirch, P. V.
  1984 *The Evolution of Polynesian Chiefdoms.* Cambridge University Press, Cambridge.

Knight, V. J.
  1981 Mississippian Ritual. Unpublished Ph.D. dissertation, Department of Anthropology, University of Florida, Gainesville.
  1986 The Institutional Organization of Mississippian Religion. *American Antiquity* 51(4): 675–687.
  1989 Symbolism of Mississippian Mounds. *In Powhatan's Mantle: Indians in the Colonial Southeast,* edited by P. H. Wood, G. A. Waselkov, and M. T. Hatley, pp. 279–291. University of Oklahoma Press, Lincoln.
  1990 Social Organization and the Evolution of Hierarchy in Southeastern Chiefdoms. *Journal of Anthropological Research* 46(1): 1–23.
  1994 The Formation of the Creeks. In *The Forgotten Centuries: Indians and Europeans in the American South, 1521–1704,* edited by C. M. Hudson and C. C. Tesser, pp. 373–392. University of Georgia Press, Athens.
  1997 Some Developmental Parallels Between Cahokia and Moundville. In *Cahokia: Domination and Ideology in the Mississippian World,* edited by T. Pauketat and T. E. Emerson, pp. 229–247. University of Nebraska Press, Lincoln.
  2001 Feasting and the Emergence of Platform Mound Ceremonialism in Eastern North America. In *Feasts: Archaeological and Ethnographic Perspectives on Food, Politics, and Power,* edited by M. Dietler and B. Hayden, pp. 311–333. Smithsonian Institution Press, Washington, D.C.

Knight, V. J., and V. P. Steponaitis
  1998 A New History of Moundville. In *Archaeology of the Moundville Chiefdom,* edited by V. J. Knight and V. P. Steponaitis, pp. 44–62. Smithsonian Institution Press, Washington, D.C.

Kopytoff, I.
  1986 *The African Frontier: The Reproduction of Traditional African Societies.* Indiana University Press, Bloomington.

Kowalewski, S. A.
  1996 Clout, Corn, Copper, Core-Periphery, Culture Area. In *Pre-Columbian World Systems,* edited by P. N. Peregrine and G. M. Feinman, pp. 27–38. Monographs in World Archaeology, No. 26. Prehistory Press, Madison, Wisconsin.

Kowalewski, S. A., G. M. Feinman, L. Finsten, R. E. Blanton, L. M. Nicholas

1989   *Monte Alban's Hinterland, Part II: Prehispanic Settlement Patterns in Tlaco-lula, Etla, and Ocotlan, the Valley of Oaxaca, Mexico.* Memoirs of the Museum of Anthropology, University of Michigan, No. 23. University of Michigan, Ann Arbor.

Kristiansen, K.

1987   Centre and Periphery in Bronze Age Scandinavia. In *Centre and Periphery in the Ancient World,* edited by M. Rolands, M. Larsen, and K. Kristiansen, pp. 74–85. Cambridge University Press, Cambridge.

LaForge, H. H., J. Smith, and M. Taylor

1925   *Physical Geography of Georgia.* Stein Printing Company, Atlanta.

Larson, L. H.

1971a   Archaeological Implications of Social Stratification at the Etowah Site, Georgia. In *Approaches to the Social Dimensions of Mortuary Practices,* edited by J. A. Brown, pp. 58–67. Society for American Archaeology, Memoir 25. Washington, D.C.

1971b   Settlement Distribution during the Mississippian Period. *Southeastern Archaeological Conference Bulletin* 13:19–25.

1972   Functional Considerations of Warfare in the Southeast during the Mississippi Period. *American Antiquity* 37:383–392.

1989   The Etowah Site. In *The Southeastern Ceremonial Complex: Artifacts and Analysis,* edited by P. Galloway, pp. 133–141. University of Nebraska Press, Lincoln.

1993   An Examination of the Significance of a Tortoise-Shell Pin from the Etowah Site. In *Archaeology of Eastern North America, Papers in Honor of Stephen Williams,* edited by J. B. Stoltman, pp. 169–185. Archaeological Report No. 25, Mississippi Department of Archives and History, Jackson.

1994   The Case for Earth Lodges in the Southeast. In *Ocmulgee Archaeology, 1936–1986,* edited by D. J. Hally, pp. 105–116. University of Georgia Press, Athens.

n.d.   Buildings. Manuscript on file, Antonio J. Waring Laboratory of Archaeology, Carrollton, Georgia.

Ledbetter, R. J.

1992   Archaeological Investigations of the Vulcan Tract, Bartow County, Georgia. Report prepared for Vulcan Materials Company, Inc., by Southeastern Archaeological Services, Inc., Athens.

Ledbetter, R. J., and C. A. Smith

1986   Lafingal Clearcut Survey. Manuscript on file, Department of Anthropology, University of Georgia, Athens.

Ledbetter, R. J., W. D. Wood, K. G. Wood, R. F. Ethridge, and C. O. Braley
  1987   *Cultural Resource Survey of Allatoona Lake Area, Georgia.* Final report prepared for the Mobile, Alabama, U.S. Army Engineer District, Contract DACW01–85-C-0183. Southeastern Archeological Services, Inc. Athens, Georgia.

Lewis, R. B., and C. Stout (editors)
  1998   *Mississippian Towns and Sacred Spaces: Searching for an Architectural Grammar.* University of Alabama Press, Tuscaloosa.

Lewis, T. M. N.
  1995   Architectural Industry. In *The Prehistory of the Chickamauga Basin in Tennessee, Volume II,* edited by L. P. Sullivan, pp. 54–78. University of Tennessee Press, Knoxville.

Lewis, T. M. N., and M. Kneberg
  1946   *Hiwassee Island.* University of Tennessee Press, Knoxville.

Little, K. J.
  1999   The Role of Late Woodland Interactions in the Emergence of Etowah. *Southeastern Archaeology* 18(1): 45–56.

McKivergan, D. A.
  1995   Balanced Reciprocity and Peer-Polity Interaction in the Late Prehistoric Southeastern United States. In *Native American Interactions: Multiscalar Analyses and Interpretations in the Eastern Woodlands,* edited by M. Nassaney and K. Sassaman, pp. 229–246. University of Tennessee Press, Knoxville.

Meyers, M., J. Wynn, R. Gougeon, B. Shirk
  1999   Vining Phase Excavations in the Chattahoochee-Oconee National Forest. *Early Georgia* 27:36–58.

Miller, C.
  n.d.   Contribution to the Archaeology of Georgia: Archaeological Explorations in the Allatoona Reservoir, Northwest Georgia. Manuscript on file, Department of Anthropology, University of Georgia, Athens.

Milner, G. R.
  1990   The Late Prehistoric Cahokia Cultural System of the Mississippi River Valley: Foundations, Florescence, and Fragmentation. *Journal of World Prehistory* 4:1–43.
  1991   American Bottom Mississippian Cultures: Internal Developments and External Relations. In *New Perspectives on Cahokia: Views from the Periphery,* edited by J. B. Stoltman, pp. 29–48. Monographs in New World Prehistory, No. 2. Prehistory Press, Madison, Wisconsin.
  1998   *The Cahokia Chiefdom: The Archaeology of a Mississippian Society.* Smithsonian Institution Press, Washington, D.C.

1999   Warfare in Prehistoric and Early Historic Eastern North America. *Journal of Archaeological Research* 7(2): 105–151.

Moorehead, W. K. (editor)

1932   *The Etowah Papers.* Phillips Academy, Andover, Massachusetts.

Morgan, J. R.

1980   An Archaeological Survey of an Area Proposed for the Development at Etowah Mounds, Bartow County, Georgia. Report prepared for the Department of Natural Resources, Atlanta, Georgia.

Morse, D., and P. Morse (editors)

1983   *Archaeology of the Central Mississippi Valley.* Academic Press, New York.

Muller, J.

1989   The Southern Cult. In *The Southeastern Ceremonial Complex: Artifacts and Analysis,* edited by P. Galloway, pp. 11–26. University of Nebraska Press, Lincoln.

1997   *Mississippian Political Economy.* Plenum Press, New York.

1998   Towns along the Lower Ohio. In *Mississippian Towns and Sacred Spaces: Searching for an Architectural Grammar,* edited by R. B. Lewis and C. Stout, pp. 179–199. University of Alabama Press, Tuscaloosa.

Nash, C. H., S. Neitzel, and J. D. Jennings

1995   The Dallas Site. In *The Prehistory of the Chickamauga Basin in Tennessee, Volume II,* edited by L. P. Sullivan, pp. 305–371. University of Tennessee Press, Knoxville.

Nassaney, M.

1992   Communal Societies and the Emergence of Elites in the Prehistoric American Southeast. In *Lords of the Southeast: Social Inequality and the Native Elites of Southeastern North America,* edited by A. Barker and T. Pauketat, pp. 111–143. Archeological Papers of the American Anthropological Association, No. 3. Arlington, Virginia.

Neitzel, S.

1995   The Sale Creek Site. In *The Prehistory of the Chickamauga Basin in Tennessee, Volume II,* edited by L. P. Sullivan, pp. 441–466. University of Tennessee Press, Knoxville.

Neitzel, S., and J. Jennings

1995   The Hixon Site. In *The Prehistory of the Chickamauga Basin in Tennessee, Volume II,* edited by L. P. Sullivan, pp. 372–418. University of Tennessee Press, Knoxville.

Oberg, C.

1955   Types of Social Structure in Lowland South America. *American Anthropologist* 57:472–487.

Pauketat, T. R.

1992   The Reign and Ruin of the Lords of Cahokia: A Dialectic of Dominance. In *Lords of the Southeast: Social Inequality and the Native Elites of Southeastern North America,* edited by A. Barker and T. Pauketat, pp. 31–52. Archeological Papers of the American Anthropological Association, No. 3. Arlington, Virginia.

1994   *The Ascent of Chiefs: Cahokia and Mississippian Politics in Native North America.* University of Alabama Press, Tuscaloosa.

1998   Refiguring the Archaeology of Greater Cahokia. *Journal of Archaeological Research* 6:45–89.

Pauketat, T. R., and T. E. Emerson

1991   The Ideology of Authority and the Power of the Pot. *American Anthropologist* 93:919–941.

Pauketat, T. R., and T. E. Emerson (editors)

1997   *Cahokia: Domination and Ideology in the Mississippian World.* University of Nebraska Press, Lincoln.

Payne, C., and J. F. Scarry

1998   Town Structure at the Edge of the Mississippian World. In *Mississippian Towns and Sacred Spaces: Searching for an Architectural Grammar,* edited by R. B. Lewis and C. Stout, pp. 22–48. University of Alabama Press, Tuscaloosa.

Peebles, C. S., and S. Kus

1977   Some Archaeological Correlates of Ranked Societies. *American Antiquity* 42:421–448.

Peet, R. K.

1974   The Measurement of Species Diversity. *Annual Review of Ecology and Systematics* 5:285–307.

Peregrine, P. N.

1992   *Mississippian Evolution: A World-System Perspective.* Monographs in World Prehistory, No. 9. Prehistory Press, Madison, Wisconsin.

1995   Networks of Power: The Mississippian World-System. In *Native American Interactions: Multiscalar Analyses and Interpretations in the Eastern Woodlands,* edited by M. Nassaney and K. Sassaman, pp. 247–265. University of Tennessee Press, Knoxville.

1996   Introduction: World-Systems Theory and Archaeology. In *Pre-Columbian World Systems,* edited by P. N. Peregrine and G. M. Feinman, pp. 1–10. Monographs in World Archaeology, No. 26. Prehistory Press, Madison, Wisconsin.

Phillips, P., and J. A. Brown

1978   *Pre-Columbian Shell Engravings from the Craig Mound at Spiro, Oklahoma,* paperback, part I. Peabody Museum Press, Cambridge, Massachusetts.

Plog, S.
1980   *Stylistic Variation of Prehistoric Ceramics.* Cambridge University Press, Cambridge.

Polhemus, R. B.
1987   *The Toqua Site: A Late Mississippian Dallas Phase Town.* Report of Investigations, No. 41. Prepared by the Tennessee Valley Authority. Department of Anthropology, University of Tennessee, Knoxville.

Powell, M. L.
1994   Human Skeletal Remains from Ocmulgee National Monument. In *Ocmulgee Archaeology, 1936–1986,* edited by D. J. Hally, pp. 116–129. University of Georgia Press, Athens.

Ranjel, R.
1993   Account of the Northern Conquest and Discovery of Hernando de Soto. In *The De Soto Chronicles: The Expedition of Hernando de Soto to North America in 1539–43,* vol. 1, edited by L. A. Clayton, V. J. Knight, and E. C. Moore, pp. 247–306. University of Alabama Press, Tuscaloosa.

Renfrew, C.
1973   Monuments, Mobilisation, and Social Organization in Neolithic Wessex. In *The Explanation of Culture Change: Models in Prehistory,* edited by C. Renfrew, pp. 539–558. University of Pittsburgh Press, Pittsburgh.
1974   Beyond a Subsistence Economy: The Evolution of Social Organisation in Prehistoric Europe. In *Reconstructing Complex Societies,* edited by C. B. Moore, pp. 69–95. Bulletin Supplement, No. 20. Cambridge.
1975   Trade as Action at a Distance: Questions of Integration and Communication. In *Ancient Civilization and Trade,* edited by J. Sabloff and C. Lambert-Karlowsky, pp. 3–59. University of New Mexico, Albuquerque.

Robinson, W. S.
1951   A Method for Chronologically Ordering Archaeological Deposits. *American Antiquity* 16:293–301.

Rountree, H.
1989   *The Powhatan Indians of Virginia.* University of Oklahoma Press, Norman.

Rudolph, J. L.
1984   Earthlodges and Platform Mounds: Changing Public Architecture in the Southeastern U.S. *Southeastern Archaeology* 3:33–35.
1985   Earthlodges in the Southeast. In *Archaeological Investigations at the Beaverdam Creek Site (9EB85), Elbert County, Georgia,* edited by J. L.

Rudolph and D. J. Hally, pp. 472–478. Russell Papers. National Park Service, Interagency Archaeological Services, Atlanta.

Rudolph, J. L., and D. J. Hally (editors)

1985   *Archaeological Investigations at the Beaverdam Creek Site (9EB85), Elbert County, Georgia.* Russell Papers. National Park Service, Interagency Archaeological Services, Atlanta.

Sahlins, M.

1958   *Social Stratification in Polynesia.* American Ethnological Society, Seattle.

Sanders, W. T., and B. J. Price

1968   *Mesoamerica, the Evolution of Civilization.* Random House, New York.

Scarry, J.

1990   The Rise, Transformation and Fall of Apalachee: A Case Study of Political Change in a Chiefly Society. In *Lamar Archaeology: Mississippian Chiefdoms in the Deep South,* edited by M. Williams and G. Shapiro, pp. 175–187. University of Alabama Press, Tuscaloosa.

Scarry, J. (editor)

1996   *Political Structure and Change in the Prehistoric Southeastern United States.* University Press of Florida, Gainesville.

Schneider, J.

1977   Was There a "Pre-Capitalist" World System? *Peasant Studies* 6:20–29.

Schortman, E. M., and P. A. Urban

1987   Modeling Interregional Interaction in Prehistory. In *Advances in Archaeological Method and Theory,* vol. 11, edited by M. B. Schiffer, pp. 37–95. Academic Press, New York.

Schroedl, G. F.

1994   A Comparison of the Origins of Macon Plateau and Hiwassee Island Cultures. In *Ocmulgee Archaeology, 1936–1986,* edited by D. J. Hally, pp. 138–143. University of Georgia Press, Athens.

1998   Mississippian Towns in the Eastern Tennessee Valley. In *Mississippian Towns and Sacred Spaces: Searching for an Architectural Grammar,* edited by R. B. Lewis and C. Stout, pp. 64–92. University of Alabama Press, Tuscaloosa.

Schroedl, G. F., and C. C. Boyd, Jr.

1991   Late Woodland Period Culture in East Tennessee. In *Stability, Transformation, and Variation: The Late Woodland Southeast,* edited by M. S. Nassaney and C. R. Cobb, pp. 69–90. Plenum Press, New York.

Sears, W. H.

1958a   The Wilbanks Site (9CK5), Georgia. *Smithsonian Institution Bureau of American Ethnology Bulletin* 169:129–194.

1958b   Excavations at Etowah. Manuscript on file, Department of Anthropology, University of Georgia, Athens.

Seckinger, E. W.

1977   Social Complexity during the Mississippian Period in Northwest Georgia. Unpublished Master's thesis, Department of Anthropology, University of Georgia, Athens.

Service, E. R.

1962   *Primitive Social Organization.* Random House, New York.

Smith, B. D.

1990   *The Mississippian Emergence.* Smithsonian Institution Press, Washington, D.C.

Smith, M. T.

1976   The Route of De Soto through Tennessee, Georgia, and Alabama: The Evidence from Material Culture. *Early Georgia* 4:27–48.

1987   *Archaeology of Aboriginal Culture Change in the Interior Southeast: Depopulation during the Early Historic Period.* University Presses of Florida, Gainesville.

1989   Aboriginal Population Movements in the Early Historic Period Interior Southeast. In *Powhatan's Mantle: Indians of the Colonial Southeast,* edited by P. H. Wood, G. A. Waselkov, and M. T. Hatley, pp. 135–149. University of Nebraska Press, Lincoln.

1994   *Archaeological Investigations at the Dyar Site, 9GE5.* Report No. 32, University of Georgia, Laboratory of Archaeology Series. Athens.

2000   *The Rise and Fall of a Southeastern Mississippian Chiefdom.* University Press of Florida, Gainesville.

Southerlin, B. G.

1993   Mississippian Settlement Patterns in the Etowah River Valley near Cartersville, Bartow County, Georgia. Unpublished Master's thesis, Department of Anthropology, University of Georgia, Athens.

Spencer, C. S.

1987   Rethinking the Chiefdom. In *Chiefdoms in the Americas,* edited by R. A. Drennan and C. A. Uribe, pp. 369–389. University Press of America, New York.

Steinen, K.

1992   Ambushes, Raids, and Palisades: Mississippian Warfare in the Interior Southeast. *Southeastern Archaeology* 11(2): 132–139.

Stephenson, D. K., A. King, and F. Snow

1996   Middle Mississippian Occupation in the Ocmulgee Big Bend Region. *Early Georgia* 24(2): 1–41.

Steponaitis, V. P.

1978   Locational Theory and Complex Chiefdoms: A Mississippian Example. In *Mississippian Settlement Patterns,* edited by B. Smith, pp. 417–453. Academic Press, New York.

1983   *Ceramics, Chronology, and Community Patterns: An Archaeological Study at Moundville.* Academic Press, New York.

1991   Contrasting Patterns of Mississippian Development. In *Chiefdoms: Power, Economy, and Ideology,* edited by T. Earle, pp. 193–228. Cambridge University Press, Cambridge.

Steward, J. H., and L. C. Faron

1959   *Native Peoples of South America.* McGraw-Hill, New York.

Stuiver, M., and T. F. Braziunas

1993   Modeling Atmospheric 14C Influences and 14C Ages of Marine Samples Back to 10,000 BC. *Radiocarbon* 35:137–189.

Stuiver, M., and H. A. Polach

1977   Discussion: Reporting of 14C Data. *Radiocarbon* 19:355–363.

Stuiver, M., and P. J. Reimer

1993   Extended 14C Database and Revised CALIB Radiocarbon Calibration Program. *Radiocarbon* 35:215–230.

Sullivan, L. P.

1986   The Late Mississippian Village: Community and Society of the Mouse Creek Phase in Southeastern Tennessee. Unpublished Ph.D. dissertation, Department of Anthropology, University of Wisconsin-Milwaukee.

2001   *Dates for Shell Gorgets and the Southeastern Ceremonial Complex in the Chickamauga Basin of Southeastern Tennessee.* McClung Museum Research Notes 19. Knoxville.

Swanton, J. R.

1922   *Early History of the Creek Indians and Their Neighbors.* Bulletin 73. Bureau of American Ethnology, Washington, D.C.

1946   *Indians of the Southeastern United States.* Bulletin 137. Bureau of American Ethnology, Washington, D.C.

Thomas, C.

1894   Report on the Mound Explorations of the Bureau of Ethnology. *Smithsonian Institution, Bureau of Ethnology, Twelfth Annual Report.* Washington, D.C.

Trubitt, M. B.

2000   Mound Building and Prestige Goods Exchange: Changing Strategies in the Cahokia Chiefdom. *American Antiquity* 65(4): 669–690.

USDA

1926   *Soil Survey Map of Bartow County, Georgia.* Bureau of Chemistry and Soils, Washington, D.C.

Varner, J. G., and A. J. Varner

1951   *The Florida of the Inca by Garcilaso de la Vega.* University of Texas Press, Austin.

Wallerstein, I.

1974   *The Modern World-System I.* Academic Press, New York.

Waring, A. J.
  1968   The Southern Cult and Muskhogean Ceremonial: General Consid-
         erations. In *The Waring Papers: The Collected Papers of Antonio J. Waring,
         Jr.,* edited by S. Williams, pp. 30–69. Papers of the Peabody Museum
         of American Archaeology and Ethnology, No. 58. Harvard University,
         Cambridge.
Waring, A. J., and P. Holder
  1945   Prehistoric Ceremonial Complex in the Southeastern United States.
         American Anthropologist 47:1–34.
Wauchope, R. W.
  1938   WPA Archaeological Survey of Georgia, Quarterly Report, for Work
         through December 31, 1938. On file at the Middle American Re-
         search Institute, Tulane University, New Orleans.
  1939a WPA Archaeological Survey of Georgia, Quarterly Report, for Work
         through March 31, 1939. On file at the Middle American Research
         Institute, Tulane University, New Orleans.
  1939b WPA Archaeological Survey of Georgia, Quarterly Report, for Work
         through June 30, 1939. On file at the Middle American Research In-
         stitute, Tulane University, New Orleans.
  1939c WPA Archaeological Survey of Georgia, Quarterly Report, for Work
         through September 30, 1939. On file at the Middle American Re-
         search Institute, Tulane University, New Orleans.
  1939d WPA Archaeological Survey of Georgia, Quarterly Report, for Work
         through December 31, 1939. On file at the Middle American Re-
         search Institute, Tulane University, New Orleans.
  1940a WPA Archaeological Survey of Georgia, Quarterly Report, for Work
         through March 31, 1940. On file at the Middle American Research
         Institute, Tulane University, New Orleans.
  1940b WPA Archaeological Survey of Georgia, Quarterly Report, for Work
         through June 31, 1940. On file at the Middle American Research In-
         stitute, Tulane University, New Orleans.
  1948   The Ceramic Sequence in the Etowah Drainage, Northwest Georgia.
         American Antiquity 47:1–34.
  1966   *Archaeological Survey of Northern Georgia with a Test of Some Cultural
         Hypotheses.* Society for American Archaeology, Memoir 21. Salt Lake
         City.
Welch, P. D.
  1991   *Moundville's Economy.* University of Alabama Press, Tuscaloosa.
  1996   Control over Goods and the Political Stability of the Moundville
         Chiefdom. In *Political Structure and Change in the Prehistoric Southeastern
         United States,* edited by J. F. Scarry, pp. 69–91. University Press of
         Florida, Gainesville.

Wharton, C. H.

1978   *The Natural Environments of Georgia.* Geologic and Water Resources Division and the Office of Planning and Research, Georgia Department of Natural Resources, Atlanta.

Wiessner, P.

1983   Style and Social Information in Kalahari San Projectile Points. *American Antiquity* 49(2): 253–276.

1984   Reconsidering the Behavioral Basis for Style: A Case Study among the Kalahari San. *Journal of Anthropological Archaeology* 3:190–234.

Williams, M.

1985   *Scull Shoals Revisited.* U.S. Forest Service Cultural Resources Report, No. 1. Gainesville, Georgia.

1994   The Origins of the Macon Plateau Site. In *Ocmulgee Archaeology, 1936–1986,* edited by D. J. Hally, pp. 130–137. University of Georgia Press, Athens.

Williams, M., and G. Shapiro

1996   Mississippian Period Political Dynamics in the Oconee Valley, Georgia. In *Political Structure and Change in the Prehistoric Southeastern United States,* edited by J. Scarry, pp. 128–149. University Press of Florida, Gainesville.

Williams, M., and G. Shapiro (editors)

1990   *Lamar Archaeology: Mississippian Chiefdoms in the Deep South.* University of Alabama Press, Tuscaloosa.

Willis, W. S.

1980   Fusion and Separation: Archaeology and Ethnohistory in Southeastern North America. In *Theory and Practice: Essays Presented to Gene Weltfish,* edited by S. Diamond, pp. 97–123. Mouton Publication, The Hague.

Wilson, D. J.

1988   *Prehistoric Settlement Patterns in the Lower Santa Valley, Peru.* Smithsonian Institution Press, Washington, D.C.

Wobst, M. H.

1977   Stylistic Behavior and Information Exchange. In *For the Director: Research Essays in Honor of James B. Griffin,* edited by C. Cleland, pp. 317–342. Anthropological Papers 61, Museum of Anthropology, University of Michigan. Ann Arbor.

Wright, H. T.

1977   Research on the Origin of the State. *Annual Review of Anthropology* 6:379–397.

1984   Prestate Political Formations. In *On the Evolution of Complex Societies: Essays in Honor of Harry Hoisjer, 1982,* edited by T. Earle, pp. 41–78. Undena Publications, Malibu, California.

Index

Agency theory, 21
Allatoona Reservoir, 29, 33–35, 43. *See also* Lake Allatoona
American Bottom, 19–21, 94
Anilco, 79
Apalachicola River, 123
Armor phase, 118
Ashley, Margaret, 33, 37

Barnett phase: definition, 32; in Etowah River valley, 92
Beaverdam Creek site, 63, 119–123
Bell Field site, 119–126
Bennett style, 122
Big Black River valley, 20
Black Mesa region, 105
Brainerd-Robinson Coefficient, 97, 102–103
Brewster phase: at Etowah, 81–83; definition, 32; in Etowah River valley, 92
Brown, James A., 1, 24, 45, 69, 70, 80, 90–93, 108, 121–124, 128, 132
Brown's Mount site, 108
Buffer zone, 17
Busk, 94. *See also* Green Corn Ceremony

Cahokia site, 16–17, 21, 96, 130
Caldwell, Joseph R., 29, 33, 85, 116
CALIB 4.3, 145, 148, 151
Ceramic assemblage: causes of change in, 93–94; changes expected with political change, 94–96; measuring diversity in,

96–97; measuring similarity in, 97. *See also* Brainerd-Robinson Coefficient
Chattahoochee River, 123–126
Chauga site, 116–118, 126
Cherokee (ethnic group), 110, 113, 137, 142
Chi square, 148, 151, 153
Chickamauga Basin, 57–58, 66, 112, 116–117
Chickamauga Reservoir, 57
Chiefdom: archaeological recognition of, 11–17, 84–85; complex, 6; group-oriented, 9; individualizing, 8; organizational variability, 4–10; paramount, 6–7; simple, 5
Citico site, 119, 123–126, 132–133
Citico style, 39
Communal, 9, 18, 54–55, 60, 86, 90, 113–115
Competition, 8, 20–21, 114, 123–125, 129–131, 141–142; factional, 19–21, 129; political and military, 134; power building through, 55, 115
Conyers Farm site, 33, 42–43, 90–91, 98
Coosa Country Club site, 39
Coosa paramount chiefdom, 21, 133, 136, 142
Coosa River, 26–38, 83
Coosawattee River, 108, 112–122, 132–134
Copper plate, 69–75, 91, 128, 132
Creek (ethnic group), 110, 137–138, 142–143, 164, 172
Creek Confederacy, 138

Dallas phase, 62, 82
Dallas site, 133
Davis site, 57, 112–116
De la Vega, Garcilaso, 80
De Soto, Hernando, 3, 79–82, 133–136, 142
DePratter, Chester B., 3, 11, 15, 21, 80–83, 93–94, 135
Diversity. *See* Ceramic assemblage
Dual Processual Theory, 3

Early Etowah period, 29; in northern Georgia, 108–115
Early Etowah phase: at Etowah, 52–60; definition, 30; in Etowah River valley, 86–88
Early Lamar period, 29; in Etowah River valley, 81; in northern Georgia, 131–134
Early Mississippian period, 29
Early Savannah period, 29; in Etowah River valley, 63; in northern Georgia, 119–126
Early Wilbanks phase: at Etowah, 63–73; definition, 30; in Etowah River valley, 89–91
Earth lodge, 43–46, 88, 110–112, 120–122. *See also* Earth-embanked building; Macon Earthlodge
Earth-embanked building, 40, 43, 88, 110, 115, 119, 120. *See also* Earth lodge; Macon Earthlodge
Etowah River Valley, 26–28
Etowah site: description, 50–51; ditch at, 1, 35, 50–51, 60–64, 71, 78–79, 91; excavation history, 33–35, 51; palisade at, 35, 59, 62–66, 71–80, 91. *See also* Mound C

Factionalism, 8–9, 21, 129–131
Feasting, 20–22, 55, 59–60, 87, 113–115
Fission-fusion process, 13
Flint River, 132
Free Bridge site, 33 41–42, 90–91, 98
French Broad River, 136
Funeral Mound, 111–112

Gorget, 39, 68–76, 91, 121–122, 126, 132–133, 136
Gramsci, Antonio, 21
Grand Village of the Natchez, 80
Greater Braden style, 132
Green Corn Ceremony, 54–55, 95. *See also* Busk
Guachoya, 79

Hamilton culture, 52–53
Hatch, James W., 11, 82–83, 123–124, 135
Hawaii, 7, 21
Hegemony, 21
Hickory Log site, 35
Hierarchy, 5–17, 113
Hightower style, 126, 132
Hiwassee Island phase, 52–57, 86–88, 108–117, 122
Hiwassee Island site, 57–59, 108–117
Hixon site, 57–59, 112–113
Hollywood site, 126
Horseshoe Bend site, 32–33, 47–49, 91–92, 98–101, 105
Hudson, Charles M., 3, 6, 15–17, 55, 79, 82, 93–95, 133, 137
Humpf, Dorothy A., 82–83, 135

Ideology, 4–10, 16, 19–22, 113–114, 128, 142
Internal African Frontier, 118, 140
International style, 8, 18, 112, 121–2, 123, 126, 135, 140
Itaba, 82, 136

Jarrett phase, 116–118

Kaminaljuyu, 96
Kelly, Arthur R., 29, 34, 38, 40, 45, 51–55, 64, 66, 68, 74, 80, 93, 96–97, 110, 113, 116, 122, 145–146, 148–151, 153
King site, 34, 82
Knight, Vernon James, 1, 4, 14, 24, 54–55, 80, 113–114, 128, 130, 132, 137

Lake Acworth site, 35

Lake Allatoona, 34, 90. *See also* Allatoona Reservoir

Lake Jackson site, 20, 123

Larson, Lewis H., 1–3, 11, 28–29, 34, 44–45, 51–55, 57, 58, 62, 66, 68, 70–71, 75–82, 89, 110, 128, 145–146, 151, 153

Late Etowah period, 29; in northern Georgia, 115–119

Late Etowah phase: at Etowah, 60–63; definition, 30; in Etowah River valley, 88–89

Late Lamar period, 29; in northern Georgia, 134–138

Late Mississippian period, 29

Late Savannah period, 29; in northern Georgia, 126–131

Late Wilbanks phase: at Etowah, 73–81; definition, 30–32; in Etowah River valley, 91–92

League of the Iroquois, 114

Leake site, 34

Little Egypt site, 132–133, 136, 142

Long Swamp site, 32–33, 45–47, 88–89, 98, 106, 115–117, 120

Macon Earthlodge, 110. *See also* Earth-embanked building; Earth lodge; Mound D-1 Lodge

Macon Plateau site, 2, 60, 108, 111, 113, 117, 121

Mayes phase: definition, 32

Midden-filled pit, 52–55, 113, 146, 153. *See also* saucer

Middle Mississippian period, 29

Migration, 111, 119

Mississippi River valley, 16

Moorehead, Warren K., 1–3, 33, 37, 42, 51, 59, 64, 66, 68, 81–82

Mound: as earth symbol, 54; as political capital, 10–11; construction of as rite of intensification, 54, 115; spacing, 11–12

Mound C (Etowah): 1, 3, 33, 44, 50, 53–62, 71–73, 81, 143, 146; burials at, 52,

68–80, 111, 125, 141; construction of, 34, 45, 66–68, 75–77, 90–91, 125; radio-carbon dates, 145, 151–154

Mound D-1 Lodge, 117. *See also* Macon Earthlodge

Moundville Engraved, *variety Hemphill,* 130

Moundville site, 20, 90, 130–131, 143

Mouse Creek phase, 136

Nacoochee site, 126

Napochies, 21

Nashville Basin, 123

Natchez (ethnic group), 80

New Archaeology, 119

Nixon site, 38–39, 85, 92, 106, 136

Ocmulgee River, 63, 132

Oconee River, 118, 126, 129. *See also* Oconee valley

Oconee valley, 63, 118–119, 132. *See also* Oconee River

Oostanaula River, 27, 37, 38, 39

Palisade, 35, 44, 59–66, 71–80, 91, 117, 120, 128, 133

Pauketat, Timothy R., 4, 19, 21, 94, 130

Peer-Polity Interaction, 20

Peregrine, Peter N., 20, 22–24

Plains, 23, 123

Plant Hammond site, 33, 34, 37–38, 91–92, 98–105

Plum Bayou culture, 21

Political change: causes of, 19–25

Political complexity, 6–7–10, 14–21, 84, 139

Political economic strategies, 7–10; ar-chaeological identification of, 17–19; corporate, 9–10; network, 8–9

Political economy, 3–5, 9, 13, 22, 60, 73, 82, 87–88, 112, 117, 120–121, 139

Powhatan paramountcy, 20

Prestige goods, 20, 22–24, 55, 70–71, 87–88, 104, 111, 115–117, 121, 130; ex-change, 20, 24, 122; system, 8, 20

Raccoon Creek site, 41, 90–91, 98
Radiocarbon dates, 113, 145, 148–153
Ramey Incised, 94–96, 130
Redistribution, 4–5
Richness. *See* Ceramic assemblage
Rogan, John P., 33, 42, 51, 64, 68–81
Rymer site, 136

Sale Creek site, 57
Sandy Hammock site, 63
Saucer, 47, 53, 62, 146–153. *See also* Midden-filled pit
Savannah River, 115–119, 126, 129. *See also* Savannah valley
Savannah valley, 19, 118–119, 125
Schroedl, Gerald F., 14–15, 52–53, 59, 86, 108, 113
Scull Shoals site, 63, 123
Sears, William H., 29, 33, 43–45, 59–63, 70, 78, 81, 88–90, 145, 148
SECC exchange corridor, 124, 141
Service, Elman R., 4, 7, 171
Shinholser site, 126
Similarity. *See* Ceramic assemblage
Sixtoe Field site, 108, 112–114, 119
Social ranking, 2–4, 21–24, 52, 60, 71–73, 83, 114, 137, 140, 141; achieved, 77, 86; ascribed, 10
Social solidarity, 9, 113–114, 129, 140
Southeastern Ceremonial Complex (SECC), 1, 24, 70–71, 91, 124–130, 135, 140–143, 151–154
Southern Cult, 1, 70. *See also* Southeastern Ceremonial Complex (SECC)

Spanish, 3, 15, 17, 21, 82, 134–135, 142–145. *See also* de Soto, Hernando
Spiro site, 45, 69, 90, 122
Stamp Creek phase: definition, 32
Stamp Creek site, 33
Staple finance, 9
Statues, 79, 80
Steiner, Dr. Roland, 39
Surplus, 5–10, 12, 19, 21–22, 134, 141

Tennessee River, 126. *See also* Tennessee valley
Tennessee valley, 116, 124–126, 133–134, 141
Teotihuacan, 96
Thomas, Cyrus, 1, 3, 33, 42, 51, 64, 68, 78
Timucua (ethnic group), 79
Tugalo site, 116–120
Two Run Creek site, 33, 39–42, 90–91, 98

Vining phase, 118–119

Wallerstein, Immanuel, 23
Warfare, 16–24, 79, 93, 114, 128, 140–141
Wauchope, Robert W., 29–33, 36, 39–49, 60, 85, 90, 97–98, 116
Wealth finance, 8
Wilbanks site, 33, 43–45, 88–91, 98–106, 115–116, 120
Woodstock Fort site, 33
Works Progress Administration (WPA), 33, 36, 108
World-system: perspective, 23–24; theory, 20, 23